CARITAS

JUAN MARÍA LABOA

CARITAS
The Illustrated History of Christian Charity

PAULIST PRESS
NEW YORK / MAHWAH, NJ

International Copyright © 2014
by Editoriale Jaca Book SpA, Milano
Libreria Editrice Vaticana
All rights reserved.
First Italian edition, *Atlante Storico della Carità*
September 2014

All rights reserved. No part of this publication may be reproduced, stored in a retrieval system, or transmitted in any form or by any means, electronic, mechanical, photocopying, recording, scanning, or otherwise, without the prior written permission of the Publisher. Requests to the Publisher for permission should be addressed to the Permissions Department, Paulist Press, 997 Macarthur Boulevard, Mahwah, NJ 07430, (201) 825-7300, fax (201) 825-8345, or online at www.paulistpress.com.

The Scripture quotations contained herein are from the New Revised Standard Version: Catholic Edition, Copyright © 1989 and 1993, by the Division of Christian Education of the National Council of the Churches of Christ in the United States of America. Used by permission. All rights reserved.

Library of Congress Control Number: 2014938722

Dust jacket design by Lightly Salted Graphics

Type and image selection by Pixel Studio, Milan

Printed and bound by Gráficas Estella S.L., Navarre, Spain

ISBN 978-0-8091-0610-3

English-language edition
Published by Paulist Press
997 Macarthur Boulevard
Mahwah, New Jersey 07430
www.paulistpress.com

CONTENTS

INTRODUCTION	6
Chapter 1 THE LOVE OF THE FATHER	11
Chapter 2 THE PARABLES OF JESUS	18
Chapter 3 THE MIRACLES OF JESUS	23
Chapter 4 THE COMPASSION AND MERCY OF JESUS	29
Chapter 5 THE DIACONATE	33
Chapter 6 MARTYRDOM: A SYMBOL OF LOVE	39
Chapter 7 CHRISTIANITY IN ROME DURING THE DECLINE OF THE EMPIRE	44
Chapter 8 THE CHURCH AND CHARITY UNDER JULIAN THE APOSTATE	48
Chapter 9 THE FATHERS OF THE CHURCH AND SOCIAL JUSTICE	51
Chapter 10 COOPERATION AMONG CHURCHES	57
Chapter 11 THE ORATORIES OF DIVINE LOVE	61
Chapter 12 ITINERANT MISSIONARIES	68
Chapter 13 EVANGELIZATION IS LOVE	76
Chapter 14 TEMPTATIONS AGAINST CHARITY	88
Chapter 15 MONASTICISM	93
Chapter 16 WHERE THERE IS SUFFERING, MARY SHINES	106
Chapter 17 SAINT MARTIN OF TOURS AND OTHER SAINTS	113
Chapter 18 THE WORKS OF MERCY	117
Chapter 19 FRANCIS OF ASSISI	122
Chapter 20 THE MENDICANTS	126
Chapter 21 PILGRIMS AND HOSTELS	131
Chapter 22 HOSPITAL ASSOCIATIONS	136
Chapter 23 LOSE YOUR FREEDOM, FREE YOUR NEIGHBOR	141
Chapter 24 HELPING THE SICK	146
Chapter 25 TEACHING THE POOR	153
Chapter 26 TEACHING THE IGNORANT	158
Chapter 27 CHRIST IN THE PRISONS	162
Chapter 28 THE SIGNS OF THE TIMES	165
Chapter 29 NINETEENTH-CENTURY RELIGIOUS FOUNDATIONS: RESPONSES TO POVERTY	170
Chapter 30 THE CATHOLIC WORKER MOVEMENT	173
Chapter 31 SAINTS AHEAD OF THEIR TIMES	177
Chapter 32 THE MYSTERY OF CHRIST IN THE POOR	181
Chapter 33 HÉLDER CÂMARA AND ÓSCAR ARNULFO ROMERO	185
Chapter 34 THE WORKER PRIESTS	189
Chapter 35 WILLINGNESS TO LISTEN	192
Chapter 36 SILENT COMPANIONS: CHARLES DE FOUCAULD'S LITTLE BROTHERS AND SISTERS OF JESUS	198
Chapter 37 MOTHER TERESA AND THE MISSIONARIES OF CHARITY	203
Chapter 38 EMMAUS AND POST–WORLD WAR II COMMUNITIES	209
Chapter 39 CARITAS INTERNATIONALIS	213
Chapter 40 JESUS AND PAIN	217
Chapter 41 POPE FRANCIS: "BUT YOU ARE NOT TO BE LIKE THAT"	223
APPENDIX: SHARED GENEROSITY	232
NOTES	234
INDEX OF NAMES	236
PHOTO CREDITS	239

INTRODUCTION

Jesus told his disciples that they would be recognized by their fruits, and little by little he indicated the precise nature of these fruits: That you love one another; do to others as you would have them do to you; bless those who persecute you; love your enemies. Jesus loved us to the extent of identifying with us, he gave his life for us, and he exhorted us to follow in his footsteps.

In announcing that God is our Father, he made the disciples understand that we are all brothers and sisters and that we should act as such. Once we are reborn and regenerated, we should assume a new attitude toward divinity, nature, society, and human beings.

The Church that he proposed to us is not reduced to a temple, a sacrifice, a commandment, or an organization, which are parts of every religion, but rather it fundamentally consists in a population that loves one another, a community distinguished by its fraternity and solidarity. With his words, he taught us that God is the Father, the Son, and the Holy Ghost, and he shows his paternity through his tenderness toward all his creatures, bestowing his gifts without distinction.

In the life and preaching of our Church, and in accordance with the evangelical texts, love is talked about constantly, both in the most appropriate and least opportune moments, out of habit or passion. All of the prayers, homilies, and official documents talk about the subject and take its importance in the life of the Church as given. However, there is reasonable doubt that the practice does not always correspond to the theory. In fact, there have never been courts of the Inquisition that condemn the lack of charity among believers, it has never been stated that the sin against charity is of only venial importance, and neither has there been an ecclesiastical

1. *Charity and monks. Miniature from the Chludov Psalter, first half of ninth century, Moscow. Charity is portrayed as a tree bearing fruit.*

2. *"God said, 'Let there be light…Let there be lights in the dome of the sky…Let us make humankind in our image, according to our likeness'…And the rib that the Lord God had taken from the man he made into a woman." Miniature based on Genesis from Petrus Comestor's* Historia Scholastica, *fifteenth century, Vatican Library, Vat.Lat. 5697. In this image as in all the others of the Creation, the Father is always embracing, exhorting, and encouraging his creatures.*

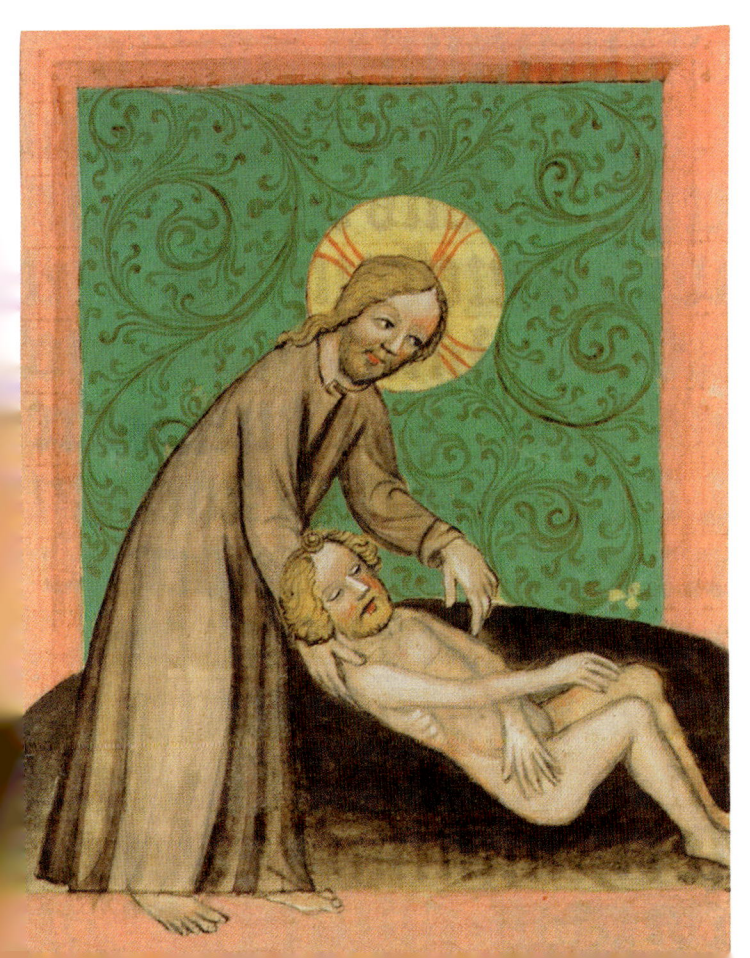

INTRODUCTION

investigation that has comprehensively dealt with those moments in which we have acted as if the end justified the means. We talk infrequently about concrete love in books on the theology and history of the Church and, while not forgetting its charitable role, little is said about the presence of reciprocal grace and love in the daily lives of God's people. Definitions of Divine grace and love are given in a metaphysical and heavenly sense, but it is difficult to find texts that compare them to the love of the mother for her child, as Saint Francis does when he describes how those who follow him should behave: Their fraternal love must be maternal; he speaks to Brother Leo like a mother speaks to her child, and in his letters he invokes a familial ideal in which the faithful are transformed into the spouses, siblings, and mothers of Christ, according to a clearly defined spiritual ascent.[1]

In our lives, we come across all kinds of suffering, but the most upsetting is the suffering of the innocent. "Whose fault is it?" Jesus' disciples asked when they met a man who was blind since birth. In his reply, Jesus uses a different logic: Do not look at the past, but at the future. He invites us to fight suffering of all kinds, attenuating its effects, eliminating it if possible, and accompanying and loving those who suffer, bearing the burden of the consequences, just as he did. The cross is the most appropriate meeting place between the human being, who is always weak, and Christ, who is innocent and just. It is the antechamber of the definitive meeting.

I have always thought that a history of Christians and of the Church that does not focus on the capacity of loving other human beings evades the fundamental nucleus of the faithful community and of the ecclesiastical institution. This history has yet to be written. In these pages, I want to slightly modify the usual stance taken by studies of the history of the Church and delicately place the accent on the love, solidarity, and affective concern that Christians have for each other. "Look how they love each other" said the pagans admiringly, referring to the early Christians. Probably the only Christian identity is charity. What does this love consist of? How is it shown? How has this feeling and this behavior existed in the course of history? These are just some of the important questions that I aim to answer.

In this book, I delve into the life of Christians, I analyze them, and I compare them to other moments and aspects of our history.[2] The result aims to be a mosaic of a life that simply and spontaneously demonstrates how tenderness, love, and compassion flow like a creek in the arteries of the Christian body. Is this always true of everyone? Obviously not. We continue to be clay vases that contain sin and grace, selfishness and generosity, lightness and regenerative passion. Our organization is excessive and we are excessively worried about it; and, like the priests of the Temple, we would prefer some people to fail if they do not interfere with our ecclesiastical organization. It is because of this temptation that the Church always has to protect its profound similarity with Jesus. It is not about words or voluntarism, but generosity. For the most part, Christians have not been great saints, eminent popes, or knowledgeable theologians, but ordinary Christians, with little theological baggage; nevertheless, they have loved and love their children, have taught them what Christ represented in their lives, and got along with their neighbor, helping in any way they could. These obscure stories make up the most beautiful pages of Christianity and these are the true heroes of this history of love: Although we only mention the names of the founders of congregations and ecclesiastical institutions, and the performers of great endeavors, the real heroes are their anonymous heirs, who have put out so many fires and reassured so many uncertainties, for they are the true architects of a more merciful and fraternal society.

The ten just men of the Old Testament have been transformed into anonymous masses who perhaps do not understand the significance of the Mass, or are unaware of the sense of the baroque world of Rome. They do not use the Internet, and they have

INTRODUCTION

3. *Peter healing a lame beggar in Lydda and raising a woman from the dead in Joppa; vision of the centurion Cornelius and Cornelius greeting Peter; Ecstasy of Peter and the christening of the first pagans. Miniature from the Bavaria Bible, 1175–1200 from the twelfth century. Universitätsbibliothek Erlangen-Nuremberg, Germany.*

INTRODUCTION

never had a pastoral letter, but as night falls, before they go to sleep in their beds, they thank God for the benefits received and talk to Christ about their sorrows and joys. They are the ones who make up the community, who acknowledge each other affectionately during the Eucharist, and who give the little they possess for Caritas initiatives: They have learned to love and give life to those around them. They are the ones who approach their neighbor, who live and work with the sick, the marginalized and the excluded, with AIDS sufferers, with problem youths, with the poor of all kinds, with those who have been rejected, and with all the untouchables in the world.

In this book, you will find the names of people, institutions, and religious congregations. In general, they represent heroic, generous, and creative attitudes and actions, as well as new ideas. For example, in a neighborhood of Madrid the Servants of Saint Joseph have installed a laundromat where women at risk of social exclusion can enter the world of work. The same community accommodates the needy people that the parish Caritas and the Women's House have encountered. I could have added innumerable other names, but I consider them mentioned when I talk generally about the actions for which they are liked, admired, and respected.

For the most part, this book is in chronological order, but it is flexible and a little unconventional. However, on reading the result, I think that the continuity of faith and generosity is highlighted. When I mention other works, I do not always indicate specific pages because I think that the sense of the work as a whole is important.

We continue to think like the prophet that, for those who love, the joyous time full of life and completeness is eternity, but the eternity that leads to the realm of heaven is already with us.[3]

4. Believers portrayed in an Exultet *from 1060–1070 from Montecassino. Vatican Library, Vat.Lat. 3784.*

1. John receiving the Apocalypse from an angel. Detail of a Miniature from the Commentario of dell'Apocalisse *by Beatus of Liébana, codex of Ferdinand I and Doña Sancha, eleventh century. Biblioteca Nacional de España, Madrid.*

Double page overleaf:
2. "He breathed into his nostrils the breath of life, and the man became a living being." Miniature based on the Genesis of Petrus Comestor's Historia Scholastica, *early fifteenth century. Vatican Library, 1Vat.Lat. 5697.*

3. Creation of Eve. By Maestro Nicolo, 1138. Detail of the left diptych on the door of the Basilica of San Zeno Maggiore in Verona.

Chapter 1
THE LOVE OF THE FATHER

Love comprises the very heart of the Trinitarian mystery and the Trinity is at the origin of the Incarnation of Christ, the creation of material, of man, of life in its entirety, and of everything that exists. Jesus' new commandment is an addition neither to knowledge nor to revelation, but it encompasses them and explains them both completely.
Let us start by claiming with conviction that both the Old and New Testaments are the custodians of the revelation of God's love for humanity. We believe that God is the author of the Bible and its true protagonist. Let us call this literary genre an autobiography. In other words, in the Bible God describes his relationships with us, which never fail to surprise in many different ways. Out of love for us, he created us in his own likeness and similarity; out of love,

4. Creation of Eve. *Detail of the bronze door of Hildesheim Cathedral, 1015.*

Double page overleaf:
5. Creation of Adam with his head on Christ's knee, and of Eve who is held almost upright by the Creator. Carving over the central bay of the north porch of Chartres Cathedral, thirteenth century.

he called upon us to maintain an ineffable personal relationship with him; out of love for us, he became involved in our history, the history of humankind, which is actually a detailed description of this never-ending meeting in a thousand different ways. God has always taken the initiative, and we have found ourselves ineffably enshrouded in his compassion.

This love is gratuitous; it depends on neither our merits nor our insistence, and it does not depend on our prayers. The initiative has always been his alone. He loved us first, so much so that he made us in his own image. Jesus reminded us that God makes it rain on the good and the bad, he understands our weaknesses and helps us with our needs; and the prophet Isaiah tells us that God has always respected our limits: "For I will pour water on the thirsty land, and streams on the dry ground. I will pour out my spirit on your offspring and my blessing on your descendants" (Isaiah 44:3).

The people of Israel felt they were loved, protected, and defended by God at all times. When Holy Scripture describes who and what we are, it says that we are those whom "God remembers," "that God loves," and that we are "the people of God." God himself says: "I shall be your God." It is to this God, who is able to love and shows such devotion, that we must answer because it is only in this response that we will find our own completeness, our sense of being, and our own happiness.

This is why our indebted reply to the first commandment consists in loving God above anything else, "With all your heart and with all your soul and with all your mind" (Matthew 22:37).

Over the past two thousand years, Christians have felt God loved them, whether in the simplicity of their lives, the happiness of their families, in remote villages, the solitude of monasteries, or in sickness, persecution, joy, and serenity. "The Lord is good to all; he has compassion on all he has made" (Psalms 145:9).

There is not one Christian church without a cross or without the daily commemoration of the sacrament of Christ. "For God so loved the world that he gave his one and only Son" (John 3:16). The gift of his Son is the very heart of Christianity, its most fundamental doctrine, the pledge of God's interest and love for his children. It is a strange Christian doctrine because it focuses its message on the weakness of God that results from his love, the sacrifice of his Son on the cross that results from this ineffable, mysterious love. Those of us who live in weakness, uncertainty, or insecurity are able to understand the purifying and reassuring power of divine love. For those of us who love, time is eternity; for a child the father's love is a compass and strength; for an adult it is a support and balance. For human beings God's love is the true reference point, the profound sense of life, and the vital horizon of existence.

Our image of God marks and determines the style, doctrine, and rites of religions. By identifying God with love, Christianity presents itself as the religion of brotherhood, of generous abundance, hope, and shared joy. "God my joy and delight" (Psalm 43:4), "the God of my life" (42:8), "My God whom I praise" (109:1), "Save me from all my transgressions" (39:8), and "God is the strength of my heart" (73:26) are just some of the definitions in the Old Testament, while in the New Testament Christ appears as a friend, a compassionate fellow man, merciful and benevolent.

Sin consists in not knowing love and of being incapable of loving. Love is the law and justice is the expression of love. If we love, we are as righteous as Christ was. When sentenced by the law, the woman caught in adultery was saved by love. The Pharisees wanted to apply the law without having experienced it as love. Christ resolved the case with forgiveness and reconciliation. In fact, just like charity solidarity is first an observation and then a duty: Feeling bound to someone, sharing their fate, putting oneself in their shoes.

In his beautiful letter about love, John the Apostle writes that those who do not love do not know God, and that God is love. The entire history of humanity

comes down to love and the lack of love, to mercy and sin, to the ability to feel one is God's child, and to those who have been unable to find companionship and who are errant, wandering around the world like a new Cain. According to the poet Paul Valéry, "all the possibilities of error lie in those who hate." If we in the Church had taken the Apostle's words to heart, our history would have been different, our communities would have been different, and our relationships would have had other characteristics; nevertheless, it must also be recognized that the history of charity has played an important role in our Christian, fraternal lives. In fact, it is delightfully revealing to see just how many Christians thought there was no better way to transmit the love of Christ than with poultices, plasters, ointments, compresses, cleansing, and tranquility. What better mission has there been in history than healing? What we ask of God is mercy and protection. Mercy, love, and closeness are what we ask of our brothers and sisters.

"I praise you Father…because you have hidden these things from the wise and learned, and revealed them to little children" (Matthew 11:25), Jesus said with gratitude, because we can all understand and love a God who talks to us about family and fraternity, love, generosity and service; a God who becomes man and suffers with us; a God who is present in our everyday life, in our human and family experiences. Christians enjoy a huge but joyful responsibility as both the instrument and witness of the creator's redeeming love; but it fails massively when estrangement transforms it into an obstacle. "Many will say to me on that day: 'Lord, Lord, did we not prophesy in your name and in your name cast out demons and in your name perform many miracles?' And then I will tell them plainly: 'I never knew you; away from me, you evildoers'" (Matthew 7:22–23).

Chapter 2
THE PARABLES OF JESUS

When talking with Nicodemus, the restless Jew who had recognized Christ as the Teacher who could answer the questions that were troubling him, to his amazement Jesus told him that he needed a new heart, to be born again (John 3:3). What he was really asking was for us to remain open to the Lord and not to follow the closed, stubborn attitude of our forefathers: "Do not harden your hearts as you did at Meribah, as you did that day at Massah in the wilderness" (Psalms 95:8). It was with this spirit that the prophet Samuel said to young Saul: "The spirit of the Lord will come powerfully upon you… and you will be changed into a different person" (1 Samuel 10:6) and the psalmist had beseeched God: "Restore to me the joy of salvation, and grant me a willing spirit to sustain me" (Psalms 51:12). The disciples knew that, thanks to the Holy Spirit, the redemptive and regenerative love of Christ transforms our lives, which are dominated by egoism and sin.

In the form of lively, disconcerting tales that are aimed at the hearts of those who will listen, Jesus' parables introduce us to figures who have acted out of the generosity, love, and compassion that come from a purified, generous heart. In this sense, the conversation with Nicodemus is a true parable: If we do not transform our hearts of stone into hearts of flesh and blood, if we do not change our intentions, and if we do not purify our desires, we can neither understand Jesus' words, nor put into practice his teachings, and we can neither receive Christ nor believe in the Lord. Put more simply, if we do not make an effort to change and let ourselves be converted to be reborn with a new spirit that is both welcoming and clear, it will be impossible to understand the true sense of Christ's message and requests. The parable that best illustrates what Jesus is proposing, and is the closest to his intentions, might be that of the Good Samaritan. While the Samaritan—

1

a member of a people the Jews regarded as impure and inferior—was walking one day, he came across a stranger who had been attacked and robbed by bandits who had left him injured and in a sorry state at the roadside. In this encounter with suffering and abandonment, we see the Samaritan as a loving person with an open heart who is moved by the needs of another person: "He went to him and bandaged his wounds, pouring on oil and wine. Then he put the man on his own donkey, brought him to an inn, and took care of him. The next day he took out two silver coins and gave them to the innkeeper. 'Look af-

THE PARABLES OF JESUS

1. Christ and Nicodemus. Detail of a miniature from the Egyptian Gospel of the Paris Institut Catholique, ca. 1249.

2. Mission of the Apostles. Miniature from the Sijsky Evangeliary, Moscow.

ter him,' he said, 'and when I return, I will reimburse you for any extra expense you may have'" (Luke 10:34–35). In this precious parable, Jesus is telling us that our neighbors offer us all the possibility to behave as we should, following in God's footsteps.

In the history of Christianity, the "Good Samaritan" has always been an example we have followed, an expression of Christian love for our neighbor, an unknown neighbor who is, nevertheless, our brother or sister. Christ himself was actually the first Good Samaritan, who "went round doing good" (Acts 10:38), teaching the good news while he healed the hearts and bodies of those he met. Following his example and admonitions, his disciples adhered to his good example from the very first time they were sent to announce the kingdom of God "proclaiming the good news and healing people everywhere" (Luke 9:6). The parable taught Christians that for Jesus we are all brothers and sisters and that everyone deserves help, affection, and protection.

The history that followed was one of generosity and egoism, sin and mercy, but I do not think I am exaggerating when I say that a great number of Christians converted over the centuries, to become Good Samaritans who worried about their neighbor's suffering and pain. Following divine exhortation, it was the faithful who identified the completeness of the Law with the love of God and one's neighbor. Countless illustrious names may be remembered over the centuries for their acts of love and self-sacrifice toward their forsaken brothers and sisters. So much poverty and injustice on earth has been extinguished and made human by the creativity, goodness, and sacrifices of many people whose names remain unknown, and whose memory lasts only in the goodness of God. The history we are familiar with and read usually corresponds to famous people, politicians, intellectuals, popes, and saints. But the world has made progress, in particular thanks to an infinite number of strangers, nameless citizens who, with their modest, silent work, have helped to improve the often difficult and laborious lives of numerous people. And it is there that we can discover countless Samaritans who have made more bearable the difficult and wretched existence of the incalculable, voiceless inhabitants living in towns, villages, and hamlets all over the world. This infinite hidden goodness cannot be narrated but it fills Heaven with saints and is the regenerating and restorative power of humanity.

With great steadfastness and confidence, Christians

THE PARABLES OF JESUS

3. Stained glass window depicting the Good Samaritan, south aisle of Chartres Cathedral.

THE PARABLES OF JESUS

4. *Stained glass window depicting the Prodigal Son,
north transept of Chartres Cathedral.*

THE PARABLES OF JESUS

5. Jesus and the woman taken in adultery. Detail from the Egyptian Gospel of the Paris Institut Catholique, ca. 1249.

1. Resurrection of Lazarus. Miniature from a Syrian Gospel book from the sixth century. Cathedral Treasury, Rossano.

have depended on God who is good and near. Thanks to the daily liturgy, we have understood the divine fatherhood, his presence in the climatic changes of the seasons, his help in catastrophes, and his concern during infirmity. We have asked him for rain during times of drought, protection during epidemics, and for him to be close to us during disasters. Everyday experiences aside, Christians have always had faith that one day God would put an end to their suffering, injustice, and death. In the meantime, true Christians were aware of the fact that they were alive thanks to the forgiveness and mercy of God; furthermore, while saying *Our Father* each day, in turn they then promised to forgive and show mercy to their neighbors, and to uphold unwaveringly their desire to help everyone to construct their own dignity.

This process of God drawing closer to his children, and his children drawing closer to each other, reaches its apex in the parable that, more than any other, describes the key characteristics of Christianity: The parable of the prodigal son or rather, of the merciful father. It is obvious that Jesus is referring to God when he describes this father: Someone who never loses hope, never ceases to love, never passes judgment even if he has every reason to do so, and who is happy when his penitent son returns in his arms. Christianity is the religion of a Trinity of love, one that selflessly loves the children it has created in its image and likeness, which recognizes their limits and loves them as they are, and which expects them to love one another like brothers and sisters, as if they were the children of the same father. "Look how much they love one another!" the Romans exclaimed in surprise when they saw the Christians' reciprocal love for one another. For Christians, this was not just their Teacher's commandment, but came spontaneously from the heart. The proclamation of good news consisted in saying that God was their mutual Father, their rock and their salvation.

In a letter to his sister Marcellina, and commenting on both the Pharisee Simon's thoughts regarding the sinner who had anointed Jesus' feet and Jesus' words to Simon, Saint Ambrose wrote: "Hair is considered to be superfluous to the body, but if it is anointed it becomes fragrant; it adorns the head but if it is not anointed, it becomes a burden. The same can be said of wealth: If we do not know how to use it, if it does not acquire the perfume of Christ, it becomes a burden. But if we help the poor, if we cleanse their wounds and purify their filth, it is as if we were drying Christ's feet." On another occasion when he was reproaching Emperor Valentinian II about the priests of a pagan cult, Ambrose said: "The possessions of the Church are the maintenance of the poor. Let them count up how many captives the temples have ransomed, what food they have contributed for the poor, to what exiles they have supplied the means of living." This text includes a list of some of the charitable works carried out by the Church, all of which were based on the Teacher's exhortations.[4]

Chapter 3
THE MIRACLES OF JESUS

The inhabitants of Galilee—farmers, small tradesmen, and shepherds—once met with Jesus as he passed through their villages, looking after the sick, driving away demons, and freeing the people of illness, lack of dignity, and exclusion. He spent three years walking from one village to the next and with his passion, words, and deeds, convinced them that God loved them, was by their sides, and worried about them. The sick got better, those possessed by the devil were released from their dark, narrow world, and many of them discovered the meaning of their lives. "How God anointed Jesus of Nazareth with the Holy Spirit and power, and how he went around doing good and healing all who were under the power of the devil, because God was with him," is written in the Acts 10:38.

The Gospels tell us that Jesus healed so many because he pitied those who were suffering physically or spiritually, because deep down he felt God's mercy for human beings. He discovered that the people were like "sheep without a shepherd" and took pity on them; he told them about the heavenly Father, assuring them that God of Israel was a God who was both close to them and compassionate. To those who listened, not only was it clear that Jesus was not simply repeating hearsay, stereotypes, or empty slogans but rather, by observing his lifestyle and tenderness, they understood that his words came from his own joyful personal experience. They felt cared for, their suffering found relief, their spirit was pacified, their life restored, and they felt they were the sons of God. These were the feelings of those who

THE MIRACLES OF JESUS

listened to him, proving that the words with which he had replied to the envoys of the Baptist were the truth: "Go back and report to John what you have seen and heard: The blind receive sight, the lame walk, those who have leprosy are cleansed, the deaf hear, the dead are raised, and the good news is proclaimed to the poor" (Luke 7:22).

The first Christians were aware that Jesus' actions focused on two complementary objectives: The proclamation of the good news that the kingdom of God was near and, at the same time, diligently healing sickness and disease among the people (Matthew 4:23). In this manner, using words and signs, he was therefore effectively proclaiming that God's saving action was already part of him. After having sent his disciples to proclaim the good news for the first time, "they set out and went from village to village, proclaiming the good news and healing people everywhere" (Luke 9:6). This was also the task Christians received over the centuries: Proclaiming the greatness of God and, at the same time, being close to the wretchedness and suffering of their neighbors, seeking their happiness and recovery, and working together on the regeneration of a society that was all too often divided and without hope.

The presence and vicinity of God never cease to produce all kinds of works in his creation: Beauty, goodness, and truth, which are always somehow present in nature and humanity. It is wonderful to experience how God's miracles are present in such abundance in our lives. Perceiving and enjoying them is one of the most joyful sensations of our existence. It is with gratitude that we Christians speak of Providence, this widespread, creative, and generous presence of the Creator of nature and life of human beings. A presence that is perceived in hope and that, in turn, induces hope. Ezekiel remembered this hope when he initially voiced his own personal experience of discouragement: "Son of man, these bones are the people of Israel. They say: Our bones are dried up and our hope is gone;

2. Healing of the blind man. Fresco in Monastery Ravanica in Serbia, 1387.

3. Healing of the man with dropsy. Fresco, 1316–1319. Church of St. George, Staro Nagoričane, Macedonia.

we are cut off" (Ezekiel 37:11). Very quickly, however, it became gratitude and a project for the future when he recognized God's loving decision: "The Sovereign Lord says: My people I am going to open up your graves, and bring you up from them; I will bring you back to the land of Israel" (Ezekiel 37:12). This hope is directed only at God, but God always uses us to spread his gifts and demonstrate how close he is. Being aware of this personal ability to take part in the divine project is one of the most gratifying experiences a human being can have.

THE MIRACLES OF JESUS

4. The Marriage at Cana. Detail of a miniature from the Egyptian Gospel of the Paris Institut Catholique, ca. 1249.

5. Exorcism of the Gerasene Demoniac. Miniature from the Hitda Codex, ca.1020, Cologne. Hessische Landesbibliothek, Darmstadt, Germany.

Throughout the nineteenth and twentieth centuries, various religious congregations added the word *providence* to their names. They devoted their attention and existence to abandoned children, the elderly, and poor but, above all, they wanted to show that it was actually divine Providence that was protecting and helping them through their deeds. In a certain sense, divine miracles continue to manifest themselves in all human domains, day after day, thanks to the love and dedication of humanity. The real human adventure lies in discovering the authentic face of love, and to do so it is essential to discover and put into practice our ability to love. All too often we limit and impoverish ourselves with narrow-minded loves and limited horizons, without perceiving the immense love around us, which is moving freely and enriching a world that remains contradictory and disconcerting.

Human thought, art in all its expressions, and different religions have all perceived the world as a splendid display and plastic expression of the omnipotence of God, but not always as an expression of his goodness and compassion. Nevertheless, God has known us from the beginning of time and his entire creation has always been in relation to our existence and conditioned by it. He knew that some would rebel against his love and mercy, but he also knew that some would love him as soon as they were capable of love, and that never again would they abandon him. Some conversions will be the source of joy up in heaven and, at the end of time, in the final glory of creation, all creatures will reunite to celebrate his love so that, at the end of time, the different fields of creation will once again turn to their Creator.

In the meanwhile, in the course of history, humans continue to discover and face the miracles that God has spread throughout the universe. These are signs that have to be studied, deciphered, and understood. Some of the more humble, more innocent, or purer souls have undertaken the mission to understand them, translate them, and make them known: "The heavens declare the glory of God; the skies proclaim the work of his hands," says Psalm 19:1, and in *The First and Second Life of Saint Francis of Assisi*, Thomas of Celano writes: "What ecstasy the beauty of the flowers aroused in him, when he admired their form and smelt their delicate perfume!… He began preaching to them, inviting them to praise and love God as if they were endowed with reason. He did the same with offshoots, grapevines, stones and the woods, beautiful countryside, flowing water, luxuriant gardens, the earth and fire, the air and

6. Miracle of the Spring, attrib. Giotto. From the Saint Francis Cycle, 1297–1300. Upper Church of the Basilica of St. Francis in Assisi.

7. Sermon to the Birds, attrib. Giotto. From the Saint Francis Cycle, 1297–1300. Upper Church of the Basilica of St. Francis in Assisi.

1. Healing of the woman with hemorrhage. Detail on the front of the Brescia Casket, late fourth century. Museo di Santa Giulia at San Salvatore in Brescia, Italy.

2. Raising of the daughter of Jairus. Detail on the left side of the Brescia Casket, late fourth century. Museo di Santa Giulia at San Salvatore in Brescia, Italy.

wind, inviting them to love and praise the Lord, with simplicity and purity in the heart."⁵

The *Canticle of the Sun* is another expression of Saint Francis' admiration: "Most High, all-powerful, good Lord, Yours are the praises, the glory, the honor, and all blessing. To You alone, Most High, do they belong, and no man is worthy to mention your name." Even today, at the beginning of October the fruits of the fields are offered in churches as thanks for the continuous miracle of the seasons and the food that nature is blessing us with. The Eucharist is an amazing act of thanks to the God who has saved us, and is offered by Christians every day in memory of Christ. When we Christians thank God for being our Father, we are also thanking all our brothers and sisters, and it is at that moment that we all become closer and more united.

As we can read in their lives, the great saints repeated the miracles of Jesus. The living, vital presence of the Lord can be seen in the lives of his saints, in their overflowing love for God and man, in the miracles they carried out, and in their ability to create peace and solidarity. They believed that there was only one universe, that of humanity, and that its evolution always culminated in God. They believed that all their deeds were guided by the principle that we have to serve those who are less fortunate before serving ourselves—first serving those who suffer more, who are needier and more alone than we are.

Chapter 4
THE COMPASSION AND MERCY OF JESUS

The Gospel according to Mark describes a particularly significant miracle, that of the bleeding woman (Mark 5:24–34). We do not know her name; she seems to be alone with neither relatives nor friends, and we are told that the doctors had ruined her. Owing to the customs of that time, her sickness not only made her sterile but also meant she was universally regarded as impure, and was shrouded by shame and dishonor. This is why she did not have the courage to voice her request openly and only dared touch Jesus' cloak without anyone seeing. According to the Jewish religion, after having touched him, he would be impure. It was Jesus' words that gave her the courage to approach the source of a blessing that could only be given for free, unlike the fortune that had been spent on doctors to no avail. Her shy, simple touch revealed her fear and all her hopes at the very moment God showed his compassion.

In this miracle, we can see the greatness of God and the Lord's merciful love. Jesus felt that healing her was not enough; he wanted to reach the very depths of her soul and was not satisfied until he had begun conversing with her and they had formed a bond. Jesus is no official, but a friend who is concerned and meets us halfway. Not only was the woman cured, she was also praised for her faith and called daughter, which was an extremely rare occurrence in the Gospels.

Jesus invites us to assimilate this woman's experience: First of all, developing an awareness of our weakness and smallness, aware that life is eluding us owing to the loss of fundamental values and the presence of conflicting aspects in our existence that make us feel sterile, while we neglect what is important and ignore the ultimate meaning of our lives. Jesus' immense sensitivity toward the pain of human beings meant he was able to relate to them with all his senses, with both mercy and compassion: He would look in their eyes, listen to their words, encourage them, and touch the person with his hands so they would be cured. When the bleeding woman in the crowd approaches him from behind and touches him, the curative power that healed sickness forever left his body (Mark 1:25–34), and when he touched a leper with his hands, he restored to a man who had been shunned by everyone dignity and self-confidence that he had believed was lost forever (Mark 1:40–45). The man who had been blind since birth was dazzled by a strange light that flooded his eyes when the fingers of the unknown Galilean caressed his eyelids and when he heard the words: "Go, wash in the Pool of Siloam" (John 9:7). The deaf mute man felt someone take his hand and pull him away from the crowd; when they were alone Jesus put his fingers in his ears, touched his tongue with saliva, and then ordered his closed ears, "Be opened!" (Mark 7:34). The strength of those words broke through the barrier of his deafness, while releasing his tongue and his entire existence that had been condemned to silence.[6]

Today Christ still serves us water, wine, bread, light, oil, friendship, and a love for healing, reviving, feeding, strengthening, and saving anyone in need. He obtains a new heart for us and, infusing us with a new spirit, he makes us abandon our routine, spurring us on to change ourselves. Despite the current crisis of Churches and religions, this might be why the generous figure of Jesus still arouses admiration and interest, and why we still attribute him with moral authority in a period that is devoid of ethical references. Furthermore, for us he is a friend who offers his life for us, one who grants his pardon with

3. Jesus and the woman at the well. Detail of a miniature from the Egyptian Gospel of the Paris Institut Catholique, ca. 1249.

4. Multiplication of the loaves. Miniature from the Reichenau Evangeliary, ca. 990. Vatican Library, Vat.Lat. 4453.

a friendly reception, who asks us to be as merciful as the heavenly Father and to change our heart. We are the disciples of a Teacher who was a master of the art of welcoming, protecting, and offering refuge in his arms to the injured lives and battered bodies of countless men and women. With our solidarity, concern, sympathy, and proximity, it is our task to transform the faithful community, the Church, into a space of communion, welcome, compassion, and common fraternity, able to embrace those who are still suffering in both body and soul.

It is terrible for us to all say the Our Father together and share the Eucharist if we are keeping our hearts closed, despising or ignoring those around us. If we act in this fashion, we only manage to weaken our affiliation to the Church and the true sense of Christian identity. On the contrary, what Jesus is doing is asking us to reshape our way of thinking, to reconstruct our

4

Next page:
5. Paul asks the High Priest for letters to the synagogue of Damascus; conversion of Paul; laying of the hands of Ananias and the baptism of Paul; Paul preaching at Damascus; Paul cures a paralyzed man in Lystra. Miniature from the Bavaria Bible, 1275–1300 (XII). Universitätsbibliothek, Erlangen.

lives, our friendships, and our faith with his teachings about the poor and small as the starting point.

According to Jesus, the kingdom of God is present where people are acting with mercy. If his presence is to be visible, we must introduce compassion into life, a sentiment that is always present in divine manifestations. We must have pity when looking at lost souls, those without work or bread, criminals who are unable to recreate a life, or victims who have fallen by the wayside. Mercy must take root in the families and lives of towns. Jesus arrived, offering the forgiveness and mercy of God, initiating a dynamic of reciprocal forgiveness and compassion while always acting accordingly, just as Isaiah hoped: "Stop doing wrong, learn to do right; seek justice. Defend the oppressed, take up the cause of the fatherless, plead the case of the widow" (Isaiah 1:16–17).

The ways in which Jesus moves are totally free from all earthly stereotypes or models of authority and arrogance, disqualifying any display of dominance between brothers: It is the beginning of a new style in which the strong do not impose their will on the weak, the rich on the poor, or those with knowledge on the ignorant. In this new kingdom, Jesus sees the fundamental bond as fellowship in reciprocal service, sharing a meal with those who seem to have "less," and are "beneath" us, and thus invalidating any pretext of believing oneself to be "better" or to be "above" others. Jesus has different priorities; he shows us what the actual substance of his proposal really consists of, and what we have to do to truly become his disciples. He repeats more than once that if we are to achieve a change in how we think, love, act, and react then we have to be reborn, just as Nicodemus taught us.

Today, now that we are aware of the inadequacy of many of our institutions, symbols, and attitudes we should be able to find other ways of embodying Christ. All too often, the Church looked at itself in earthly mirrors and not enough in the mirror of the Gospel.

It is first with his life, followed by his doctrine, that Christ has taught us what God is, and what he wants us to be; this is what his disciples understood from the very beginning.[7] Teresa of Avila began her autobiography with the desire to "sing the acts of mercy of the Lord," while Thérèse of Lisieux decided to write in the steadfast conviction of "doing just one thing: To start singing what I shall repeat later in all eternity: The acts of mercy of the Lord." In a certain sense, the history of Christianity is the history of this mercy and of the gratitude that we feel as its receivers.

Chapter 5
THE DIACONATE

In classical Greek, the word *diákonos* means "waiter" or "servant." In this sense, Jesus claims that he did not come to be served but to serve, giving a new dimension to the meaning of his own person and teachings. This idea of serving has pervaded the practice of the ecclesiastical ministries, Christian vocation, and relations with its followers at its best moments. However, when those in charge of the organization or administration of the community are driven by power or control, one of the most important teachings of Christ is warped.

We Christians frequently are overcome by the contradictions between the concepts we use, and the methods of governance used to implement them. Pope Gregory I disapproved of the patriarch of Constantinople for assuming the title "ecumenical," so as a rebuke, he called himself "Servant of the Servants of God." However, history has taught us that at times, in the shadows of this definition, the oppression and ill-treatment of the Lord's servants and children have continued, the shepherds transformed into transgressive wolves in Christ's flocks. The Lord was very clear when he taught his disciples. They were not to behave in the same way as those who held earthly power: His admonition was, "the last will be first." We have to be willing to share, participate, forgive, and help at every moment, with the active construction of that kingdom in heaven that is already in some way in our hearts: "You know that the rulers of the Gentiles lord it over them, and their great ones are tyrants over them. It will not be so among you; but whoever wishes to be great among you must be your servant" (Matthew 20:25–27). In the past, when consuls were sent on a mission, they were given the following piece of advice: "Do not act as a judge, but as a bishop." However, all too often over the centuries we have gone from service to domination and tyranny.

We know from experience, however, that the diaconate has always remained alive in ecclesiastical memory. There is no doubt that one of the most important activities carried out by the Church of Jerusalem in its earliest years was, socially speaking, the *diakonía kathemeriné*, helping widows, orphans, the poor, the sick, prisoners, those who were hungry and thirsty, or those who were naked or had been abandoned. The new doctrine concentrated on the acts of Jesus—the authentic good news that was being proclaimed—but Jesus appeared to his disciples as truth and life, making it impossible to separate his teaching from his closeness to and love for the blind, the lame, and the poor, and from his unceasing concern for the suffering people who remain calm in spirit when faced with calamity.

In their description of the lives of the early Christians, the Acts of the Apostles tell us that, "All who believed were together and had all things in common; they would sell their possessions and goods and distribute the proceeds to all, as any had need" (Acts 2:44–45). This division and distribution of goods frequently caused conflicts and possibly inequality. Disciples speaking Greek began grumbling against those who spoke Hebrew because they thought that their widows were being neglected in the daily service. Well aware that their specific task was to preach and teach, the Apostles decided to select seven men who were to devote themselves to serving at the altar and administrating charitable work. The most famous of these was Saint Stephen (Acts 6:1–6).

Although they were not called "deacons" anywhere in the New Testament, in his famous book *Against the Heresies* Saint Irenaeus (135–200) wrote that

THE DIACONATE

1. Works of mercy. Detail from Judgment Day, *1061–1067. Tempera on panel by painters from the Roman school Nicolò and Giovanni from the Oratorio di San Gregorio Nazianzeno. Vatican Museum.*

3. Fra Angelico. Saint Lawrence distributing alms, 1447–1448. Niccoline Chapel, Vatican Apostolic Palace.

2. Division of Rome into civil and ecclesiastical areas in the third century AD.

"the Apostles elected Stephen as the first deacon," thus establishing a tradition that still survives today, of relating the diaconate to the Christian need and practice to love and help the less fortunate. Around the year 57 for example, in Rome, Ephesus, and Philippi, ecclesiastical functions were divided among the bishops who presided and taught, and the deacons who served and distributed goods to other Christians, all members of a priestly and regal people.

However, the sacramental context of the election of these seven men (via the imposition of hands) gave them both liturgical prominence and a dedication to serving their brothers and sisters (Acts 6:3), which was to be the same for deacons throughout history. According to the texts extant, the deacons managed all the material assets of the Church and were in charge of organizing charitable acts, in particular for the sick. In the middle of the third century, following the significant reorganization of the administration of the Roman dioceses, Pope Fabian divided the city into seven districts, which were responsible for their respective districts and charitable work. Several decades later, the Council of Caesarea issued a law limiting the number of districts in a city to the same number, regardless of its size.

At the banquets (agápe), which the early communities organized relatively often for charity, the deacons had the task of coordinating the liturgical organization with the social aspects, and distributing the money and gifts they had received to the needy. Before long, the deacon had become an important assistant to the bishop so that, although the diocesan bishop had the final responsibility for charitable work as well as for the other diocesan functions, the deacons maintained a direct relationship with the social needs of the community and were the bishops' eyes, ears, hands, and hearts. Furthermore, the deacons usually acted as intermediaries between the congregation and the bishops, a role that grew in importance as the number of Christians increased and the extra-ecclesiastical tasks of the bishops grew, making them even more important in society. According to the *Didascalia apostolorum* from the third century, the good of the community depended on the smooth cooperation between the bishop and the deacon.

We must bear in mind that most charitable work was established and regulated in the tiniest detail, and it was in this framework that deacons carried out executive tasks that were of the utmost importance. They received and distributed donations from the faithful, in particular donations and legacies that the Church was receiving with growing frequency.

Under Constantine, the State entrusted the Church with the supervision of conditions in prison and assistance to widows, orphans, and abandoned children; in other words, a considerable part of public social deeds. The clergy became the defender and intermediary between the people and government. Soon the diocese was looking after millions of needy people. Describing his own diocese, John Chrysostom spoke of 3,000 widows and virgins in addition to the sick, lepers, and foreigners, not to mention the people who usually received food and clothes. The same can be said of the bigger cities.

In the sixteenth century, both Luther and Calvin wanted to change this diaconate system and tried to restore the functions that deacons had had in the early Church, in other words, working with the poor and playing a significant role in social charity. This was fulfilled only partially and not everywhere, although there is no doubt that a certain presence or at least some nostalgia remained in the diverse Christian denominations for a diaconate with charitable responsibilities. On the other hand, in mostly Protestant countries the churches often lost control of their property, which passed into the hands of state institutions so that charity and education soon became the responsibility of the modern state. In the Anglican Church under Elizabeth I, although helping the poor fell to the parishes, the queen would not allow the diaconate to be established.

During the twentieth century in Europe, several illustrious Catholic figures tried to revive the diaconate as a permanent ministry. Pius XII wanted to establish the permanent diaconate but there were sufficient bishops in Europe and the matter was left open. It was brought up again with greater urgency in several American and African countries, so that during the preparations for the Second Vatican Council, ninety bishops asked the pope to deal with the subject during council deliberations. During the second session, the council fathers discussed the diaconate, and a majority voted in favor of its re-establishment. On November 21, 1964, the re-establishment of the permanent diaconate was proclaimed in the Dogmatic Constitution on the Church in the Modern World (*Lumen Gentium*). With papal approval, national bishops' conferences were allowed to decide whether to restore the diaconate in their respective regions. According to these new laws, married men who were at least thirty-five years old, or unmarried men who were at least twenty-five years old, could become permanent deacons. In 2003, there were at least 30,000 permanent deacons in 105 countries, almost half of which were in North America. Ordained at a mature age, often married, and usually with work experience, deacons are an accessible, committed presence in the ecclesiastical organization in the life of laypeople. Where they do exist, they have managed to become a bridge between two worlds that are not always very close.

4. Martyrdom of Saint Stephen. Fresco from the Crypt of Epiphanius, 824–842, San Vincenzo al Volturno. Saint Stephen the Deacon is the first Christian martyr.

Chapter 6
MARTYRDOM: A SYMBOL OF LOVE

1. Martyrdom of Saint Lawrence. Fresco from the crypt of Epiphanius, 824–842, San Vincenzo al Volturno.

2. Martyrdom of Peter and Paul. Miniature of a troparion from Prüm Abbey, Rhineland-Palatinate, ca. 995–1001. Bibliothèque Nationale de France, Paris.

Those who do not fear death are immortal. Believing in the resurrection of Christ means believing in everlasting life; it means believing that God is the God of the living, that God is the way and is life. The example set by martyrs became fertile seed for Christians who believed that Christ was God on earth and that believing in him would guarantee them eternal life. This is where we find the Christian paradox: Those who lose their life save it forever.

Martyrs became fundamental reference points for the new communities: Peter and Paul in Rome; Ignatius in Antioch; Irenaeus in Lyons; Polycarp in Smyrna; Perpetua and Felicity, and, later, Cyprian in Carthage; Fructuosus in Tarragona; Eulalia in Mérida; and Dionysius in Alexandria. In the first three centuries, thousands of Christians were martyred for their faith. Martyrdom forged the true union with Christ. Blood constituted an authentic baptism that led to the pardoning of sins: The figure of Christ suffering was present in the Holy Communion and therefore martyrdom was the Holy Communion, in which we drink the chalice of Christ's sufferings. The presence of Christ in the martyr represented the Church's most important charismatic presence in the first centuries. Since the French Revolution, persecutions against the Church and cases of martyrdom have occurred repeatedly. We find bloody de-Christianizing processes during the National Convention and Reign of Terror (1792–1795), the Paris Commune (1870), the

Mexican Revolution (1926–1938), the Communist regimes in Eastern Europe, the Spanish Civil War, and in China, the cause of a harsh and bloody persecution. Between 1917 and 1941, 600 bishops, 40,000 priests, and 120,000 monks and nuns were killed in Russia. At least 75,000 places of worship were destroyed until the 1960s. It was the longest religious persecution in history.

Loving to the point of sacrificing their life, being consistent and faithful until their dying breath, self-immolation, and suffering all the pains for the love of those with neither a voice nor rights: Martyrdom was a contemporary reality for Christians of the first centuries and it still is today in the age of defending human rights and freedoms. Today we have a more complex and realistic idea about the causes of martyrdom, beyond the traditional one of a death endured out of loyalty to a belief. "A martyr is also someone whose death will often be the result of their participation in the struggle for justice and other Christian realities and values," wrote Karl Rahner. "The fate of greatness is suffering," said Pavel Florensky, who was shot in 1937 in the large Soviet gulag on the Solovetsky islands. We can add that in many cases the practice of charity extends to giving one's life for one's brothers and sisters, whether from disease, depletion of strength, or violence suffered in maintaining one's commitment to the weak, the marginalized, and the oppressed. The reason for these deaths has not always been due to hostile forces against the Christian faith, but to personal devotion and remaining faithful to the demands of a doctrine and an identity forged from evangelical generosity in situations of risk and social or economic injustice.

This was the case of the two Franciscan missionary sisters, Maria Javier and Guillermina, who volunteered to work in the hospital of Totoras during the bubonic plague epidemic that spread across Argentina in 1919. They were aware of the risk they took in staying with and nursing the sick, but they did not hesitate in their devotion. The entire twentieth century is full of stories like this. Countless religious men and women died for the love of the sick, demonstrating that for them life was meaningless if protecting it meant abandoning those in need of their help. They showed that remaining with the poor was more important than protecting themselves. In

many cases, working with the sick implies an incumbent risk of losing one's own life, and many people from religious orders have chosen this route. This was a common occurrence in previous centuries, mainly due to plagues and contagious diseases.

In many countries today, assisting the poor means being exposed to extremely harsh political or social conflicts in dangerous environments. In some situations, Christians are aware that practicing charity and defending the weak means risking their lives. The story of Christianity has thousands of examples of this, but in the twentieth century, this devotion to the poor became intolerable for certain economic or political powers. More than once, we come across

MARTYRDOM: A SYMBOL OF LOVE

3. Detail of the cemetery in the Potma forced labor camp, Russia.

4. View of the wooden huts in the Auschwitz concentration camp, Poland (photo Auschwitz Museum).

5. The huts in the quarantine section of Auschwitz (photo Comité International d'Auschwitz).

6. Father Maximilian Kolbe.

the evangelical principle that states true recognition or the adoration of God cannot exist where justice is oppressed and mocked.

Maximilian Kolbe is one of the most moving examples of charitable martyrdom in a Nazi death camp. For John Paul II, he was a "martyr of love": "A prisoner of the concentration camp, [he] defended in that place of death an innocent man's right to life." Father Kolbe declared, "he was ready to go to death in the man's place, because he was the father of a family and his life was necessary for his dear ones." Arrested and deported to Auschwitz in 1941 for being the head of the Franciscan community of Niepokalanów, he saved the life of one of his fellow prisoners, dying in his place in a "Starvation Bunker" on August 14, 1941, after two weeks of suffering. Another example of consistency and of the love for truth and one's own brothers and sisters is the German Protestant pastor Dietrich Bonhoeffer, founder of the Confessing Church ("only he who cries out for the Jews can sing Gregorian chants"), who was hanged by the Nazis in the Flossenbürg concentration camp in 1945. The life of love is consistently shown, even if it is hidden. Even in the most dreadful situations this permits our faith in both God and humanity to shine through, in the sense of faith in solidarity and the dignity of the human being.[8]

Father Valerian Cobbe explained how his untiring so-

7. Dietrich Bonhoeffer, pastor of the German Lutheran Confessing Church, for whom he headed the Finkenwalde seminary.

8. Still from Xavier Beauvois' film Of Gods and Men, *which recounts the ordeal of the Trappist monks of Our Lady of Atlas in Tibhirine, Algeria. The scene shows the monks and their kidnappers disappearing into the fog.*

cial activity in Bangladesh was linked to the spread of the Gospel: "Basically there remains one single fact, that we are here to preach the evangelical message 'until we all attain to the unity of the faith and of the knowledge of the Son of God, to mature manhood, to the measure of the stature of the fullness of Christ' [Ephesians 4:13]. The missionary's contribution to the development of peoples comes from the Gospel. Jesus spoke to the people, but when the people were hungry he had compassion and gave them food. Furthermore, we need to be aware that in this land dominated by Muslims the only Christian message we can spread is that of our example, of our social work, of our human and Christian charity."

Driven by these ideas, he organized hugely successful agricultural cooperatives that provided work for numerous people, but he provoked the wrath of the men who had traditionally profited from those poor people. He was murdered on October 14, 1974. One of his companions wrote that he had been killed because the flag of the oppressed had been raised too high. We find other missionaries murdered for similar reasons in Brazil, the Philippines, Honduras, and Peru.

Among the numerous victims of the military dictatorship in Argentina in the 1970s were the religious leaders of the parish of St. Patrick in Buenos Aires, a gathering place for people who opposed the climate of illegality and repression that had broken out in the country. They were killed by a group of armed men who then disappeared without a trace. In October 1976, in the diocese of São Félix do Araguaia, in Brazil, the Jesuit priest Joao Bosco Penido and Bishop Pedro Casaldáliga tried to free some women who had been tortured by local police. One of the policemen killed the Jesuit with two shots to the head. Many other priests, religious people, and laypeople died for the same reasons. The Jesuits of the Universidad Centroamericana in El Salvador are among them.

One of the most famous and touching cases from the end of the twentieth century is that of the Cistercian monks of the Our Lady of Atlas Abbey in Algeria, who were deeply involved in creating a dialogue and living harmoniously with the Muslim world. The local people loved the monks, who served as dispensing pharmacists (one of the brothers was a doctor), and who had a great ecumenical sensitivity. A head of the GIA, the most extremist Islamic organization, ordered the monks to abandon the monastery. However, after serious reflection, they decided to stay with the people of the area who helped the monastery with all its needs. They did not want to die, but they thought that abandoning the monastery meant abandoning the people they lived with. Their love for Islam and for the Algerian people was one of the reasons that led them to stay. Brother Michel Fleury wrote: "The word 'martyr' is such an ambiguous term here….If something happens to us, which I hope it won't, we

want to experience it together with all of these Algerian men and women who have already paid with their lives, in solidarity with all of these innocent forgotten people. It seems to me that the one who is helping us today is he who called us. I am full of wonder."

The Trappists of Our Lady of Atlas, monks and martyrs, show that it is possible to conjugate monastic life, hospitality, and dialogue with the acceptance of martyrdom, which in reality indicates the realization of boundless generosity, even at the risk of one's life.

"No one has greater love than this, to lay down one's life for one's friends," said Jesus to his disciples. Following his example and in his name, numerous disciples have offered their lives for their brothers and sisters; they include Shahbaz Bhatti, the only non-Muslim minister in the Pakistan government, who was assassinated on March 2, 2011. He was Federal Minister for Minorities and opposed the blasphemy law used as a weapon against non-Muslims. Endowed with deep religious convictions, he died defending both his ideals and the rights of minorities and women, totally aware that he was putting his life at risk. In his spiritual will we find this confession: "Since I was a child, I was accustomed to going to church and finding profound inspiration in the teachings, the sacrifice, and the crucifixion of Jesus. It was his love that led me to offer my service to the Church. The frightening conditions into which the Christians of Pakistan had fallen disturbed me. I remember one Good Friday when I was just thirteen years old: I heard a homily on the sacrifice of Jesus for our redemption and for the salvation of the world. And I thought of responding to his love by giving love to my brothers and sisters, placing myself at the service of Christians, especially of the poor, the needy, and the persecuted who live in this Islamic country. I have been asked to put an end to my battle, but I have always refused, even at the risk of my own life. My response has always been the same. I do not want popularity, I do not want positions of power. I only want a place at the feet of Jesus. I want my life, my character, my actions to speak of me and say that I am following Jesus Christ. This desire is so strong in me that I consider myself privileged whenever—in my combative effort to help the needy, the poor, the persecuted Christians of Pakistan—Jesus should wish to accept the sacrifice of my life."

I would like to mention other forms of self-offering, of silent martyrdom so to speak, by many other people whose charity for others over the years has led to conditioning their own existence: Young people who do not marry in order to care for invalid parents or siblings struck down with serious disabilities; people who lose their jobs because they stood up for coworkers who were unjustly punished; those who are marginalized at work because they are too honest to get involved in financial scams; mothers who do not abort even when they know their child is suffering from serious malformations that would seriously limit their life; cloistered nuns who are ill-treated without ever complaining or rebelling. A life of moral consistency or compassion for others often produces painful consequences that mark an existence, an existence sacrificed for love and for faith.

Chapter 7
CHRISTIANITY IN ROME DURING THE DECLINE OF THE EMPIRE

Roman Christians belonged to all the ethnicities of the known world, and their mother tongues and cultures were just as different as their origins. All the contradictions of a global empire could be found among their numbers, who belonged to different social classes and lived under very different economic conditions. It was the Gospel, the Good News announced by Christ, that would shape their unusual identity and make them feel like members of the same community, a united community with one faith and a common hope.

In Eusebius of Caesarea's *Ecclesiastical History*, we read that at the time of Pope Cornelius (251–253) the Church of Rome helped 1,500 people, including the poor, widows, and the sick. Given the rise in conversions over the next two centuries, we can calculate that the number of people given alms grew proportionally. Every Christian document of the first two centuries speaks of the constant concern of the communities in helping the most needy and weakest among them.

The Church obtained the money needed for its charitable works primarily thanks to collections from the faithful. The most famous day was undoubtedly "collection day," dedicated to collecting a considerable sum of money, enough to answer the needs of the poor of all kinds living in the diocese. The Roman Christians celebrated this holiday of generosity annually between July 5th and 15th, on the same days and with the same aim that pagans traditionally celebrated the *Ludi Apollinares*. According to Saint Leo the Great, the Christian version of this holiday was the older of the two, but it was probably copied from the pagan holiday.

This pope insisted on adding alms and charitable deeds to the fasting and prayer of Lent: "We are committed to defending the widows, helping the orphans, consoling those in tears, reconciling ourselves with our enemies, providing lodging for pilgrims, aiding the oppressed, clothing the naked, and caring for the infirm." This was an exhortation to the faithful to be personally committed to cooperating with the works of the diocese.

Christian Rome approved and supported the institution of public granaries to sustain the lower classes. Wheat was not sold in these granaries, but was stored and distributed among the needy. Representatives of the Bishop of Rome administered the agricultural properties that the Roman Church owned in Africa and in Sicily, and they had the task of sending the harvests to Rome. On numerous occasions the popes, even when enjoying neither independence nor the powers of government in the city, were the only ones capable of finding a solution to the problems of food shortages or famine, earning a universally respected moral authority and the grateful trust of the Romans.

Two centuries later, at a time of greater decline, Gregory the Great (590–604) oversaw and organized the daily provision of food for the Roman population, which had suffered the calamities and chronic disorganization of the age. He imported the necessary food, particularly wheat, from the Sicilian lands owned by the Roman Church. He also restored the buildings of a city in ruins and in obvious degeneration.

Rome and the local churches in general kept a complete list of the needy in their communities, which provided a glimpse into their parish's situation. Thanks to this index, the bishops and deacons knew in minute detail the needs of each indigent and tried to respond to them according to each situation. Rome was a wealthy diocese, with a considerable

1. Last Supper. Mosaic, 493–ca. 526. Basilica of Sant'Apollinare Nuovo, Ravenna. There are few depictions of the Christian community, the iconography mainly depicting scenes from the Old Testament and the Gospels. However, we do have representations of the Eucharist banquets in the catacombs. The image of the Last Supper with the Apostles is the representative example of the Christian community.
The Early Christian mosaic in Ravenna is particularly expressive: the large fish on the table recall the miracle of the multiplication, responding to the needs of everyone.

2. Pope Cornelius and Saint Cyprian. Sixth-century fresco in the Catacomb of Saint Callistus, Rome. Saint Cyprian, the Bishop of Carthage, supported the merciful attitude of the pope towards those who had renounced the faith under persecution.

3. Saint Melania the Younger. Modern icon.

4. Raphael (and workshop), The Meeting of Saint Leo the Great and Attila. *Fresco, 1513–1514. Room of Heliodorus, Vatican Museums.*

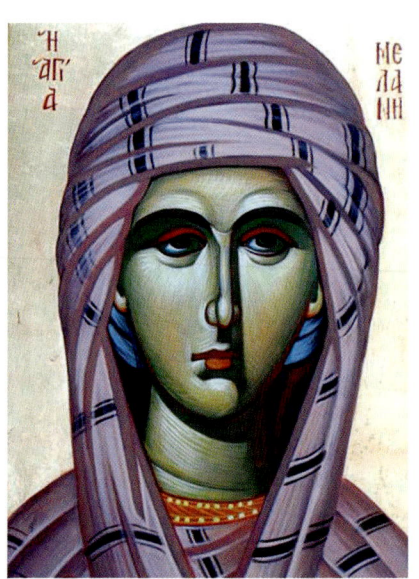

sum of well-administered assets, starting with the wealth of the basilicas and ending with the legacies of the main families and the bequests of numerous Christians. An example of this generous devotion is Cyprian, Bishop of Carthage, who, having converted to Christianity at the age of forty-five, distributed a large part of his fortune among the poor. Two centuries later, around 409, Roman society was moved when Melania the Younger, one of the richest heiresses of the Empire, happily married to Pinianus, a man as rich as she, decided to donate all of her wealth to the poor and to embark on a life of chastity. They were not the only ones: The poor were the constant recipients of significant amounts or even all of a donator's wealth.

These were not simply actions to help the more unfortunate out of pity or humanitarian sentiment; in Christianity, there was a new model of human relations and fraternal society. A community that loves its brothers and sisters because it believes that God is common to all should demonstrate it through words and actions. Maximus the Confessor wrote: "He who shows himself worthy of God drives out self-love through charity, and simultaneously makes all of the folly of vices that by now no longer have reason to be nor foundation in him disappear. This man no longer knows pride, a sign of arrogance toward God, a multifaceted and innate evil;… befriending other human beings with a voluntary benevolence, he consumes envy, which in turn would consume first of all he who feels it; he eliminates choler, homicidal desires, anger, deceit, falsehood, derision, rancor, greed, and everything else that divides humankind."[9]

Christian identity lies not just in the Creed and in the canon of the Scriptures, but is also and predominantly manifested in the fraternal relationship of Jesus' disciples: "And if…I have all faith, so as to remove mountains, but do not have love, I am nothing" (1 Cor 13:2). In the new society, Christians will obey Jesus' exhortation: "Do to others as you would have them do to you." He does not ask us to treat others as they would treat us, as in the concept of an eye for an eye, but as we, who love ourselves

very much, would like to be treated. This decision to take the initiative ourselves is translated into the Our Father with the risky task of asking the Lord to forgive us our debt, as we also have forgiven our debtors.

The liturgy maintains the principle that for Christ all humans have equal dignity. Slaves could be baptized and take the Eucharist just like free people. This was a revolutionary decision, since pagan slaves could not participate in official worship and had to organize worship among themselves. In the catacombs, we never find the word *servant*, because for those Christians everyone was equal, even in death. Leo the Great tried to save Rome from the barbarians, the barbarians from themselves. His principal task was to rescue the children of God from anything that threatened their life and their freedom. Throughout the centuries, we see this repeated. Europe sprang from this ecclesiastical work of integration. Christianity, pronouncing the universal paternity of God and the humanizing and saving presence of Christ, created a culture from an amalgam of peoples, cultures, and traditions that integrated with Roman traditions and the peculiarities of each people. To achieve this result it was undoubtedly essential for Christianity not to be rooted in any particularly racial, geographical, social, or political context. It was genuinely catholic. In this sense, it was important to appreciate the elements of continuity as much as those of discontinuity between the Roman world of Saint Augustine and the Christian-Barbaric world that followed. Elements of continuity include the charitable ministering that the bishops and ecclesiastical institutions invariably maintained in the cities, caring for the weakest of the different communities. Like an echo of Julian the Apostate's admonition, the new models maintained the imprint of charity and concern for the welfare of citizens that had characterized the first Christian communities.[10]

Chapter 8
THE CHURCH AND CHARITY UNDER JULIAN THE APOSTATE

Julian (331–363) was the son of Julius Constantius, brother of Emperor Constantine. At the age of six, he witnessed the extermination of his family as Constantine's children murdered potential rivals during their rise to power. For the next twenty-four years, he lived in fear of being assassinated by his cousin Constantius, who went on to die heirless. At the age of thirty, Julian was declared emperor.

During his youth, he studied philosophy, and he thought himself predestined to restore the ancient Roman values that he felt were degraded by his uncle's imposition of the Christian religion. He ended up hating Christianity as much as he hated his relatives. For him, Jesus of Nazareth, far from embodying the final and full expression of the Word, was nothing more than an illiterate peasant whose teachings, completely lacking truth and beauty, were illogical, without any common sense, and socially subversive. After personally experiencing the cruelty of his cousins and their capacity to assassinate without punishment or remorse, it is possible that Julian found it hard to swallow the doctrine of love proclaimed by Jesus and openly practiced by his disciples, but discredited by his royal relatives who were confessed Christians.

If we reflect on this story, we realize that the conversion of power in all its dimensions was extremely difficult. Christianity was accepted as a personal religion, but those in power continued to be selfish, violent, rash, and aggressive toward anyone who was considered an enemy or a competitor. The Capetians, Bourbons, Hapsburgs, and Braganzas supported the Church and were even endowed with personal piety, but they usually believed that the ends justified the means. Constantius was undoubtedly sincerely Christian, but as emperor, he was as violent and immoral as were any of his pagan predecessors. "But you are not to be like that," Jesus exhorted his disciples. Unfortunately, it turned out to be very complicated to reconcile power with love and service.

Dominated by the desire to recreate the classical past and to reinstate the gods of Mediterranean polytheism, when he became emperor in 361, Julian aimed to move the Empire from Christian revelation to Greek reason. He therefore wanted to return to the spirit and method of classical philosophy, but his concept had little structure or system. The historian Edward Gibbon observes that "the genius and the power of the emperor were unequal to the enterprise of restoring a religion which was destitute of theological principles, of moral precepts, and of ecclesiastical discipline," but Julian tried with audacity, moved by resentment for Constantine and Christianity, identifying the latter with the former.

Despite this rejection of and aversion to Christianity, Julian was extremely sensitive to the characteristics of the new religion that attracted people and reinforced its presence and expansion. In a letter to a high priest, he wrote, "…when it came about that the poor were neglected and overlooked by the priests, then I think the impious Galileans observed this fact and devoted themselves to philanthropy. And they have gained ascendancy in the worst of their deeds through the credit they win for such practices. For just as those who entice children with a cake…by the same method, I say, the Galileans also begin with their so-called love-feast, or hospitality, or service of tables,—for they have many ways of carrying it out and hence call it by many names,—and the result is that they have led very many into atheism."[11]

As he slowly continued, enacting his decision to renew paganism, Julian decided it was better to copy

1. *Triumph of Cybele and Attis. Silver bowl of Parabiago. Civiche Raccolte Archeologiche, Milan. The cult of Cybele came to Rome from Greece at the beginning of the second century AD. Often called "the great mother," magna mater, by the Romans, her cult was taken up by Julian because Cybele protects nature and thus the agricultural activities that provide humanity with vital resources.*

the very thing that had helped Christianity triumph. He wrote to the high priest Arsacius: "Why, then, do we think that this is enough, why do we not observe that it is [the Christians'] benevolence to strangers, their care for the graves of the dead and the pretended holiness of their lives that have done most to increase atheism?....In every city establish frequent hostels in order that strangers may profit by our benevolence; I do not mean for our own people only, but for others also who are in need of money. I have but now made a plan by which you may be well provided for this; for I have given directions that 30,000 modii of corn shall be assigned every year for the whole of Galatia, and 60,000 pints of wine. I order that one-fifth of this be used for the poor who serve the priests, and the remainder be distributed by us to strangers and beggars. For it is disgraceful that… the impious Galilaeans support not only their own poor but ours as well, all men see that our people lack aid from us."[12]

These hospitals and hostels, which Julian so admired, were houses for the needy who found themselves homeless, a place of refuge for the poor, pilgrims, the infirm, and the homeless, cases in which Christian charity and aid were performed under the more or less direct guidance of the bishop. Once freedom had been obtained and as the number of Christians gradually increased, these cases multiplied. It should therefore not seem strange that the pagans identified Christianity with an organization that reached numerous different pockets of society. Julian's intention to renew paganism was unsustainable. Although it is impossible for us to know what would have happened had his reign been longer, Christian practices and organization had actually obtained such wide success it is difficult to imagine an alternative. Above all, the Christian presence in fulfilling the needs, poverty, and desires of the world would have been almost impossible to duplicate under the decrepit pagan religion, despite every lavish effort to revitalize it. Christianity offered consolation and generated enthusiasm, two spiritual states necessary in that time and in ours. God was close, merciful, and paternal, and had nothing to do with the reinstatement of paganism as promoted by Julian and other philosophers. Despite the fact that sin and weakness were always present, the love experienced in the Christian communities continued to be their strength and their glory.

For the people of the fourth century, Christianity did not present itself as a doctrine or a dogma, or as an association of mutual assistance, not as a theology or an institution, however original, but rather as a radical life style, the ideal of a renewed person and society. Worship, liturgy, devotion, and, above all, its way of understanding others and putting itself in relation to them, were the expressions of this transformation of the psychology, sensitivity, and behavior of Christians. The practices of penitence, mortification, charity (from fraternal love to almsgiving), and the perception of being part of the mystical body of Christ determined new social relations and a group feeling that transcended both time and space. Clearly Julian did not understand the importance of this transformation if, having reduced his modernization of paganism to new doctrines and a renewed social organization, he thought that this cosmetic update of paganism could fatally wound Christianity. In his project, Julian forgot that only Christ is love and that he is the generator of the love and generosity of Christians.

2. Bust of Emperor Julian the Apostate. The Louvre, Paris.

Chapter 9
THE FATHERS OF THE CHURCH AND SOCIAL JUSTICE

Most of the Fathers of the Church came from well-off families, had had a good intellectual education, and an intense evangelical spirit that shaped their personalities and works. They were all extremely generous, sharing their wealth among the needy and becoming famous for their charitable deeds.
They were exceptional interpreters of the Holy Scripture, which they kept with them constantly, accentuating and proclaiming their deep social consciousness, demonstrating that the roots of this were inseparable from Christianity. In their writings they dealt with such fundamental themes as the essential equality, dignity, and primacy of human beings, which was always to be respected; private property and its social nature; wealth and the exchange of goods; work and its dignity; economic development and the deference to be given morality. According to the Fathers, the duties of the rich did not consist solely of personal formality, but, fundamentally, in sharing their wealth with those lacking basic necessities, not only to enable their survival, but also to help them develop their potential. It was not merely about being generous, but being just; and in their writings, they did not hesitate to use bold and insistent language. In fact, as they gradually developed structures to assist the poorest and progressively became the protectors and benefactors of individuals and cities, the bishops exhorted their congregations to put their personal wealth in the service of the needy and the Church. Starting with the Gospel, their arguments went beyond recommending charity and assistance, and they eventually developed a doctrine of the substantial equality of humankind and human rights, based on the Creator's pronouncement that all earthly goods should be shared.
Here are what I consider some of the most significant texts by the most important Fathers:

Saint Basil (330–379), the most modern of the Greek Fathers, frequently highlighted the social and community nature of the evangelical doctrine regarding property and wealth. "Charity submits free men to each other and simultaneously accentuates and maintains the freedom of will." "God's decree does not teach us that we should refuse and shun material riches as though they were ills, but he tells us how to administer them. If we condemn someone, under no circumstances should it be because they possess riches, but because they have used them dishonestly or because they have been incapable of making good use of them." "You who dress your walls, and let your fellow-creatures go bare, what will you answer to the Judge? You who harness your horses with splendor, and despise your brother if he is ill-dressed; who let

THE FATHERS OF THE CHURCH AND SOCIAL JUSTICE

your wheat rot, and will not feed the hungry; who hide your gold, and despise the distressed?"

"It seems to me that the infirmity of this man's soul is like that of the gluttonous, who prefer to burst with too much food rather than give their leftovers to the needy. Remember who gave you that which you possess, remember who owns what you administer, from whom you received it, why you were favored and not others. You were made to be God's servant and administer those who are, like you, servants of God. Do not think that your riches are exclusively for your stomach. Remember that what you hold in your hand belongs to others. Riches can be pleasing for a while, but they are fleeting and disappear, and in the end you will be asked for the exact tally of each thing."

Saint Cyril of Jerusalem (313–386) is known and admired for the catecheses he preached in 358 to the newly baptized, in which he methodically explained the creed of the Church of Jerusalem, without forgetting any of the articles dedicated to generosity in the distribution of wealth. "Whatever matter thou receivest from God to administer as a steward, administer profitably. Hast thou been put in trust with riches? Dispense them well. Hast thou been entrusted with the word of teaching? Be a good steward thereof. Canst thou attach the souls of the hearers? Do this diligently. There are many doors of good stewardship."

Saint Gregory of Nazianzus (330–390) underlines the social aspect in all his works, particularly in his discourse *On Love for the Poor*, which he probably preached in Caesarea in 373. "There is nothing more divine in man than doing good." He indicates the following as motives for compassion for the deprived: "If you are healthy and rich, alleviate the need of whoever is sick and poor; if you have not fallen, go to the aid of whoever has fallen and lives in suffering: if you are glad, comfort whoever is sad; if you are fortunate, help whoever is smitten with misfortune. Give God proof of your gratitude for you are one who can benefit and not one who needs to be benefited; for you are one who does not look at the hands of others, and the others look at yours. Be rich not only in possessions but also in piety; not only in gold but in virtue, or rather in virtue alone. Outdo your neighbor's reputation by showing your-

self to be kinder than all; make yourself God for the unfortunate, imitating God's mercy."

Saint John Chrysostom (344/354–407) was known for his fervent charity. As the Archbishop of Constantinople, he devoted his income to building hospitals and helping the poor. His dedication to the

On page 51:
1. *Saint Basil the Great celebrating the eucharist. Eleventh-century fresco. Cathedral of Saint Sophia, Ohrid, Macedonia.*

2. *Saint John Chrysostom. Tenth-century mural. Coptic Museum, Cairo.*

3. *The holy bishops Basil the Great, Athanasius of Alexandria, and John Chrysostom. Late twelfth-century fresco. Monastery of Saint Moses the Abyssinian, Nabk, Syria (restored by the Central Institute of Restoration, Rome).*

4. Scenes from the life of Ambrose in which his political and social commitment is also depicted on the back of the famous golden altar of Saint Ambrose in Milan, created by Volvinius in the Carolingian age (824–859).

5. Detail of the tile showing the baptism of Ambrose.

needy and the oppressed, and his interest in a more equal and just sharing of wealth was so intense that he could be called Advocate of the poor. In almost all of his homilies we come across the ardent defense of the needy and their right to alms and assistance; he reminds the rich of their duty to share what has been given to them, and, without beating about the bush, censures their lack of social conscience, their luxuries, and their acts of injustice.

"Let us do the same and strive for the health of all our brethren. Not hesitating to offer any sacrifice for the salvation of all is not inferior to martyrdom. There is nothing that pleases God more. Once again I go back to saying what I have said many times before. Christ did the same thing, exhorting forgiveness: 'Therefore, if you are offering your gift at the altar and there remember that your brother or sister has something against you, leave your gift there in front of the altar. First go and be reconciled to them; then come and offer your gift' (Matthew 5: 23–24)."

Saint Ambrose (339–397) affirms in his writing that the foundation of society lies in justice and beneficence. He insists on the importance of communal wealth and on the communitarian nature of wealth. In all of his texts he recalls the universal dominion on earth conceded by God to all humanity and the right of everyone to share its fruits. "Mercy, also, is a good thing, for it makes men perfect, in that it imitates the perfect Father. Nothing graces the Chris-

tian soul so much as mercy; mercy as shown chiefly toward the poor, that you may treat them as sharers in common with you in the produce of nature, which brings forth the fruits of the earth for use to all. Thus you may freely give to a poor man what you have, and in this way help him who is your brother and companion." These authors relativize the right of ownership, with the aim of imposing a systematic character to the practice of almsgiving and the criteria stating precisely how much should be given. Saint Augustine urged the faithful to distinguish between the superfluous and the necessary, and considered it an obligation to give the superfluous to the poor.

Saint Augustine (354–430), the great North African writer, underlines the preeminent role of justice and charity in the social order and in peace, which is the human order par excellence.

"Brothers, where does charity begin? You have heard that it leads to perfection: 'Greater love has no one than this: to lay down one's life for one's friends' (John 15:13). The Lord shows us in the Gospel the perfection of charity and in this reading he exhorts us to reach it. But you ask: when can we practice such charity as this? Do not despair too soon in your abilities. Perhaps it is already present, but it is not yet perfect: take care that it is not extinguished. But you will ask me: How will I know? We have seen how it leads to perfection, now we feel how it begins. Saint John continues, saying: 'How does God's love abide in anyone who has the world's goods and sees a brother or sister in need and yet refuses help?' This is where charity begins. If you are not yet capable of giving your life for a brother, at least be capable of giving him your goods. Let charity penetrate your heart so that you do not do good for ostentation, but for its own value of mercy, becoming capable of taking you into their heart those who find themselves in need."

"The good that charity does has no limits! If you have material goods, give what you possess; if you do not, demonstrate your good will and, if you can, give advice and help; finally, if you can neither advise nor help, give voice to your good intentions and pray for the afflicted, and without doubt God will listen to this prayer before the one that consecrates our daily bread. Those who have their heart full of charity always have something to give."

6. *Vittore Carpaccio,* Saint Augustine in his Study. *Tempera on wood, 1502. Scuola di San Giorgio degli Schiavoni, Venice.*

In other chapters, we have touched on the central importance of charity in the life of early Christianity, a thread that runs through its entire history. In Saint Augustine's writings and pastorals we see how frequently he underlines its importance: "Furthermore, there exist in the inspired Word many other testimonies that show the enormous power of charity in extinguishing and canceling out sins."

Chapter 10
COOPERATION AMONG CHURCHES

The Roman community's generosity toward the less fortunate communities was well known among the first Christians. Saint Dionysius of Corinth writes to Soter, Bishop of Rome: "For this has been your custom from the beginning of Christianity to do good to all the brethren in many ways, and to send alms to the many Churches in different cities, now relieving the poverty of those who asked aid, now assisting the brethren in the mines by the alms you send. Romans keeping up the traditional custom of Romans, which your blessed bishop, Soter, has not only maintained, but has even increased, by affording to the brethren the abundance which he has supplied, and by comforting with blessed words the brethren who came to him, as a father to his children."[13]

One hundred years later, Dionysius of Alexandria recounts how Rome regularly had aid sent to the Churches of Arabia and Syria, while in Cappadocia, at the time of Basil, they had not forgotten that under Bishop Dionysius (259–269) the Church of Rome had sent them money to ransom the Christian prisoners from their heathen capturers. Naturally, there were numerous wealthy families in Rome, but the esprit de corps and fraternity that held sway in a community so intent on helping others moves us even today.

Over the centuries, charity developed and spread in the Church in three ways: proclaiming the Word, which talks about God's love for his children; in the celebration of the sacraments, when this love spreads into the heart of the faithful; in the exercise of charity, through which God's love creates communion with one's neighbor. This neighbor belongs to one's own closest community or to the different communities around the world that make up the Father's family. All of them are equally neighbors, brethren, and God's children. This is why some bishops were concerned with the internal problems of other communities, counseling them and providing the means for solving them. During the Eucharist of each diocese, the names of the bishops with whom they were in communion were read out, demonstrating their good relations and fraternal disposition toward cooperation.

It should be said that the Christian Church (Christianity) has permanently shown three traits that define its constitutive essence: Its communitarian spirit, its charity, and its universality.

From the very start, Rome became the center of communion of the Churches, not only because Peter had been there and it was where his tomb was, but also thanks to the generous aid given to the Churches that found themselves in difficulty, thus earning it fame and the gratitude of the weaker and less privileged Churches. It was neither the only nor the first community to concern itself with the situation of those it considered its brothers and sisters; we can find numerous examples of aid and cooperation between wealthy Churches and communities in difficulty.

These early Christian communities are like a union of workers who share the fruits of their labor to help their poorer brothers and sisters. In effect, Paul organized collections that underlined the fraternal solidarity of Christians of the various Churches. In this sense, we know of the apostle's concern with urging his disciples from the different communities to be generous with the Christians of Jerusalem, who found themselves in a difficult situation. This collection and the journey from one Church to another, which he undertook with seven companions who had helped him in his request, show his interest in maintaining a continuous relationship between heathen communities and the Mother Church, even

COOPERATION AMONG CHURCHES

in complex situations, but above all it highlights his evangelical solidarity with those who believed in Christ.

In cases of catastrophes, famine, and pestilence, which were extremely frequent in those times, Christian altruism had no limits. When the nomadic Barbarians devastated Numidia and captured numerous Christians (253), Cyprian of Carthage, whose congregation was not very large, collected 100,000 sestertii for the victims (Epistle 62). He did the same during the plague epidemics in Carthage, Alexandria, and other places. After the fall of Adrianople (378), the ruin, devastation, and damage was heavy, but more important was the number of prisoners that had fallen into the hands of the Goths. Although some of his faithful were against this, Saint Ambrose decided to have the gold vessels that had not yet been used in the liturgy melted down. Using this gold, he bought the freedom of numerous prisoners. For his part, Saint Basil built an entire complex of shelters in Caesarea of Cappadocia, which became a virtual city known as Basiliade, with pavilions for the sick, foreigners, the poor, and orphans, and housing for the doctors and nurses, accommodation for visitors, schools, and workshops.

Cooperation between Christian churches was not limited to charity, but was expressed in an exceptional way through doctrinal and institutional unity. The conviction of creating a single body grew along with each bishop's awareness of his collegial and fraternal obligations, in other words, of his responsibility toward the good of all the Churches and not just his own. The minutes of the regional meetings were exchanged, therefore demonstrating the interest in understanding and discovering different experiences, and in maintaining a considerable unity of doctrine and action. Christianity thus understood that a global society, which encourages its members to exchange confidences, love, commitment, shared projects, and horizons of belonging, is stronger and more compact. In this sense, the regional and general councils created wonderful opportunities to understand, exchange, and expand ideas, and to enjoy reciprocal development by entering into contact with other traditions, sensitivities, and theological methods. The Latin, Greek, Armenian, Syrian, and African worlds were different in their rituals and theolog-

1. The first Christian communities and the journeys of Saint Paul.

COOPERATION AMONG CHURCHES

2. Image from the Caritas Internationalis website (www.caritas.org./anaut/index.html).

ical schools, but more things united than separated them. With time, psychological and political factors more often led to a separation than theological differences did.

Today, the Churches of wealthier countries maintain aid organizations to help countries in the so-called third world, for example Manos Unidas (United Hands), Adveniat, Misereor, Catholic Relief Services, and many other national institutions, and it is through these that the Catholic Churches have made a gigantic act of generosity toward these countries. A large part of the offerings of Christians of each church goes to them. Parishes and dioceses take dioceses and regions of other continents under their patronage, helping them in their most urgent need. This should not be considered extraordinary, but a natural consequence of the existing fraternity. Probably the most complete and universal charitable organization that exists in the Catholic Church is Caritas, which helps the needy directly in various national communities while providing means and personnel in the rest of the world.

Amongst its principle chapters, the social doctrine of the Church contains the "universal destination of wealth," a principle that certainly does not oppose the right to private property or to the right of nations, but neither does it recognize them as absolute or untouchable. On the contrary, it considers them means that always have to consider the needs of the common good. In this sense, it is Christianity's duty to develop an awareness of solidarity in society and in countries. Given the current level of globalization, this awareness needs to extend to the entire world with a clear aim of real cooperation between peoples.

This Christian offering and offering oneself to those in serious need should be immediate and free, according to the evangelical obligation and the examples of the saints who worked around the world. The credibility of God's love for humanity depends largely on these Christian donations. It has been like this since the beginning, based on the maxim "you received without payment, give without payment" (Matthew 10:8).

Chapter 11
THE ORATORIES OF DIVINE LOVE

Just as Jesus promised, the Spirit has revitalized and guided Christians in all ages and seasons, even in the darkest times, when they appeared to be narrow-minded in spirit or without religious concern. For example, in the fourteenth and fifteenth centuries, laypeople and clergy seemed to have abandoned themselves to frivolity and moral intemperance, seeking nothing other than unrestrained enjoyment and ignoring any moral demands. But even then, there was no lack of Christians who wanted to respect the precepts of the Gospel, and they would unite to study Jesus' doctrine, pray to the Lord, and perform charitable deeds together. Encouraging mercy, religion, and charity became interwoven objectives that received equal attention. In his *Table Talks* Luther describes an experience he had in Florence when he saw many women leave their homes to go and look after the sick in clean, well-supplied hospitals.

This was how the so-called Oratories of Divine Love—secular associations driven by profound religious concern—were established in various Italian cities. The Oratory of Saint Jerome was founded in Vicenza, and it was this model that was copied in various Italian cities: "A large enterprise of mercy, famous throughout Italy, exists in this highly religious city. In fact, under Saint Jerome's protection many laypersons are devoted to mortification and other acts of piety, living freely in their own homes; once a week twelve of them visit all the sick, the poor and the needy, district by district, comforting them with words and provisions and bringing them the sacraments of the Church. There is neither merchant nor nobleman they do not appeal to, and no door they will not knock on to ask for alms. In all, seventy people are involved in this assiduous undertaking."[14] They were aware that serving Jesus Christ in this fashion meant following a path that was anything but easy. However, overcoming their doubts and difficulties, they showed they were able to do so. We can read their objectives in the statues of the Oratory of Genoa (1497): "Brothers, our Company was founded with the only objective of letting divine love, charity, be planted and take root in our hearts….Those who wish to be a good member of this Company must be humble of heart…, direct their whole mind and every hope toward God, and place all their love in him; should this not be the case, the member will be false and a liar who will bear no fruit in this fraternity, from which no profit is to be made unless it concerns compassion toward God and our neighbors." In their everyday lives, these laypeople experienced the infinite compassionate love of our Father and felt themselves driven to act mercifully toward those in need, in particular after having contemplated the passion and death of Jesus Christ. Unlike those who reduce the religion of love to a series of formal deeds and feel better for having done them, despite not having charity in their hearts, many believers experience the importance and need of loving their neighbors, and it is this that strengthens their love for God.

The outcome of this company's commitment and generosity was the Hospital of the Incurables in Genoa (1499–1500), which took care of those suffering from syphilis, spread by Charles VIII's soldiers when they invaded Italy. Because they were believed to be incurable, the danger of contagion, and the repugnance their sores caused, hospitals refused to admit them and they were abandoned in their wretchedness. The Oratory of Divine Love decided to build a hospital only for them, and a company of members was founded to take care of its upkeep and administration. The institution was much admired, and similar hospitals were founded in other cities. In

THE ORATORIES OF DIVINE LOVE

*Next three pages:
1–4. In the fourteenth century, an area called the* **Pellegrinaio** *or "Pilgrims' Hall" was built in the hospital of Santa Maria della Scala in Siena. It was along the route of the Via Francigena where so many pilgrims traveled through the city. It was skillfully frescoed by Domenico di Bartolo between 1441 and 1444, giving us an amazing depiction of a hospital and hospice of that period: (1) feeding the poor, (2) distributing alms, (3) welcoming mothers and children, and wedding of one of the girls from the hospital, (4) tending the sick.*

1   2

THE ORATORIES OF DIVINE LOVE

5. Giovanni Cignaroli, The Virgin and Child appear to Saint Cajetan. *Chiesa di San Gaetano, Vicenza.*

6. View of Venice: In the foreground on the left is the old building of Ospedale degli Incurabili (today Accademia delle Belle Arti), overlooking the Giudecca Canal. This important building is comparable in importance to Saint Mark's Square and the Doge's Palace.

5

Venice, Saint Cajetan of Thiene began work on the new Hospital of the Incurables, intended for people suffering from infectious illnesses; the hospital also had a separate section for abandoned girls and boys, and another for prostitutes who had left their trade. The oratories were created by well-educated laypeople and often had considerable assets that were available to the confraternity. They were joined by priests who were willing to follow their vocation to the fullest; and the reason for these institutions was none other than to "sow and plant charity in our hearts." The origin of the Hospital of the Incurables in Rome was similar to that of the other Italian hospitals: "Every day on the roads and in the public squares of Rome we can see a multitude of wretched people covered in sores, some in wheelchairs, others on the ground, all terrible to look at and to smell, the source of repeated outbreaks of the plague in Rome. Raising their voice, a member of the aforementioned company asked someone to lend them one hundred ducats, with the promise of paying it back one-hundred-fold." This was how the hospital of San Giacomo degli Incurabili was founded: An authentic concentration of both human pain and the good will of countless people who spent their time and fortunes taking care of those stricken with diseases that were highly repugnant or difficult to cure, while remembering that the Creator of all things gave them the same possibility of happiness and salvation.

While a detailed history of the Church must take into consideration periods of decadence in its institutions, progressive deterioration of religious congregations, and the ignorance of a considerable part of the people, it must also note the continuous reappearance of people who, driven by Christian love and seriously concerned about the state of their own souls, never stop trying to improve the condition of their neighbors' bodies and spirits. Even in the darkest hours of the Church, when its organization was contaminated by the corruption and violence in the rest of society, we can still find the fruits and consequences of the evangelical seed, which took root in the most unlikely people, who initially seemed to be less committed or prepared.

Over the centuries, the charity of laypeople has developed with different characteristics and in different organizations. It constantly rearranges itself in order to remain united and more effective in the creation of charitable work for the needy. At times, the confraternities' charitable deeds were a substitute for the clergy's lack of pastoral action. In certain parishes that had become little more than administrative districts, and in a hierarchy that was all too often light years away from the lives of the people, confraternities became the only place where laypeople could experience the ecclesiastical dimension of Christianity. In modern times, many religious congregations offered such spaces but at no time was

there any lack of groups of laypeople who were willing to offer personal support in situations of pain, sickness, and hunger.

It is extremely difficult for the unfortunate to feel that God is near, even if they need it more than anything else. Believers can and must show them, through their lives and actions, that God is their Father and, paradoxically, that he loves them in a special way. Christians have to make an effort without sparing themselves in their encounters with others, in particular with those who feel they have been most discriminated against, left on the fringes of society, and humiliated because of their lack of ability and the ill treatment they have suffered. No matter what they do, Christians have to consider what consequences their actions will have for those who are most limited: The poorest. When demanding greater justice, they have to ask themselves: For whom? Many people will ask them to concentrate their efforts on people who are more able and whose future is more certain, but Christ devoted himself to those who appeared less able, and to those who contributed less to society; in other words, to the incurables. In some hospitals in the Middle Ages and Renaissance, patients had to confess and receive communion before they could be cured. Nevertheless, God never asks for an identity card, and he never asks for a certificate saying we have fulfilled our Easter duties. Christ's life appeared ineffective, but for more than two thousand years, thousands of people have found the meaning of their own lives thanks to him.

Chapter 12
ITINERANT MISSIONARIES

The Third Letter by John the Apostle describes his admiration for those who set out in the name of Christ (see 3 John 1:6–8), with "no staff, no bag, no bread, no money" (Luke 9:3), and who we have to welcome, look after, and help so that we are contributing toward the truth. Ever since then, countless Christians from all over the world have wandered from church to church, community to community, and country to country, to announce the Gospel and bear testimony to Christ.

Christian history tells us all about them. After Lawrence's death, the Hellenists crossed Judea and the Samaria, announcing Jesus. Others evangelized in Cyprus, Phoenicia, and Antioch in Syria. We also know about other laypeople who preached the Gospel in Asia Minor, wandering through the countryside and villages, sometimes accompanying itinerant bishops who created new communities in poor surroundings. Those who played a role in the history of the spread of Christianity include merchants, soldiers, adventurers, bishops, and priests who wandered the streets, visited the cities and countryside, announcing the good news and establishing communities that expanded until they became dioceses. The intense itinerant life of the heads of the earliest communities is surprising and certainly a sign that constant evangelization was one of their main concerns.

Medieval Anglo-Saxon monks are another famous and passionate example of those who traveled in Christ's name. They abandoned their homes and countries to spread the Gospel, teach, and civilize people, creating communities and establishing the Church. This is one of the most beautiful and evocative examples in European history. They gave the new Christians a vital, decisive, and fruitful impulse that bore fruit in the figures of the new central Eu-

ropean people and in Christian culture during the Middle Ages.[15]

With their prophesies of imminent catastrophe, merciless criticism, and proclamations full of hope, these travelers found fertile ground in the Middle Ages. The teachings of the Cathars, Waldesians, and other heterodox groups were heard by ears open to mes-

1. Basilica of St. Francis, Assisi.
The churches and their friaries were built in the city by the Franciscan, Dominican, and Carmelite orders to welcome the faithful and to allow the friars to visit the people from the city and countryside. The first majestic example of a Franciscan church is the Basilica of Saint Francis in Assisi—it seems to embrace the entire city.

sages that seemed to solve all their problems. However, it was Francis of Assisi, Dominic de Guzmán, Anthony of Padua, and countless other Franciscans, Dominicans, Carmelites, and members of other new communities, who brought peace and joy to people who were living in ignorance and desperation. Saint Vincent Ferrer (1350–1419) was one of the greatest itinerant missionaries in Western Europe, and tens of thousands of people would listen to him with admiration.

The preachers who wandered across Central Europe opposing Protestantism were much more aggressive and eager to share the doctrine proclaimed by the Council of Trent, but they were also much clearer

2. *Ruins of the Jesuit mission in Trinidad, Paraguay. The remains of the natives' houses are visible.*

and focused on spiritual care. Using a variety of methods such as sermons, lessons, and conferences in schools and universities; letters, conversations in confessionals and during debates; or with their writings and advice, these itinerant preachers carried out a surprising reconstruction of Christianity, clarifying concepts, listening to the fears and concerns of contemporary Christians, solving problems, and distinguishing the true message of Jesus from the error and scandal that had disfigured it.

America was the backdrop for a fantastic proliferation of itinerant preaching in the five hundred years since Christianity first reached its shores. The distances to be covered were vast and the colonies surprisingly well organized. However, because the population was spread over such vast areas and was not always easy to reach, it was not always possible to guarantee sufficient regular religious attention. This resulted in the so-called *Reducciones* by the Franciscans and especially the Jesuits, where they relocated scattered populations that were difficult to reach in villages. Religious or lay catechists would set out on foot to visit these dispersed inhabitants who had no contact with religion for long periods.

In the sixteenth century, countless itinerant Jesuit missionaries systematically traveled through different South American cities such as Córdoba, Santiago del Estero, and Santa Fe. Jesuits, Franciscans, and

3. Map of the Jesuit missions in the province of Paraguay, 1726.

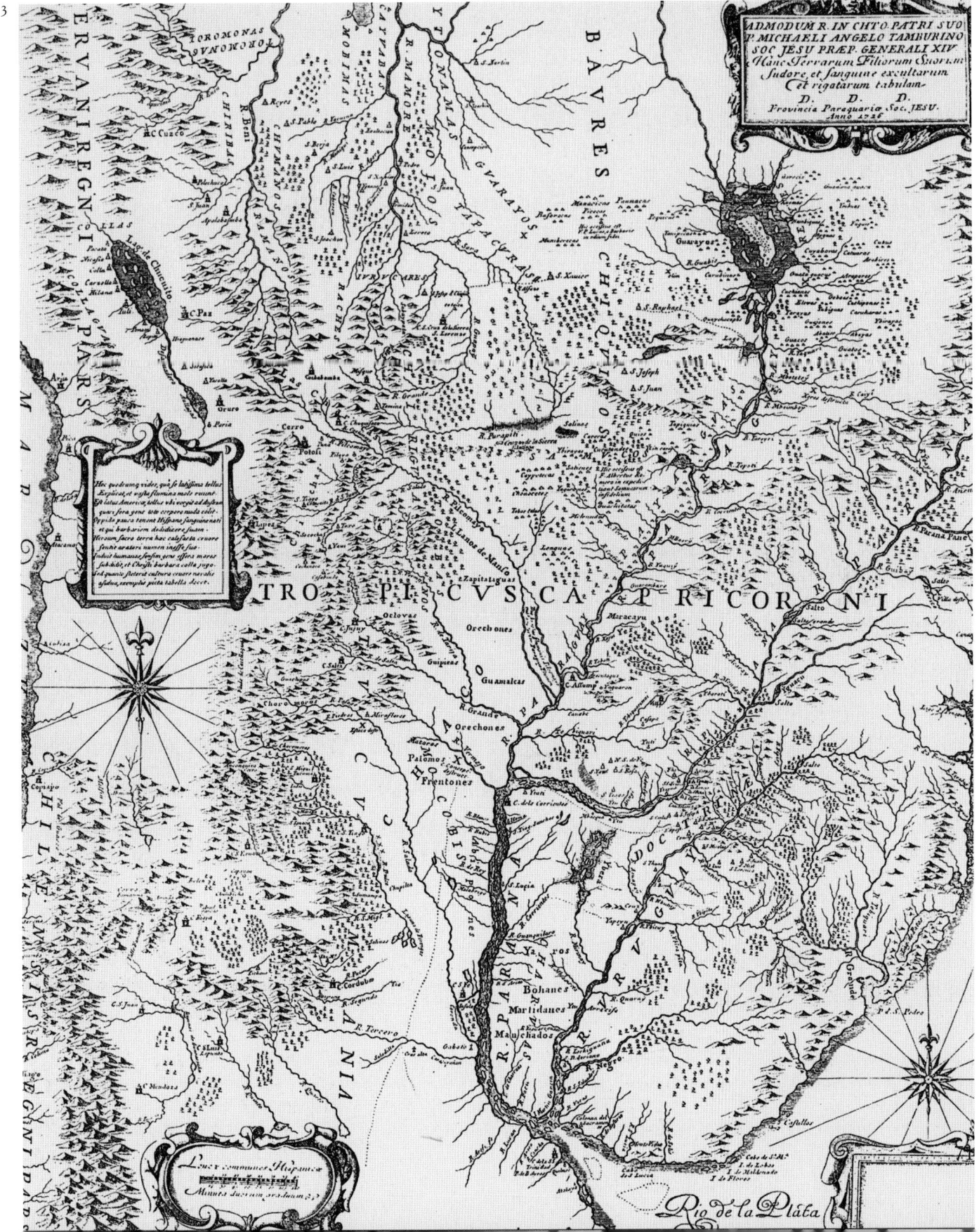

5

members of other religious congregations would occasionally visit the inhabitants of these distant places, either because summoned by the local priests or because it was part of their own apostolic programs.

In order to fill the needs of groups that were neglected by political powers, or living in difficult geographical or social conditions, some congregations formed select groups of itinerant preachers. Endowed with personal skill and following institutional programs, they preached on feast days or other important occasions when the local people called them or they were driven by their own apostolic restlessness. The Franciscans would periodically visit the Indians' villages without settling, just staying long enough to see how the Christians there were living, and giving them an intensive revision course. We know of teams of preachers based in Querétaro who left their homes and headed toward a specific region they had chosen where they systematically carried out their missionary work, population by population, in both Central America and Mexico.

The missionaries' baggage was minimal: a pallet, a screen for the confessional, a crucifix, a painting of the Virgin Mary, and vestments for services. They either carried it all on their backs or used mules. The Franciscan Saint Francis Solano is a great example of an itinerant missionary. He traveled from Cartagena de Indias to Tucumán in terrible conditions, while tirelessly maintaining his pace of preaching and administering the sacraments.

One of the Franciscans in these groups was Father Hierro and he writes, "Walking just over two leagues, he reached La Labor de los González, where he visited

4. Church dedicated to Saints Domenic and Francis in the Franciscan mission of Santa Maria de Agua, founded in Sierra Gordo, Querétaro, Mexico.

5. Cloister in the Monastery of Saint Claire, Cartagena de Indias, Colombia, departure point for the mission of Saint Francis Solano.

6. Portrait of Giovanni Battista Scalabrini. His sensitivity towards those emigrating developed in 1880, starting with Milan Central Station and the deplorable conditions of the immigrants in the port of Genoa.

7. A family of Italian immigrants arriving in New York. Photo by I. Nole, 1905.

8. Medical examination that immigrants underwent on arriving in America from Europe. Ellis Island, 1905.

the house of a poor man who with much devotion and charity offered him eggs and milk and was very happy to have given hospitality to Jesus Christ in the person of the needy."[16] What a beautiful but simple description of Christian love in its most evangelical sense!

As we know, at the end of the eighteenth century, the French Revolution inflicted catastrophic consequences on some European churches. During this period of persecution, many laypeople hid priests and acted as emissaries in diverse religious missions where they preached and distributed the Eucharist. Something similar happened during the Spanish Civil War, in particular in Madrid and Barcelona, where laypeople would pay visits and carry out the missions that the priests were unable to organize. At the end of the revolution, new congregations were established with greater impetus, with the aim of reviving the badly damaged religious network. In France, Louis-Marie Baudouin formed and trained groups of itinerant missionaries with the aim of reconstructing the Christian communities and parishes that had been destroyed during the persecution. In this way, he founded the Sons of Mary Immaculate. Itinerant missionaries were of the greatest importance for Brazilian Christians during the difficulties of the nineteenth century; after the separation from Portugal they lived for decades without any priests or other religious figures owing to the anti-clerical policies of those years that suppressed religious orders and for the most part transformed the Brazilian church into a church of laypeople. In countless communities, religious life continued, thanks to catechists and devout laypeople who moved from one community to another, keeping the religious fervor

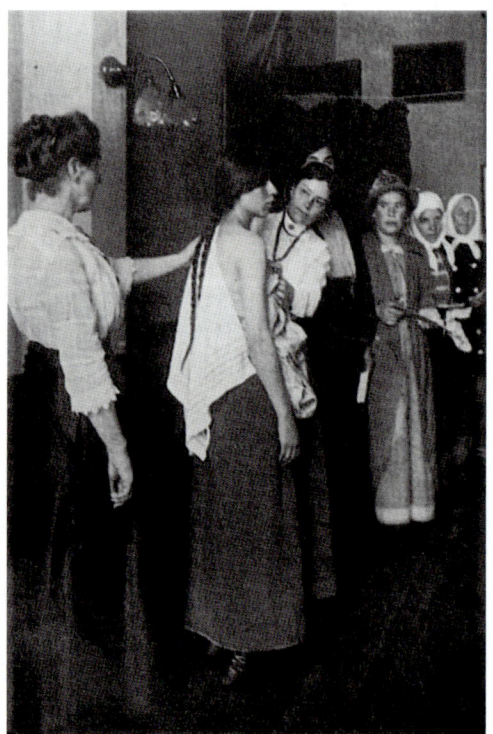

of the population alive and turning secular confraternities into important religious centers. As a result, a popular piety developed, with all kinds of liturgical and devotional displays. Sometimes these were complicated and questionable and ran the risk of syncretism. However, there is no doubt that in regions that lacked priests for long stretches of time, it was thanks to these laypeople that Christianity survived. Established at the end of the nineteenth century to work with Italian immigrants in Argentina, Chile, and the United States, Giovanni Battista Scalabrini's missionaries were in the large communities founded by their compatriots, where they would teach the catechism and traditional Italian religious customs, offering psychological support and the preservation of ties and roots with family traditions. They were also in charge of the pastoral care of the ten largest ports on the continent.

We all know that we are constantly asking ourselves questions about everyday or transcendent matters. Itinerant missionaries, people who have met God or who are seeking him unceasingly and decisively, offer answers even if they are not asked and, they also raise questions because it is with their lives and words that they give meaning to our lives. This is their greatest contribution: They explain why we are on this earth and what our objective is. Giving meaning to our existence is not only a gift and light for us, it is a sign of living, expansive love.

A more recent example is that of the African catechists who are the true heirs of the earliest itinerant missionaries that the Comboni, Consolata, Xaverians, Marianists, and many other religious communities created to fill important positions in the African churches. Catechists are the first witnesses of Christ and the first pastoral agents of the Church. They prepare us for the sacraments; they lead our prayers without priests, and reply to the countless questions of their neighbors based on their personal experience. They visit the sick and those in difficulty, and organize charity for the poor. They often work as guides and interpreters of local dialects for missionaries. Furthermore, thanks

9. *The travels of Daniel Comboni, founder of the missionary institutes named after him, in preparation for his mission project in Africa. In 1877, Comboni was made Bishop of Khartoum, Sudan.*

to them, African Christianity is becoming more mature and creative. On the other hand, in a world that is becoming globalized at an alarming rate, a world in which the countries of the North and those of the South tend to oppose one another (Davos versus Bombay), it would be a good idea for young people in the rich countries—especially those who will hold more important posts—to have an opportunity to get to know and understand the needs of the poor countries since they comprise three quarters of humanity.

Chapter 13
EVANGELIZATION IS LOVE

"Therefore go and make disciples of all nations" (Matthew 28:19), were Jesus' words when he took his leave for the last time and, from that moment on, the Apostles and their followers devoted all their efforts to proclaiming Christ's Good News to the world. In reality, this was the most demanding consequence of the disciples' love for Christ and their brothers and sisters. Their faithfulness to their Teacher and their unfailing commitment to the Jews, Greeks, and Romans meant they spent their lives preaching the Gospel, the proclamation of God's love for us.

The history of Christianity is the history of the heralds of life and the doctrine of Christ. The Apostles were the first to narrate their personal encounters and experiences with Christ, events that changed their lives and that they had to describe to others: James in Jerusalem; John in Patmos and Ephesus; Peter in Antioch and Rome; Paul who wandered throughout the Mediterranean and ended up in Rome; Thomas in India. In a very short time, the disciples spread throughout Africa, Europe, and part of Asia, founding communities in the main cities of the known world. Each act of evangelization had the same objective and the same impulse: The urgency of proclaiming to others the love and peace felt in their hearts. To do this, one will face any obstacle.

The barbarians posed a serious threat to the Empire but for Christianity they offered a new opportunity to expand the kingdom of Christ and tell other peoples of the divine calling and project. We can see this contradiction when we read Saint Augustine's *City of God*. Saint Augustine was proud of being a Roman citizen and probably distrusted the invaders of the Empire, but he was also aware of the challenge that the possibility of expanding the knowledge of Christ posed for Christians.

This is the story of Clovis and the Franks, Reccared and the Visigoths, Saint Martin and the Germanic Suebi, and Theodelinda and the Lombards. The beginnings of Western civilization are to be found in the community of different peoples united by Christianity, created at the very moment the Roman Empire collapsed and after various barbarian peoples had converted to Christianity. In their eyes, the Church presented an aura of refined civilization that was reinforced by Roman laws and culture, and it thus became their educator and legislator. During the profound religious and cultural changes that occurred in these centuries of barbarism, bishops and parishes played a fundamental role. They had to create Christian communities that were capable of becoming meeting places for both old and new Christians, in a social fabric that united different populations in their religious and cultural lives.

The center of Christian culture, which continued to play a significant role in the lives of these peoples, was the liturgy, pervaded by an extensive tradition of poetry, music, and artistic-religious symbolism. In fact, neither Byzantine nor medieval art, popular culture or theatre can be understood without a certain knowledge of the origins and historical development of liturgy. Portrayals of the passion and the nativity as well as celebrations of Christianity and the saints are at the basis of rural culture, acting as a bridge toward the higher ecclesiastic and literary culture of the time. The people saw churches not only as a place of prayer and personal encounter with God, but also as a school, theatre, or art gallery. The new Christian was characterized by their doctrinal principles and evangelical morals, and a culture that was being created in the background. As a result, we can see the rich, varied liturgies of Visigothic Spain,

1. When the Visigoths arrived in Spain at the beginning of the sixth century, they were a minority compared to the Hispanic-Romans, and preserved their traditions. The clasp preserved in the Museo Arqueológico, Madrid, is a clear example of the characteristics of Ostrogoth goldsmiths' craftsmanship.

2. Visigoth crowns, votive objects offered to the saints during official ceremonies. The religious unification of Spain took place in 576 under the Visigoth King Liuvigild, later ratified by the third Council of Toledo, the new capital in 589. For the Visigoths, Arians who had converted to Catholicism, precious jewels had important public functions.

EVANGELIZATION IS LOVE

3. Square lantern tower in the center of the Church of San Pedro de la Nave, seventh century, Zamora, Spain. A characteristic example of Visigoth architecture.

4. After King Clovis' conversion, the Franks remained Christians. The sarcophagus is exceptional, and is linked to Abbess Theodechilds' brother, Agilbert, Bishop of Paris, one of the most important men of the Church in the seventh century. At the top is a beardless Christ enthroned, seen from the front and with the open book, enclosed in the heavenly space according to Ezekiel's vision; he is surrounded by the symbols of the four Evangelists. The sacredness and the hieratic character of the image evoke Eastern iconographic designs, transmitted either directly or indirectly.

4

EVANGELIZATION IS LOVE

5. *Cover of Theodelinda's Gospel book. Museo del Duomo, Milan.*

6. *The Annunciation and the Visitation. From an important fresco cycle from the Lombard period or just afterwards, dedicated to the life of the Virgin Mary. Church of Santa Maria Foris Portas, Castelseprio, Lombardy.*

EVANGELIZATION IS LOVE

7. *The Lindisfarne Gospels, created around the year 700 by the scribe and illuminator Eadfrith. The art shows the influence of naturalism from the models imported from the Mediterranean. British Library, London (Cotton MS Nero D IV).*

Merovingian Gaul, the Ambrosian rite of Northern Italy, and the solemn Roman tradition that went on to establish itself in Central and Northern Europe in different ways.

Of course, we must not forget that our lives consist in a journey that tends to perfection, but is conditioned by the clay with which we are shaped. "Already and not yet" is the motto of our terrestrial journey.[17]

Saint Gregory the Great sent the Benedictine monk Augustine and forty companions to England to evangelize the Anglo-Saxons, after seeing a young slave from there who did not know of the existence of Christ. They were undaunted by the difficulties and dangers facing them as long as they saw peoples converted to the true religion. It had nothing to do with obtaining power or prestige, but rather with making sure God was recognized and spreading the knowledge of the truth. Nor did it have anything to do with conquest and colonization; the impulse came from the desire to tell people about the glory of God so they could recognize him, rather than live in error and ignorance. The joy of loving Christ drove them to share their own experiences with those who were still isolated.

During the Middle Ages, there was no lack of bold expeditions toward distant countries in the East, with Franciscans, Dominicans, or diocesan bishops who wanted to penetrate unknown, closed societies to preach the Gospel. They nearly always failed and, all too often, these courageous messengers lost their lives, but they were still appreciated for their generous intentions.

The urgency of proclaiming the Gospel led Saint Francis to travel to Egypt where he boldly spoke to Sultan Al-Kamil himself about the Savior, telling him that he had come to talk to him about God to save his soul. Later, a Third-Order Franciscan from Majorca, Ramon Llull, took this as the inspiration for devising subjects and methods suitable for preaching to Muslims ("I saw that the knights went overseas and to the Holy Land, thinking they would be able to recapture it by force, until they wore themselves out without having fulfilled their proposal. This is why I thought that this conquest should be carried out as You had done, Lord, with your apostles, that is, through love, prayer and the tears spilt). Subsequently, John of Montecorvino became the first missionary to preach in Peking, then capital of the Mongol Empire.

In the Counter-Reformation Church, America offered an unexpected opportunity to renew the apostolic adventure and spread the Good News, teaching the multitudes who had never heard of Christ and baptizing them. Unfortunately, the evangelization of both the Americas in the sixteenth century and of Africa in the nineteenth and twentieth were tainted by elements that distorted the work of the Church and its missionaries. With their military and administrative presence, the colonization processes of the different empires appeared so global, invasive, and totalitarian that it was impossible to avoid confusing this political presence with the religious presence, with clearly negative consequences for any appreciation of religious work. No matter how universal they may be, the extremes of avarice, greed, bias, and violence are anything but consistent with evangelical requirements. As early as the twentieth century, the examples in the early years surrounding the colonization of the Congo and the extraction of the natural rubber in the Peruvian and Brazilian Amazon rainforests were terrible. Nearly all the protagonists were Christian and although most historians have spared the missionaries' work, we cannot help but ask ourselves how the tragedy of so many people could be compatible with the proclamation of a compassionate God. Yet again, sin and mercy, generosity and concern for the rights of indigenous people, and the most atrocious egoism and cruelty live side-by-side in the Christian community.

Nevertheless, if we disregard weakness and complicity with injustice and oppression, it is not difficult for us to recognize the true desire to evangelize, consisting of a pure desire to help, guide, heal, and save people who find themselves abandoned in misery and poverty, both before and after a conquest. Bartolomé de Las Casas, Turibius of Mogrovejo, Peter Claver, José de Anchieta, Martin de Porres ("fray Escoba"), António Vieira, Jean de Brébeuf, Junípero Serra, Daniel Comboni, and Albert Schweitzer are just a few examples from generations of missionaries who guided different peoples—who, without realizing it, were in a key moment of their history—creating

8. Bartolomé de Las Casas was an encomendero *or slaveholder in what is now the Dominican Republic. Once he realized how brutal slavery was, he abandoned it in favor of his mission for the natives. In the photo, you can see the cathedral and bridge over Yayabo River in Sancti Spíritus, Cuba.*

9. A detail from the illustrated frontispiece of the Brevísima relación de la destrucción de las Indias *(A Short Account of the Destruction of the Indies), written by Bartolomé de Las Casas, Seville, 1552. For the Dominican priest, this account of the massacres and seizures that took place during the Spanish colonization of Latin America was part of his role as a "protector of the Indians."*

schools and hospitals, defending their cultures and rights for five centuries, only hoping to help those in need, driven by the desire to act as Christ's messengers.

Not everyone was equally generous and free of prejudice or self-interest. Certainly not everyone was able to see the reflection of divine beauty in every human face, but there is no doubt that it is thanks to them that the history of these people was repeatedly made more humane and free. In fact, the missionaries defended our equality with valor, but also our ability to recognize the mystery of God and Christ, our sharing in the original sin and redemption of Christ, and equal rights for all of human beings. They did not believe in the enlightened utopia of the "noble savage" but neither did they accept that natives were subjects with less means and rights than others.

The Christian invasion and colonization of many populations is probably the most painful and contradictory but passionate theme in the history of Christianity. With their actions and relations with the inhabitants of conquered lands, these Christians showed the relationship that existed between sin and grace, faithfulness and incoherence, fraternity and egoism. At the same time, the Christian presence led to greater respect for the human person, higher levels of education and coexistence, a purer conception of morality, and a more sublime and charitable notion of religion. It also meant oppression, manipulation, and voracious egotism, no more than in the past, but more unjust and unacceptable. We must not forget Hélder Câmara's protest: "How many did not treat the black people like animals without souls that could be deceived, exploited, beaten and even killed without the slightest regret?"

Charles V called bishops "defenders of the Indians" and they certainly were, many times, as were other religious figures and many other Christians who were concerned with the well-being of their souls, although perhaps not quite so worried about their physical well-being. The history of this evangeliza-

EVANGELIZATION IS LOVE

10. San Luis Rey Mission, California, founded in 1798 after the death of Junípero Serra. The Franciscan monk Junípero Serra was the main founder of the famous missions in California, which were places that welcomed the natives. This missionary work began in California in 1774 with a group of brothers; the names of many cities there correspond to the names of the missions.

EVANGELIZATION IS LOVE

11. *Painted terracotta architectural model from the Han dynasty, second century AD. William Rockhill Nelson Gallery of Art, The Nelson-Atkins Museum of Art, Kansas City, Missouri. This can be considered a traditional Chinese architectural model. China was to repeat the same stylistic features for centuries.*

12. Fan with painting of the Church of the Assumption (Namban Dera, or foreign southern temple) in Kyoto. Municipal Art Museum, Kobe. This is an example of architectural acculturation because this church echoes other Japanese religious buildings. The figures in the court are Jesuits. Started by Saint Francis Xavier and Matteo Ricci, the acculturation of the East also found its fullest expression in the construction of a church in China by the Jesuits.

tion gives us countless beautiful pages of generous creativity, guidance in everyday life, and institutions that gradually made what had always been a hard life slightly easier, educating and helping people who had lived their entire existence in subhuman conditions to make progress. There is no doubt, however, that very often countless Americans and Africans did not find the love they would have expected from those who claimed to believe in and follow the doctrine of Christ. The love of God did not shine on many occasions because sin abounded in both the new and old Christianity, and injustice, which had been denounced in the old European countries, was repeated harshly in the more recently discovered continents.

On Ignatius of Loyola's advice, Francis Xavier set sail for India when he was thirty-five. Mindful of the testimonies of Antonio de Montesinos and Bartolomé de las Casas, the young Jesuit preached the Gospel and baptized, but he made sure he respected the existing beliefs and social structures. He did the same in Japan, a country with a refined culture. He took his time with the stages of conversion, he dressed in the Japanese style, and he asked the authorities for permission to preach the Christian faith. He was probably the pioneer of a form of preaching that showed greater respect for people and cultures. Two centuries later it was applied by Roberto de Nobili in India and by Matteo Ricci in China.

Chapter 14
TEMPTATIONS AGAINST CHARITY

At the end of time, when the Lord judges the uncertain path of our lives, what will he judge us for? What will Jesus think is important? And what will have been important for us? Although it might seem that I am straying a little from the more limited field of history, I am actually still within the bounds of serious reflection based on the lengthy vicissitudes of Christian communities over the centuries, with its multitude of members who will be studied and recognized depending on their ability to love. This reflection has to take into consideration our situation, culture, and sensitivity at each specific moment, just as, when considering the history of Israel, we judge human action in accordance with the slow evolution and purification of the lifestyle and religious sensitivity, while always accompanied and guided by the prophets and decrees of God.

Over the centuries certain priorities and options that helped structure the ecclesiastical organization and community life have been left by the wayside, and there is no doubt that during this laborious and discontinuous process, doctrinal orthodoxy, liturgical norms, and ecclesiastical laws were absolutely essential. Although there is no doubt that, in theory and practice, charity has always been proposed and defended in preaching and doctrine as a fundamental element of Christianity, we have to ask ourselves how fundamental and widely practiced it really was. In fact, deviations in the doctrine and liturgy were repressed both severely and rapidly, but this urgency and need does not seem to have been that strong in the field of charity; rebukes, punishments, or excommunication for acts against charity were scarce. Charity was the subject of much preaching but putting it into practice does not seem to have been of equal importance in institutional life. There were several aspects and occasions when the substance of charity seems to have been mistreated, cast aside, or sidestepped without either the religious authorities or community doing anything immediately (I am well aware that we can all remember plenty of examples).

A religion such as Christianity, which has experienced the cruelty of the intolerance of the Roman Empire authorities, should not have shown the same intolerance—this time against paganism—after having become the main, protected religion. Neither should it have acted with intolerance and violence toward different sensitivities and interpretations that came from its own breast.

Even if we take into account all possible explanations, the Inquisition was a contradiction to a religion that defends freedom of belief and relationships based on fraternity and the reciprocal love of its members. Although only the Spanish Inquisition has remained in the historical memory, the truth is that the inquisitional attitude and mechanism remained active in all Christian churches, while its organization remained in the Catholic Church for four centuries. This intolerance also existed in other religions and in other circles of society, and it is still present in many places today, in what are regarded as democratic parties for a start. However, we Christians have to ask ourselves whether our religion does not compel us to act differently. Obviously, this is not a case of not having a defined identity but rather of understanding and considering other stories and other dynamics, which were recognized by God himself when he became incarnate in a concrete people without meaning that the value of salvation was no longer universal.

In fact, this intolerance has often led to fundamentalism and integralism, the internal divisions in sects and sectarianism that impoverish, so that Christianity,

TEMPTATIONS AGAINST CHARITY

1. Peter Paul Rubens (1577–1640), Triumph of the Church. *Museo Nacional del Prado, Madrid.*
Holding the Eucharist and with the tiara held above her by an angel, a woman is being transported on a chariot, the horses of which are led by the Virtues, the weight of which is crushing Heresy. An angel on horseback gives the keys to Saint Peter who is under an awning, a baldachin in the liturgical language and symbol of the basilicas, as a clear indication that this is the exaltation of the Roman Church.

TEMPTATIONS AGAINST CHARITY

2–3. Two starkly contrasting images. In the first (2) Vincenzo Carducci depicts the expulsion of the Moriscos from Spain. Following the Reconquista in 1492, the Muslims from the South of Spain were forced to convert. One century later, those who refused would be expelled. The same happened with the Jews. These are examples of the inability of different cultures and religions to live together. The second image (3) shows the celebration of the feast of Saint Anthony in Guarayos, Bolivia. The Catholic Church values the local traditions of the Indians, in full compliance with the teachings of the Second Vatican Council.

a fundamentally universal religion, has often been reduced to subjective visions and an irrevocable condemnation of other religious sensibilities, interpretations, and religious experiences. All too often Christians in different conditions have identified their own psychology and judgment with the absolute truth, despising and persecuting those who they thought were different.

This fratricidal fight amongst Christians was clearly against the Gospel. For centuries, more importance was given to the cultural model or Church model than to Christ, the true source and foundation of our faith. On the other hand, Christ's admonition that those who are not against us are with us was ignored. For a long time the Orthodox preferred to suffer the tyranny of the Turks rather than tolerate the Catholics, Protestants thought that Catholics were worse than atheists, and Catholics believed that Protestant churches were filled with wickedness and lies, convinced they had disfigured and corrupted the Christian doctrine. There is no doubt that this tribal, parochial spirit was also present in nations, clans, and populations with different languages or customs, but we are convinced that the Gospel is calling us all to unity and community, regardless of these differences. Once again, Jesus' command, "But you are not to be like that," forces us to judge and act differently. Nevertheless, it is clear that on many occasions the spontaneous ways in which we act have had more effect than Evangelical advice.

The treasures of the Church, the gold and precious stones, the lavish liturgical fittings in churches and cathedrals, raise serious questions about their actual necessity and extravagance when too many people have barely enough means to survive. The argument that nothing is too excessive for God is spurious. Christ chose not to have a place to lay down his head at night, and it is unacceptable that his followers remain idle in the face of their own brothers' misery while the vessels of the temple are full of gold and precious stones.

It is difficult to reconcile these clerical principles, which were so quickly established in the Church and have remained as such today, with a society of equals, in which we are all meant to be the children of the same God, have the same rights, and in which the person in charge has to be at the service of the community. The clergy quickly acquired many privileges so, as in the rest of the world, the community split into different classes and categories.

In *Lumen Gentium*, the Second Vatican Council seems to have changed direction, emphasizing the fundamental importance of the people of God in the conception and description of what the Church actually is, in contrast to a tradition that originated from hierarchy as the founding element of the community of believers. Moving in this direction the Church is focusing on the Christian as a baptized figure and therefore on the substantial element that is common to all believers, prior to any diversity of either function or vocation. In this way, it is easier to claim that power is identified in the Church as service, and being at everyone's disposal. Nevertheless, although the doctrine has become clearer, the practice has still maintained many ways of government and leadership that are difficult to reconcile with the teachings of Jesus.

In other words, there is no doubt that within the community of believers, in its organization and ways of operating, we continue to find too many forms, habits, and customs of power that appear mundane and not at all evangelical. In his letter, James the Apostle had already drawn attention to the tendency that existed in those years of giving the best places in the liturgical assembly to those who had greater means and prestige and therefore neglecting their more humble brothers and sisters.

The rediscovery of the importance of *diakonía* in council discussions, not only for the personal life of Christians but also for the approach and organization of the community, had enormous consequences. Regarding the internal structure of the Church and its relations with society, the idea of *diakonía* requires a reassessment of the attitudes and meaning of ecclesiastic institutions, beginning with a critical study of temporal models in which such institutions actually meet social needs. Centuries of accumulating material wealth led St. Robert Bellarmine to compare the Church to the Kingdom of France, with the terrible consequences we are familiar with. On the other hand, the introduction in the documents of the Second Vatican Council of the concept of communion in the conception of what the Church is, together with the concept of service and *diakonía,* should have led to a change in the conception of the structures, the excessively juridical connotation of its relations and its conception of moral. "Power and Love" was the title of a letter Jacques Maritain sent to Paul VI. Everything in this world would change if power were conceived as love and service, as Jesus had advised.

Furthermore, I would like to point out that one of the temptations against charity is the strength of inertia within the Church. We are all aware of how hard it is to change centuries-old customs that have become a lifestyle hardly consonant with the Gospel, but how can we preserve interior freedom and spiritual and material poverty in an organization that has more than a billion members? It is also difficult to accept that we can live coherently with the mystery of poverty under the appearance of prestige and luxury.

In reality, the most serious temptation for charity is mediocrity. Remaining lukewarm, being neither hot or cold, out of fear of losing something that seems to offer security and confidence, we feel we must not expose ourselves, we must not makes ourselves ridiculous or let ourselves be seen as we really are. This is the temptation to hide behind the law, behind regulations, and traditions to free ourselves of the need to be generous, creative, and radical in the expression of our faith. With this attitude, we are unable to face the fundamental problems besieging us: The fall in vocations, the role of women, the inability to attract young people, the particularism of the communities, and the gerontocracy of authorities. In fact, those who are mediocre and lack humility are unable to listen. They hide behind a tradition from the past because they do not feel they are capable of responding to the signs of the times with greatness.

If we are to contemplate history with serenity, we need to be able to appreciate the countless cases in which Christians showed they were the Teacher's faithful followers, overcame the temptation of power and egoism, and acted as good Samaritans, good citizens, and Christians who loved their brothers and sisters, like the children of God who distributed his gifts without any favoritism. For the same reason, we have to recognize the dark pages in our history. We believe that Jesus is in the Eucharist because he told us so, but we do not always accept in practice that Jesus is also in every poor person, although he told us very clearly. Unconsciously, we accept the words of Jesus that cost us less, even though it would make more sense to ask him: "Lord, what do you want me to do?"

In *The Betrothed* the protagonist Renzo is fleeing from his persecutors when he meets three people "as pale as death," holding hands in silence. Renzo gives them the little he has left. The author, Alessandro Manzoni, says that at this moment he felt great confidence in the future (ch. 17). Generosity is always a project of the future.

Chapter 15
MONASTICISM

Being in the world without being of the world. This is the remarkable paradox of monasticism, of those Christians who have abandoned the world so they are more able to follow Jesus, put into practice the teachings of Christ, and apply the Lord's advice to Nicodemus to their own lives: "No one can see the kingdom of God unless he is born again." Being born again, changing the criteria and values that seem the most natural to us, that protect our egoism and often our wrongs, and becoming a new person: This is God's project for us. Obviously, this does not mean they despise the world God created, but are showing him the love that God has for us.

They withdrew into the desert, where they fasted in solitude. They stopped participating in the economy, and neither used nor were interested in money; they had no possessions and lived in total austerity. We cannot all live like this, but these monks in the desert showed us that a different way of living is possible: without regarding things as yours or mine;

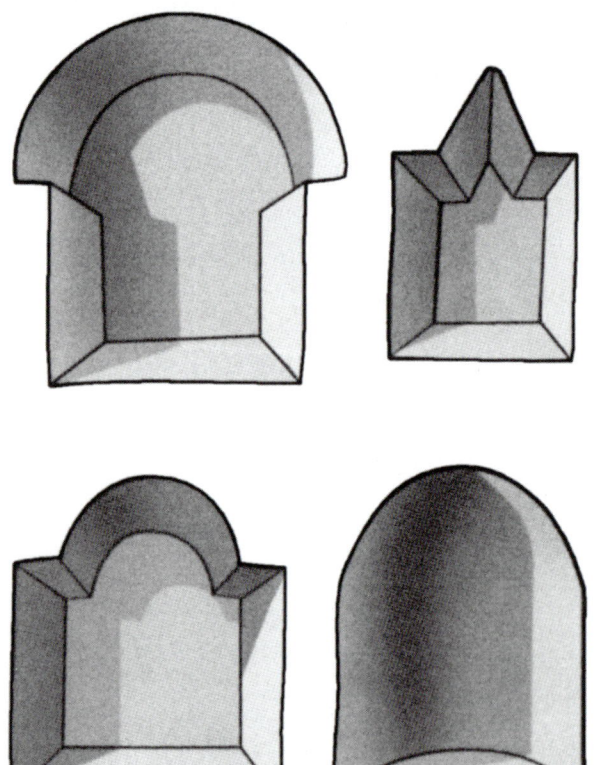

2

1–3. Aerial view of the ruins in the Kellia desert, south of Alexandria in Egypt (1). Based on the ruins, it has been calculated that there were 1,600 hermitages, each with several cells. The hermits began to arrive around the middle of the fourth century, initially living in bare cells that were then later better designed (2–3). The monks' disciples could stay in nearby cells. The life was a mix of solitary and community life, the monks coming together for the Eucharist.

3

4

5

4–5. Fifth-century architecture was less simple and more developed. The hermitages became more complex and had high walls to protect them against the desert winds.

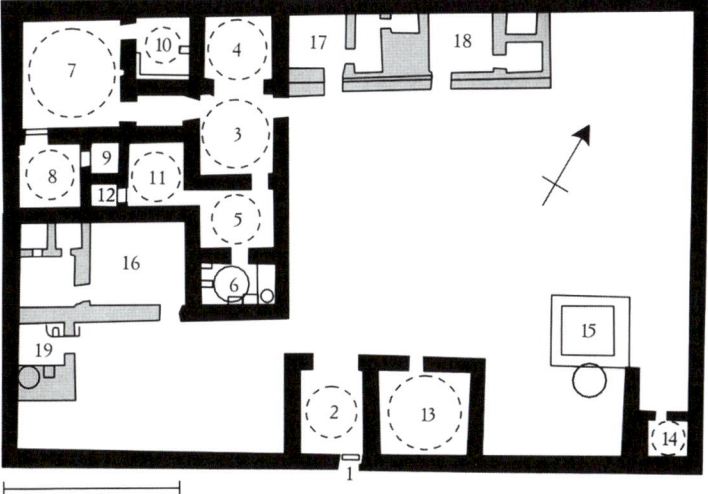

6

6. Plan of the Qusur al Izayla 48 hermitage.
In black: First phase (sixth century).
In gray: Second phase (seventh century).
1–2. Entrance and vestibule
3–4. Reception rooms
5. Service room
6. Kitchen
7. Abbot's oratory.
8. Abbot's bedroom.
9. Storeroom
10. Abbot's workroom
11. Disciple's room
12. Storeroom
13. Warehouse
14. Latrines
15. Well
16–18 Hermits' living area
19. Kitchen

7. *Saint Benedict assisted by the angel, with a book of the* Rule *presented by Abbot Giovanni I. Miniature from the manuscript handwritten in Capua over the years by Abbot Giovanni (914–934) with* The Rule of Saint Benedict *and other texts. Montecassino, Abbey Archive, cod. Casin. 175, p. 2.*

without feeling the need to accumulate objects or goods out of fear for the future or ambition, even more aware of the fact the God our Father was with them, perhaps because they devoted more time to him or perhaps because they could listen to him without being disturbed by the noise of this world. Those who shared this life would pray together and welcome visitors with the intention of showing them the path that led to Christ. They were conscious that those who came because they were attracted by their fame yearned to find a world in which they could purify and renew themselves: tranquility, fasting, silence, and solitude. This is why, although visitors disturbed their concentration, they devoted some of their precious time to teaching them the path to salvation.

"But you are not to be like that," Jesus said to his disciples, as an individual but common criterion for their behavior. If you want to follow Jesus, you have to be born again, so that while we are living in the world, we can dominate it without letting it influence us. This is the huge Christian paradox, the danger or task that is constantly present in the life of the Church: Being immersed in the world without being worldly, and without worldly things dominating us. It was against this temptation that the Fathers of the desert fought, and throughout history monks have continued to fight, showing us the possibility and importance of being evangelizers without falling into the trap of the mediocrity of the values that dominate the world.

When monks pray that God's will be done, on earth as it is in heaven and in Christ, it is at that very moment that the smallest and most ordinary human being becomes something inexpressible and magnificent. At that moment, our lives are transformed and the love of God shines in them. And it is this transformation that reveals the Epiphany and presence of God in the world.

These statements are not theories but the history of Christians. In a series of short rules, Saint Basil (329–379) established the guidelines monks had to follow if they were to put into practice their love for God and for their neighbor. On the one hand, they had to display this love by offering a good example and praying, and on the other, through manual labor, teaching, helping the sick, and so on. Saint Basil wanted his monks to do charitable works, helping the sick, assisting travelers with lodgings, looking after orphans, and educating children. *Ora et labora* is the motto Saint Benedict offered his monks. For monks, these two names have therefore always played a key role in their lives. Their work expanded to various sectors and is expressed in different ways, but what they all have in common is the well-being of those in need. Saint Augustine concludes his *Rule* with a prayer to the Lord that the monks observe it with love, "not as servants living under the law, but as persons living in freedom under grace." "With love," *cum dilectione*, is the characteristic of a monk's life that is lived under the sign of Christianity.

Saint Benedict (480–547) devoted chapter 53 in his *Rule* to how visitors should be welcomed and this went on to have considerable influence in the history of Christianity, "Let all guests who arrive be received like Christ, for he is going to say: 'I came as a guest, and you received Me.' And to all let due honor be shown." Extending hospitality to guests, in particular to the poor, became extremely important in monastic life. In the papers regarding the foundation of Cluny (909), William of Aquitaine says, "I wish that, with the best intentions, every day works of compassion be carried out toward the poor, the needy, guests and pilgrims." Hospitality has characterized Benedictine life ever since the sixth century. Not only do the guests receive, they also give. They give life to the monastery, saving it from the danger of being barrenly turned inward.

Monasteries become places to welcome the poor, especially in times of disaster, for example during the frequent, terrible famines that reduced large numbers of the population to absolute misery; their only hope lay in the monks' help. The monks' relation-

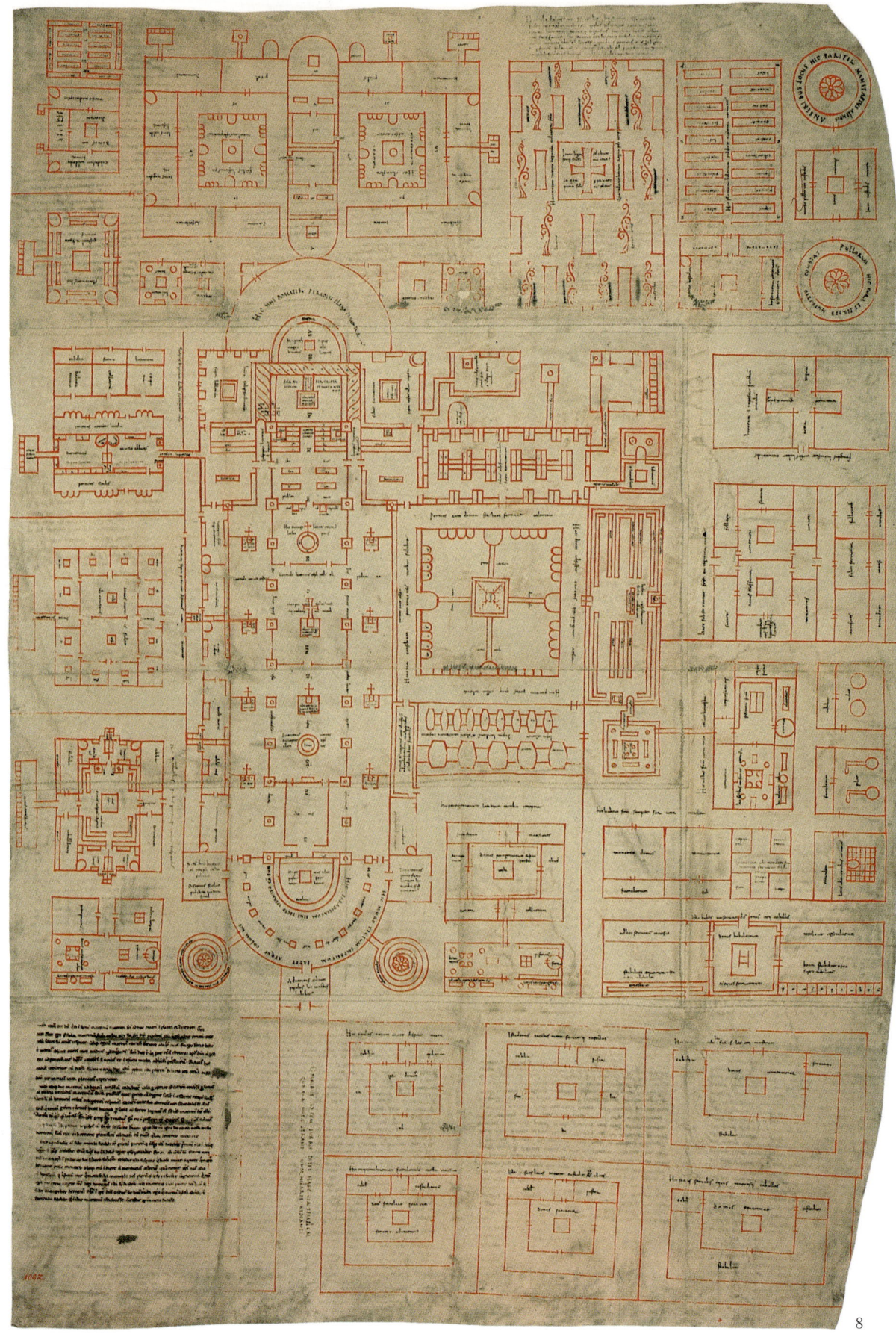

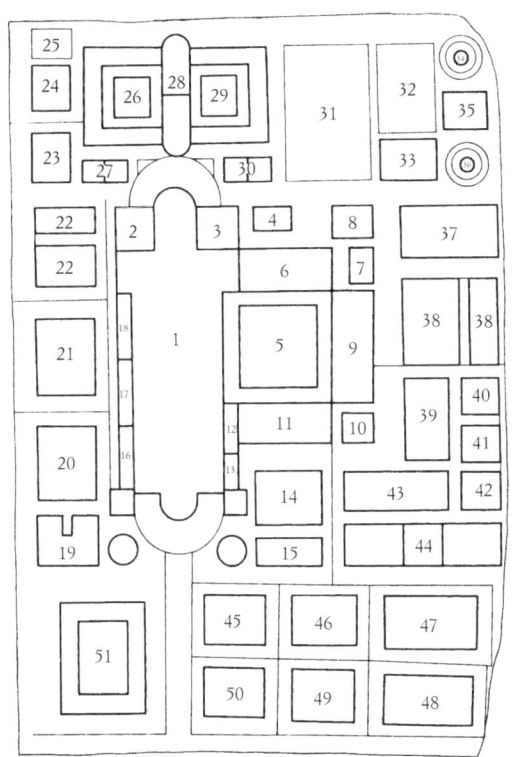

8–9. *A plan on five sheets of parchment sewn together, (8) datable to 820–830 (cod. 1092) from St. Gall's in Switzerland. It is believed to be a plan of the monastery. The functions of the various buildings are identified (9). The monastery is the true center of social life, helping those who are both spiritually and materially in need.*
1. Church; 2. Scriptorium, above: Library; 3. Two-floor sacristy; 4. Room for the preparation of the hosts and oil; 5. Cloister; 6. Chapter house; 7. Heated area and dormitory; 8. Thermal room and bathrooms; 9. Refectory, above: Vestibule; 10. Kitchen; 11. Cellar, above: Pantry; 12. Parlor; 13. Room for the monk responsible for the poor; 14. Pilgrims' hostel; 15. Brewery and the hostel oven; 16; Janitor's room; 17. House for the school headmaster; 18. Accommodation for brothers who are travelling; 19. Room to prepare beer and the guest oven; 20. Guest accommodation; 21. External school; 22. Abbey; 23. Building for bloodletting; 24. Physician's building; 25. Herb garden; 26. Hospital; 27. Kitchen and thermal room for hospital and building for bloodletting; 28. Double chapel for the hospital and novitiate; 29. Novitiate; 30. Kitchen and thermal room for novitiate; 31. Cemetery and orchard; 32. Vegetable garden; 33. Gardener's house; 34. Courtyard for geese; 35. Janitor's house; 36. Courtyard for chickens; 37. Granary; 38. Workshops; 39. Kitchen and monks' brewery; 40. Windmill; 41. Mortar room; 42. Drying room; 43. Granary and cooper's room; 44. Shed for bulls and stables; 45. Sheepfold; 46. Towers; 47. Barn for goats; 48. Cattleshed; 49. Stable; 50. Barn for pigs; 51. Servants' accommodation.

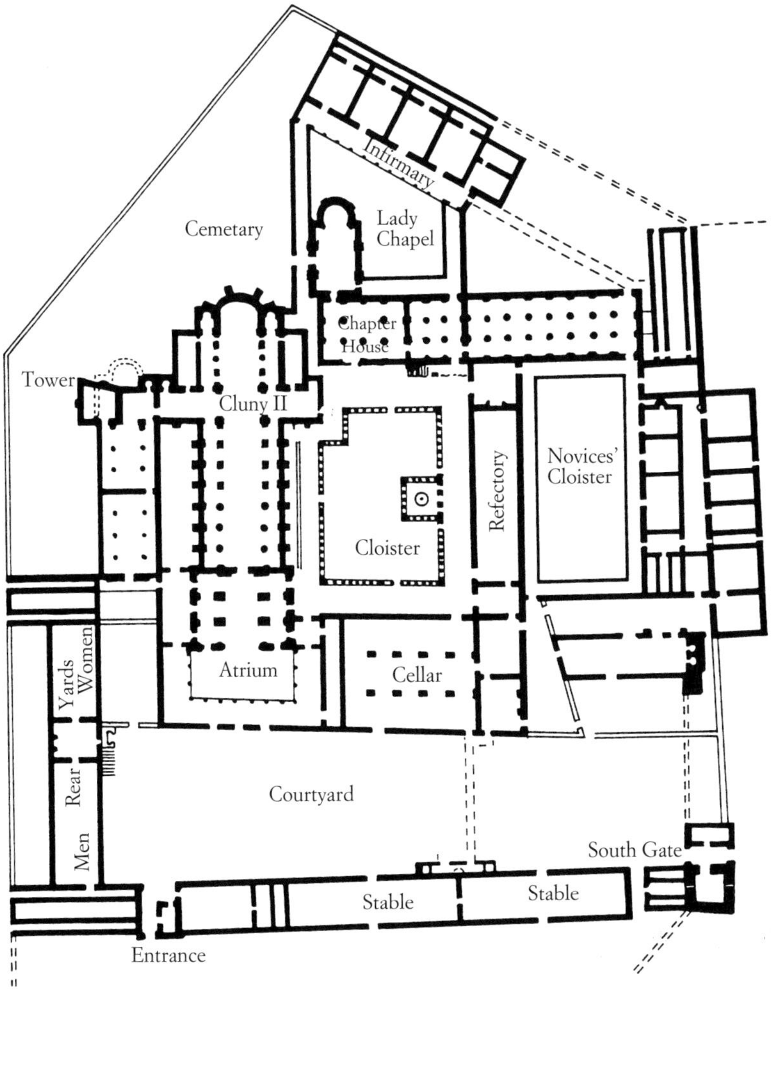

10. *Reconstruction of Cluny Abbey in 1043 by Kenneth J. Conant.*

11. *Bird's-eye view of reconstruction with the consecrated church in 1130 (Cluny phase III).*

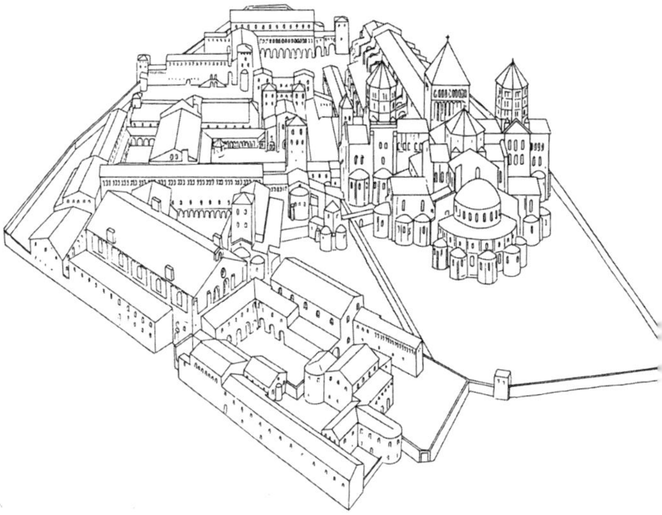

12. *Benedict heals a plague-stricken man. Fresco, early tenth century. Basilica di San Crisogono, Rome, right aisle of the lower church. The fresco highlights charitable acts, an integral part of the monks' duties.*

13. *Saint Michael's Abbey, Val di Susa, Piemonte. This is on the path the pilgrims followed from Italy to Santiago de Compostela, and that, vice versa, leads from France to Rome. Monasticism has always encouraged and assisted pilgrims, since its earliest history. In the Middle Ages, when it became prohibitive to go to the Holy Land, Cluny was the main promoter of pilgrimages to Santiago.*

MONASTICISM

14. The Certosa in Pavia was originally built by the Carthusians and was later home to several orders, including the Carmelites and Benedictines. Today it is inhabited by Cistercian monks. The alternation of religious orders has kept this extraordinary site of Western monasticism alive. We can clearly see the two-story cells where the monks lived and worked, a true example of a "monastic city."

14

15. Tent in El Abiodh Sidi Cheikh, Algeria, used by Magdeleine of Jesus, founder of the Little Sisters. Attracted by the example and spirituality of Charles de Foucauld, in 1936 Magdeleine Hutin set out for Africa, where she experienced love for Jesus and the desire that people of different religions could be friends. She returned to Europe where her congregation was approved in 1964, and established the motherhouse on land owned by the Trappists of Tre Fontane in Rome.

16. Magdeleine of Jesus dedicated the last part of her life to Russia and dialogue with the Orthodox Churches. We can see her here in a photo from 1972, against the door of the sisters' van that they called "Shooting Star," true fraternity on wheels, which they used on their travels throughout Eastern Europe when it was still under Soviet rule.

ship with the poor consisted in a voluntarily poor person wanting to help an involuntarily poor person. Obviously not all monasteries could count on the same resources but in general, they worked to collect alms, reduce their own consumption, and find additional aid they could use to run the guesthouse and distribute alms when necessary. Saint Fructuosus of Braga's *Rule* established that when the monks received new garments, shoes, or sheets, the abbot had to give their old things to the needy. On the other hand, in accordance with the *Common Rule*, anyone wanting to become a monk was obliged to get rid of any possessions and give them all to the poor. In more extreme situations, some monasteries sold their "treasures" with the aim of supporting those in more dramatic circumstances. Abbot Odilo's biography defines it as "the walking stick for the blind, pantry for the hungry, hope for the desperate, and comfort for the afflicted."

Italy offers a particular example of the interaction that existed between monasteries, ecclesiastical and social life, and the country's cultural development. We can see its religious, social, and civil influence in all regions and periods, in particular during the Middle Ages. It was in this period that some of the most interesting reforms began; some popes from these cenobia intervened in the large movement of the institutional transformation of the Church and had considerable influence on the expansion of Christian participation in religious life. Furthermore, in Italy, monasticism was the main reference point for laypeople who wanted to live their lives in a more direct relationship with God, who wanted to become poor for Christ, and take part in the apostolic life.

All along the itineraries leading to Rome or Santiago, monasteries prepared the accommodations, hospitals, or refuges used by those walking in what were often difficult conditions, both physically and spiritually. The work carried out by Anglo-Saxon and Irish monks in Northern and Central European countries and in Italy (Saint Colombanus in Bobbio) was amazing. These monks evangelized nearly all of today's Netherlands, Germany, parts of Poland, Bohemia, Denmark, and Sweden. This was not only an act of evangelization, but also of civilization. The monasteries became centers of religious-ecclesiastical life and breeding grounds for cultural dissemination. The libraries, the immense undertaking of copying manuscripts that managed to save and preserve a good deal of Greco-Roman culture, the monks' writings, and chronicles of the age were all the result of overwhelming cultural fervor. It was clearly not just a case of interest in culture, but rather of human love for God's presence in creatures and the introduction of his kingdom into peoples' hearts. This love transformed the customs and lifestyles of peoples who, in this fashion, became part of European history by introducing laws and traditions that made their conditions more human and less harsh.

Even today, in a very different world and Church, monasteries attract Christians who want to retreat to places suited to prayer and introspection, to participate in carefully prepared liturgies; they attract anyone seeking silence and the chance to meet God. In a noisy world filled with more questions than answers, many people wish to face the great questions of life and death and retreat to the monastic "deserts" to see if they will be able to find the answers to their questions there. There are fewer monks in monasteries than in the past, but they have more visitors than ever before. In general, these are not just simple tourists, or the curious. Although many would be unable to say why they go to a monastery for several days, it would not be far from the truth if we say that many of them hope to find an answer to their own unease, therefore confirming the motto we can see in several monasteries: "God is here."[18]

17. Brother Roger Schutz talking before a large assembly in Taizé in France. After the Second World War, the monastic community of Taizé helped many young people understand the communitarian aspect of Christianity. The existence of just one, small monastic community became an invitation to everyone to rediscover a fundamental dimension of Christianity.

MONASTICISM

Chapter 16
WHERE THERE IS SUFFERING, MARY SHINES

The procession of the sick across the immense esplanade in front of the large basilica marks the difference between faith and incredulity. What some people might see as a pathetic and paranoid gathering, for others is the discovery of the ineffable meeting between love and mercy, between the mystery of pain and anguish, and the human capacity for closeness and compassion.

Lourdes is disconcerting. Below the surface of shops selling aesthetically awful objects, of restaurants and hotels, cut through by the river and trees that line it, is a surprising place of silence and prayer. The people thronging in front of the grotto pray, open their hearts to the Lord, pour forth their anguish and pain, beg, and give thanks. Most of them are full of their own infirmities or those of others, reflecting on the misfortunes that afflict them, their families, or friends, and the sickness that surrounds them. It is surprising to think of so much immense human pain concentrated into such a small space; the pain of the soul and the body, our own pain and that of our loved ones; the pain of the world that only a handful face either from a sense of vocation or generosity. Everyone knows they are accepted for what they are and everyone discovers the tenderness of a God who frees them from their personal misery and sense of guilt.

When the monstrance containing the Blessed Sacrament is carried down the corridors flanked by the sick, their companions, and healthy people who are full of their painful limitations, the scene recalls Christ's encounters with the bleeding woman, the possessed, the invalids at the pool of Bethesda, the tax collectors, and the dead such as Lazarus. It is a fascinating, timeless moment that evokes feelings hard to define; God's love proliferates and generates a concentration of human love. Thus children grow, the disconsolate find encouragement, orphans are embraced, and the sick are comforted. Limited love grows thanks to the immensity of true love. It is here that God finally encounters his creation. In this meeting of glances between the Everlasting and his children, between the Generator and the generated, Mary attracts the glances and sighs of those who understand that she is made of the same clay as them, but is already in the hands of the Potter.[19]

This is what happened in Fatima, in Tepeyac, in Częstochowa, in Luján, and in thousands of other places over the centuries where humans have wept over their miseries and smiled with faith. Human misery, the poor, and the abandoned are concentrated in these chapels, sanctuaries, and basilicas: Those who have given birth to many children without seeing one of them live, those who have lived with their stomachs always empty, and those who have experienced injustice without knowing what justice is. Yet, despite this, with hope in their hearts, reserves of love in their mistreated lives, and much tenderness they draw closer to the Virgin, the only security in their downtrodden lives!

In these different shrines of the Virgin, this valley of tears seems to transform itself into a space of peace. Everything is possible there: Health, happiness, an encounter and, above all, love. They do not know how to read, but they know the story of the holy representations in which God's love for his children and the Virgin Mary's concern for her followers are recounted. They are well aware that Mary appeared to people like them: Ignorant shepherd boys, the girl Bernadette, Juan Diego, the Indian who found the image of the Virgin on his cloak. They are not important, neither are they literate, or theologians, but people for whom God is important and welcome in their lives. They only know how to love with sim-

1. *Our Lady of Fatima. Image in blue ceramic placed on the side of the capelinha (chapel), in the heart of the sanctuary dedicated to her. The image is inside the church where the apparitions occurred.*

2. *The Black Madonna of Częstochowa. The scars on the painting are considered symbolic of Poland's suffering.*

3. *Juan Diego with the Virgin. Ceramic tile, Puebla, Mexico. The image of the Madonna appeared on Juan Diego's tilma, or tunic. The inscription* non fecit *means that the image of Our Lady of Guadalupe was not painted by human hand, but was miraculous.*

4. Eucharistic procession in Lourdes.

5. Pilgrims in front of the Grotto of Massabielle, sight of the apparitions in Lourdes. The River Gave flows in front of it.

6. A pilgrim puts some Lourdes water in a bottle shaped like the statue of the Madonna.

7. A Mexican sport association procession, bearing images of the Virgin of Guadalupe.

8. Dancers wearing native costumes in front of the Basilica of Our Lady of Guadalupe, Mexico. The large bell tower complex in the background is in front of the two sanctuaries of the Virgin of Guadalupe, the old one and the new.

plicity, spontaneity, and generosity. This is why they confide fully in the mother of Jesus.

Many brothers and sisters take time off to accompany those who are unable to reach Lourdes alone. Thousands of volunteers take care of the sick on the way to Lourdes, around the city, and in the sanctuary; doctors and nurses; stretcher-bearers in the grotto, in the esplanade, and in the pools. All of them are mobilized to help the sick in their desire to reach the Virgin. The ritual bath is one of the obligations normally prescribed to the pilgrims who arrive at the end of their journey. The symbolism of water and immersion has existed since time immemorial in the history of humanity. The holy texts talk of water as symbolizing the primordial substance from which all creatures are born. Water constitutes the source and the origin, the matrix of the cosmos, and the foundation of creation. Water cures us, reinvigorates, and guarantees life. It purifies and regenerates because it annuls, dissolves, and cancels. By immersing ourselves, symbolically we die and are reborn purified and renewed. Christ chose and developed this immemorial symbolism: It is the Christian baptism. At Lourdes the bath is an important symbolic element.[20]

From the very beginnings, the Christian population understood that human love was entwined with divine love and that it flowed spontaneously from the humble and young Mary, who found a baby at her breast despite having only loved God in her short life. This is why there was always a statue, painting, or mosaic representing the Virgin and Child in chapels and small churches. She welcomed those who approached her, while her Child smiled. Christians, usually poor and subjugated to powers greater than they could stand, asked Mary for help, and God was with them.

Medieval literature in Christian countries contains beautiful stories about Mary's maternal love for her children. The miracles of Mary contain recurrent scenes of the sick, the crippled, or blind, of cruel accidents or violence suffered at the hands of evildoers; prisoners are ransomed or the repentance of sinners is obtained. They are usually ordinary, humble people, invalids and orphans, unable to react or to defend themselves. They have been abandoned and seek protection. The Virgin intercedes, helps, saves, and cures. It is the Virgin who recites the hymn of the poor to her cousin Elizabeth and who belonged to the poor both by birth and by vocation. Gonzalo de Berceo's *Los milagros de Nuestra Señora* or *Cantigas de Santa María*, collected by Alfonso X, are examples that are repeated in all Medieval European literature.

This explains the immense Marian fervor found in all Christian settings. All the Cistercian abbeys are consecrated with the sweet name of Our Lady, and even in the eleventh century, Gothic cathedrals were consecrated with the Flower of Jesse, manifesting a cult of intercession without equal. The reconstruction of Le Puy Cathedral underlines the importance of the great Marian pilgrimage: It is included in *The Pilgrim's Guide to Santiago de Compostela*, bestowing it with a fundamental importance as part of one of the routes. Actually, the pilgrimages to the Marian sanctuaries were full of love and hope that spread across the entire map of Medieval Christianity.

Mary represents the presence and closeness of the mother in a world that continues to be a mystery to us. "Here is your mother" is the promise and the conclusion. When ordinary Christians have experienced the sacred in Christian history there have been two reference points in their need to be loved and saved: Christ and Mary. They are aware that Christ is God, the Alpha and Omega of the life of the world and of human life; their savior is the absolute reference point, while Mary is their mother, Christ's, and our own, in whose arms we seek shelter, we nuzzle, we moan, we cry, and we hope. This is why, in the votive Mass to the Virgin Mary, we pray: "Grant unto us, Thy servants, we beseech Thee, O Lord God, at all times to enjoy health of soul and body; and by the glorious intercession of Blessed Mary, ever virgin, when freed from the sorrows of this present life, to enter into that joy which hath no end."

9. Musicians from the illustrations in the Cantigas de Santa María *attributed to King Alfonso X of Castile, in manuscript b.i.2, preserved at the Real Biblioteca del Monasterio de El Escorial, Spain. The manuscript was written in Seville during the reign of Alfonso, between 1280 and 1283. The numerous instruments depicted were not necessarily used to accompany one song or another, but merely serve to evoke the idea of music. However, it is possible that all or many of the players were minstrels at the service of the king.*

9a

9b

9c

9d

9e

9f

111

10. *Charity of Saint Martin. Façade of the Dome of Saint Martin, Lucca. This is a copy of the thirteenth-century original, which is now on the interior façade wall.*

1. *Detail of the mosaic containing a view of Ravenna during the age of Theodoric, showing the beauty of the palaces. Basilica di Sant'Apollinare Nuovo, Ravenna, fifth to sixth century.*

Chapter 17
SAINT MARTIN OF TOURS AND OTHER SAINTS

Christianity originated in the Roman Empire and spread beyond its borders. Numerous peoples that the Romans considered barbarians penetrated the empire and settled either peacefully or violently in many of its regions, destroying the unity and organization of its European lands. This is how one of the most fascinating pages in human history opens: The birth of Europe, of new nations with their own personalities, languages, and cultures, the result of aggregation and integration between the Roman population and invaders. Christianity and the Roman culture assimilated by Christians was a decisive element. It is interesting to consider this subject in light of the conception of Christian charity.

Sulpicius Severus wrote the *Life of Saint Martin* in 397 before the holy bishop's death (335–400). It depicts a soldier who abandoned his military career after twenty-five years of service to become a soldier of Christ, retiring to live his religiousness in solitude. Elected Bishop of Tours, he had to reconcile his role with his spiritual needs. "Martin, poor and insignificant on Earth, has a rich entrance granted him into Heaven," wrote his first biographer at the end of the work. In his *Life*, Sulpicius rates Martin as being equal to the martyrs due to his renunciation of the world, his humility, patience, and charity. Martin obtained a *martyrium sine cruore* (without shedding blood), having been given miraculous virtue by God.

There is a story about him that has become renowned in the history of Christianity. He shared his military cloak with a freezing beggar he had met in Amiens. Shortly afterward, he had a vision of Christ wearing the part of the cloak he had given away. This surprising miracle has been depicted over the centuries in churches, cathedrals, and chapels around the Christian world to remind the faithful of a portentous miracle due to an act of generosity, and a doctrine that has not always been understood but is integral to the Gospel: The identification of Christ with humanity, particularly with doubtful people full of limitations who will never manage to be self-sufficient,

2. Gregory the Great aided by an angel and talking with Peter the Deacon. From a manuscript (ca. 1022–1030) of Gregory's Moralia in Job *(Commentary on the Book of Job). Montecassino, Abbey Archive, cod. Casin. 73, pp. iv–v.*

In the mid-sixth century, Caesarius of Arles (470–543), who had constructed a large building next to his home to accommodate the sick, met thousands of prisoners from his land while in Ravenna, the capital city of Theodoric's realm. He paid their ransom by selling everything he owned, including the gifts that Theodoric had given to him. One of his contemporaries said of him: "A man among barbarians, a man of peace in the midst of war, a father to orphans and the needy." Both Martin and Caesarius were Roman citizens, but they had relationships with the barbarians and tried to create a *modus vivendi*, a cooperation and pacific coexistence between different peoples that would transform their antagonism into integration, thus laying the foundations of the new Europe.

Gradually, these extraordinary ascetics, monks, and bishops began to be considered saints even if they had not suffered martyrdom because they were considered lifelong devoted imitators of Christ. Particular attention was given to their asceticism, solitary life, and prayer, but also to their charity and capacity for understanding and integration. The devotion for these saints spread throughout Europe and they were admired and imitated by various peoples, creating new customs and traditions that would shape the life of new populations.

Saint Gregory the Great (590–604), one of the greatest popes in history, thought it natural that charity was the source of a better understanding of the Scriptures, because primarily it teaches us to love God and our neighbor. It goes against the very nature of the Scriptures to assume we understand them and expound them only to satisfy our desire for knowledge: This is Gregory's main reproach against the heretics. He believed that, although the discourses of the heretics referred to the Bible, they were ignorant of its most profound truth. The Word of God invites us to love each other and not be proud of our intelligence or create a division between believers. Reading the Scriptures is the doorway to spiritual progress. When we are contemplating the Word of

3. The Dialogues, *attributed to Gregory the Great, includes the Life of Saint Benedict. The* Codex Benedictus *(Vat. lat. 1202) is a famous illustrated version. In this page we can see six scenes, from left to right and from top to bottom: 1. Pope Gregory tells the story of Benedict to Peter the Deacon; 2. The young Benedict at school in Rome; 3. Benedict's nurse cries over the broken sieve; 4. Benedict prays until the broken sieve is mended; 5. Benedict, fleeing from the fame that his miracle has produced, meets the monk Romanus, who clothes him with the monastic habit; 6. Romanus brings bread to Benedict, lowering it in front of the cave and ringing a bell, but the devil breaks the bell.*

God, knowledge is nothing if our intelligence does not lead to action. This polarity is translated into countless antitheses that demonstrate the harmonious coherence between word and action, thought and action, faith and action, prayer and action. "It is only with the heart that one can see rightly," wrote Antoine de Saint-Exupéry in 1943; centuries earlier, Saint Thomas explained that to understand fully we have to love. Our theology and our preaching are often focused on faith and orthodoxy, without constantly referring to the love they center on and through which every relationship between God and humanity is explained. Despite this, the Christian population has perceived that love is the most important thing, just as Saint Paul did.

Of the many characters who have enriched history, we recall the figure of Saint Colombanus (543–615), who founded and inspired the monastery at Bobbio in Italy. It was a center of great cultural value, but also of great social standing thanks to the close relationships with the peasants, to whom the monks offered material help, opportunities, and rituals to live and die as Christians while shaping their moral and social conscience. A powerful network of monasteries and diocesan churches gradually occupied the peninsula, teaching the population to live with dignity, to pray, and to work, while in the synods the bishops created rules for the lives of the people, establishing social norms, recognizing political authority, and strengthening the influence of the papacy in the various regions. These monasteries cultivated the transmission of ancient knowledge and of Roman culture, but at the same time they created, protected, and taught people a way of life during those hard and calamitous times. They were shaping what would much later become the European population, teaching them the Christian doctrine and morality through rituals and catechism.

Saints are presented in European history as the most important exponents of this synthesis: They love, they care for others, they create institutions dedicated to encouraging the material and spiritual progress of human beings, and they live for their faith and their love of Christ. After their death, healings and wonders of every kind multiplied in the sanctuaries dedicated to them. Sick people visited these sanctuaries, but the oppressed and the persecuted also found protection and refuge there. The importance of the reverence of saints has been extraordinary, for both the most sophisticated and the most uneducated. In fact, some traditional pagan cults that had been firmly rooted among the people disappeared when they were deliberately replaced with the veneration of local saints. The world of divine power and mystery, capable of overcoming the ills and anxieties afflicting the population, was imposed. The Inquisition, on the other hand, was obsessed with orthodoxy and frequently forgot the conditions of those it judged, their weaknesses, and their need to hope and to grab onto what could help them in the uneven battle against the powers of evil and human egoism. For modern people, it is sometimes hard to understand this world of popular imagination, but there is no doubt that it was an expression of genuinely human and Christian spirit, generated by those fears and anxieties that have always been present throughout history.

The Church has always recognized the value of popular piety. The population has an almost innate sense of the sacred and of transcendence. It has an authentic thirst for God and an acute sense of his profound attributes: Paternity, providence, a loving and constant presence, and mercy.[21]

The entire history of salvation constitutes the vast movement of the lives of thousands of people that the Book of Revelation writes about; the story of the Church is the river of life of many protagonists known and unknown to us but not to God, a movement of people capable of integrating the finite with the infinite, the divine with the human, the eternal with history, and death with resurrection.

If God chose the personal dimension, if he favored biographies or human experiences for his revelation, then the decisive importance of these testimonies in the Christian experience is clear. The Bible is not a book of theories, philosophy, or theology, but is about men and women, prophets, sinners, disciples, and witnesses, who live and speak of Christ. Only God knows the majority of these witnesses, but it is also—it is above all—thanks to them that the Word of God has reached us and that we are Christians.[22]

Chapter 18
THE WORKS OF MERCY

Along with the solemn and universal commandments in both the Old and the New Testaments, in Christian tradition we find a group of recommendations, methods, and practical means of behavior found in everyday pastoral teaching. Its aim was to teach them about customary relations with other human beings in accordance with the life and teachings of Jesus. From the thirteenth century, almost all the synod statutes made it obligatory to teach the faithful the seven works of mercy together with the seven sacraments and the mystery of the Trinity and the Incarnation.

These works were to be expressed in an indeterminate number of ways, but once again, tradition reduced them to seven: Seven spiritual and seven corporal works of mercy. In no way was this a sentimental approach to the needs of humans but rather a way of understanding human nature, its needs, and its limits. Above all, they promoted the personal commitment to achieving a more human, just, happy, and united society. Precedence is given to the spiritual works of mercy, with which we offer a spiritual good deed and thus come to the aid of a neighbor's soul. These spiritual works are more important than the corporal works, since the spirit endures for eternity. Nevertheless, sometimes a corporal work of mercy is preferable: For example, before giving spiritual advice to a starving person you should give them something to eat.

Advise the doubtful. Jesus advises teaching those who aspire to perfection. The Christian must show those who act against the brothers and sisters and the community the right path to follow with patience and tenderness, and counsel those who want to follow Jesus more closely. The life of Christ was effectively a constant corrective to a wrong turn on the path for anyone who listened to him or who asked his opinion. We recall the figure of the young man who asked Jesus what he should do to be perfect. The Lord gave him some advice, which would become one of the classic foundations of Christian spirituality. Spiritual direction was a very ancient method that the Christian communities closely followed on the road to perfection. Ignatius of Loyola, Thérèse de Lisieux, and Hans Urs von Balthasar are examples of spiritual teachers who continue to show the path leading to God.

Teach the ignorant. Christianity is a religion that we listen to and learn from, we learn and assimilate it, interiorizing it in such a way that it is transformed into a way of life and action. From its very beginnings, Irenaeus, Origen, and other famous figures from early Christianity established schools of doctrine or Christian theology, which were not merely sources of learning but also of action and behavior. Their aim was to teach the truth that is Christ and in showing the good way of the Gospel. Centuries later, the cathedral and monastery schools spread the subjects and learning that they taught. Alcuin, Bruno, Thomas Aquinas, Bonaventure, and many others are renowned teachers of knowledge and learning. Education for the poor as a means of social advancement sprang from humanism and, above all, with the advent of Baroque spirituality, was marked by a generalized sensitivity toward the disinherited. Numerous religious congregations originated from the desire to impart these teachings to the poorest, starting with the one founded by Saint Joseph Calasanz. After the French Revolution and, above all, during the Industrial Revolution, men and women suffered the anguish of seeing their children growing up in inhumane conditions. They wanted to offer them education and the means to escape their closed and strictly partitioned environments,

THE WORKS OF MERCY

1. *Catechism lesson in an Andean village in Peru. Christian teaching must respect local cultural traditions and consider them a help rather than a hindrance when spreading the Gospel.*

whose barriers could only be broken by money or education.

Admonish sinners. Jesus offered a series of rebukes and corrections that had to be taught to those who err, sin, or infringe the laws. Every believer has to help the sinful or those who behave illicitly because, in a certain sense, we are all responsible for everyone. In extreme cases, the whole community works as a single body, first with words, advice, and persuasion, and lastly, if the sinner shows no sign or repentance, with the definitive castigation of excommunication. Saint Alphonsus Liguori (1696–1787), Saint John Vianney (1786–1859), Pier Giorgio Frassati (1901–1925), and countless priests and laypeople of high reputation directed and cleansed the conscience of many believers who turned to them either in the confessional, in spiritual direction, or in conversations about personal problems.

Comfort the afflicted. We cannot forget the disappointment and sadness that oppress many people around us, sometimes because they cannot sense the transcendent. The revelation of the evangelical

Good News is essentially joyous, happy, and full of hope. Christ explains our origins and our goal. He is the Alpha and Omega of humanity. In reality, Christians should not be sad, because we are full of a deep happiness. Blaise Pascal writes: "Only the Christian religion renders humans amiable and happy at the same time." This is why all sadness is inexplicable in a Christian, and needs to be healed, overturned. "Rejoice in the Lord always; again I will say, Rejoice. Let your gentleness be known to everyone. The Lord is near" (Phil 4:4–5). Every believer has to give reason for their happiness and transmit it to others.

Forgive offenses. "An eye for an eye" represents one of the most deeply rooted reactions. Faced with a spontaneous need to respond to every act of violence, every insult, and every assault blow for blow, Jesus expresses one of the most arduous principles of human anthropology: Forgiving seventy times seven, turning the other cheek, responding to ill with good. Forgiveness is an attribute of God and a way of judging in accordance with the Our Father.

Patiently forbear tiresome people. The Mystical Body implies a constant ebb and flow between its members. Each one of us possesses our own peculiarities and has received different talents. At no time should we become proud of our qualities, because they are gifts and are not due to our own merit. It is therefore fitting that we accept the pettiness and limitations of others with patience and fraternal love. In reality, nobody is so perfect that they do not have their own faults.

Pray to God for the living and the dead. The Our Father is a choral, community prayer. We ask for something for ourselves and we give thanks for the gifts received. We pray to God for our dead, and those of the community; by name The Eucharist is always the Christian people's prayer for itself, a prayer to the Father through the intercession of the Son. Prayer for the dead is one of the oldest rituals of humanity, but in Christianity the death and resurrection of Christ is its reference point, an image and a foreshadowing of our own. In each Eucharist we pray in the name of the living and the dead and give thanks to God for being the Living, the God of the living, in whose arms we are all reunited.

Works of corporal mercy echo the exhortations of Jesus in chapter 25 of the Gospel according to Matthew regarding Judgment Day, in which Jesus is identified with the sick, the hungry, the naked, and the outsider. Corporal works reflect the conviction that Christians cannot live by keeping our own spirit and concerns far from the sufferings and difficulties of others (Ps 72 [73]), because those who abandon others abandon God.

The expression of this theme in art is limited to some of the schools of the north, generally created for hospitals or the seats of charitable confraternities. Caravaggio's canvas for the Pio Monte della Misericordia in Naples is unique in its conception and realization, as it illustrates in a single image the seven corporal works of mercy with the aid of examples taken from daily life, from the Bible, and from the lives of saints.

Feed the hungry. "And the crowds asked him, 'What then should we do?' In reply he said to them, 'Whoever has two coats must share with anyone who has none; and whoever has food must do likewise'" (Luke 3:10–11). In the course of the history of Christianity, parishes, monasteries, and religious houses have fed those in need. In numerous churches, bread was distributed to the hungry who attended the catechism lesson and who behaved well.

Give drink to the thirsty. In the bible, the desert is a symbol of the human condition. When they were without water, the people of Israel complained to Moses because they were dying of thirst and hunger. God procured water and manna, saving them from their distress. The Christian community imitates God's action, not permitting anyone to suffer from hunger and thirst, the main impediments to human development, to perish.

Clothe the naked. Thanks to the association Caritas, parishes in many cities collect used and new clothing

2. *Charity of Saint Anthony,* attrib. Maestro dell'Osservanza. *Detail of the Altar of Anthony the Abbot, ca.1440, from the Church of Saint Augustine, Siena. National Gallery of Art, Washington.*

3. *Colantonio. Detail of one of the panels of the altar step of the* Polyptych of Saint Vincent Ferrer, *fifteenth century. From the Church of Saint Peter the Martyr in Naples, the work is housed in the National Gallery of Capodimonte. Ferrer, a Dominican, was famous for his miraculous charitable works. We can recognize him thanks to his raised right hand, a gesture of the preacher.*

in order to give a coat or some bedding to those in difficulty. Saint Martin shared his cloak with a pauper, and Saint John of God did the same. Human dignity requires us to be dressed with dignity. Our fraternal sympathy means we ensure that our neighbor does not suffer from the weather.

Accommodate pilgrims. Accommodations for pilgrims and travelers were established first in Jerusalem and Rome, and then elsewhere on commonly used routes. Every Christian had the right to be housed by the communities they passed through. In our predominantly Christian world, this urgency seems to have disappeared, although the obligation not to allow any person to sleep on the street for lack of welcome remains lodged in the subconscious of believers. Many cities have homeless shelters that often are run by religious or laypeople of Catholic Action.

Visit the sick. Jesus assiduously visited and cured the sick, who were the weakest at a time when doctors were rare, and home cures were often ineffective. In our parishes today, we make sure that the sick are

treated, cured, and protected, convinced that abandonment and solitude are one of the most painful ills of our society. In Seville, Saint Angela of the Cross (1846–1932) founded a congregation with the aim of ministering with joy, piety, and simplicity; many other nuns in other places have devoted themselves to the same task.

Ransom prisoners. Slaves or people kidnapped for money were often ransomed. During the barbarian invasions, many bishops, starting with Saint Ambrose, offered all the money they had to free these people. At the time of the Saracen incursions, ransoms were paid and some Christians even offered themselves in exchange for those who had been captured. In 1941, the Franciscan Maximilian Kolbe exchanged his life for that of the father of a family held in the same concentration camp.

Bury the dead. Throughout history, too many dead have been left exposed to the elements, with nobody taking care of them. Christians believe in the resurrection of the dead and have veneration for their mortal remains, preparing burial in the hope of Judgment Day. Christian communities saw to it that all the dead had a Christian burial and that they would not be forgotten. The cult of the dead is an important part of Christian liturgy. There is hardly a place in Europe that does not have a cemetery next to the parish church. In 1975, Isidoro Lezcano established the Brothers of the Resurrection in Tangiers, with the mission of burying the dead. José María de Jesús Crucificado established the Hermanos Fossores de la Misericordia in 1953 in Guadix (Granada) with the same aim.

Chapter 19
FRANCIS OF ASSISI

Francis of Assisi, the pauper and universal brother who experienced most vitally the filial relationship with the Father, "the most faithful image we have ever had of Our Lord" (Benedict XV), has left in the memory of Christianity the most complete human reflection of God's love that illuminates human existence. He enriched Christian spirituality with a dynamic ecological dimension, manifested in religion, literature, and art, able to express his acute and brilliant sense of nature and creation with a happy and joyful language.

On the morning of September 17, 1224, on the splendid Mount Alverno, Francis felt pierced by multiple, agonizing, and exquisite pains: Visible and bleeding wounds of the Passion could be seen on his hands, feet, and chest. Christ's most ardent follower bore the stigmata of his God on his body, and in a mysterious but real and perceptible way he found himself united with his crucified Lord in his pain and agony. On that day, Francis, who identified with the poor Christ, with the Christ who was close to all, with the Christ who admired meadow lilies and birds, bore on his body the signs of his Master's death on the cross. It was doubtless a disturbing and portentous sign of his identification with Christ.

Events leading up to this began years before in a square in Assisi, when the young Francis responded to the demands and threats of his father by stripping and announcing that God was his real father, to those who witnessed the scene in stupefaction. He did not disown those he loved, but announced that his absolute priorities were God and poverty, in other words, a total refusal to possess even the smallest things of this world, which always end up possessing and conditioning us. Poverty was the means and the ends of sanctity, and consisted in the hunger for the realm of God and his justice. "I shall go naked to meet my Lord." From that moment on, he was hidden in the light of the poor Christ and was at the complete disposal of his brothers and sisters.

He dedicated himself to the poorest, particularly lepers. Before, his instinctive reaction was revulsion. One day he met a leper on the street. Francis leapt from his horse, went up to the leper, took his hand, and kissed his putrefied flesh. Having conquered his fears, he embarked on his great adventure. From that moment on, Francis opened himself fully to Christ. He would continue to be a man, but Christ lived within him.

He set about repairing the Church with evangelical simplicity, in a great renewal of love, the love that Jesus preached. He understood and interpreted the Scriptures with spontaneity and cheer, *sine glossa*. The Jesus who had called him was immediate and close. For Francis charity for one's neighbor was not an abstraction but an indefatigable engine of the soul, with which he offered other Christians his total openness and the ideal proposed by God in the Scriptures.

The story of the first Franciscan community is one of an overflowing love for God and for humans of equal intensity. These friars did not make their mark in history because of their acts for the poor, but due to their identification with and love for those who found themselves on the bottom rungs of the ladder of human society. They had nothing, they could give nothing; they practiced humility, poverty, and chastity in order to identify with the lowest of this world. This is why clerics and laypeople had the same importance in the fraternity. They did not study and possessed nothing either personally or communally. In Saint Francis' new community, differences of

1. Saint Francis and the pauper. A miniature from a manuscript of Saint Bonaventure's Legenda Maior. *Istituto Storico dei Cappuccini, Rome, fourteenth century. Historically, the reform of the Church happened due to a deliberate return to evangelical poverty, which includes helping the marginalized. The figure of Saint Francis, whose greatness in humility would be recognized by Protestant tradition, is an example that has endured for centuries.*

2. Giotto, The Dream of Innocent III. *From the* St. Francis Cycle *frescoes depicting the life of Saint Francis, 1295–1300. Upper Basilica of the Basilica of St. Francis, Assisi. The fresco illustrates a dream in which the pope sees Francis supporting the Church. It is perhaps one of the most significant images of the "Franciscan revolution." The saint, his work, and his order, in their absolute poverty, are the support, in other words, the reformers, of the Church.*

condition and origin did not play a role, invalidating the medieval idea that social classes of the earthly city were due to God's will.

Having left everything to the poor, they led a life in which there was perfect equality among the brothers, who presented themselves as "ignorant" and "submitted to all." They led their lives as transients, they were committed to manual labor, and rejected privileges, churches, and dwellings that did not conform to "holy poverty." This stripping down of the individual represented a gesture of friendship and fraternity toward the poor, the smallest, a rejection of any barrier that separated them from the disinherited and the sick. This attitude, which Francis and his first companions took to extreme consequences, was transformed into a real testimony of the Christ who has nowhere to rest his head, a traveling companion of all the disinherited there have been in the world. Saint Francis exhorted his disciples to "rejoice in the company of mean and despised persons, the poor and weak and infirm and the lepers and those that beg in the street."

Francis' aim was to teach people by example rather than words: "All the friars should preach by their deeds!" he wrote in the rules of the order, and he always observed this precept. Thomas of Celano, who knew him well, wrote that Francis remained unchanged "in his life and in his words."[23] However, for Francis poverty was neither the goal nor an end in itself, but the journey toward Christ and participation in his realm. The most rigorous poverty is not the ideal of the order, but an objectification, albeit a highly important one, of life according to the Gospel of Jesus Christ. This radical poverty stimulated so much love that it made one serve the other, worry for them, and procure the bare necessities. This concrete and spontaneous fraternal love is one of the decisive traits of the Christian model that Saint Francis demonstrated to his followers. Disregarding everything earthly and no longer loving themselves with an egoistic love, they transformed others into the object of their love; they tried to dedicate themselves wholly to satisfying the needs of their brothers and sisters.

His concept and his life ("the model of the little brothers") have remained in the minds and ideals of Christians and non-Christians as the best approximation of Christ's fraternal, joyous, and generous love, and as the real possibility of putting into practice the radical nature of Jesus' proposals. For Francis, life according to the Gospel meant retracing Christ's path, following in his footsteps, without being distracted by anything or anyone. The following note is probably his last will, transmitted to the Poor Clares, the sisters who lived in San Damiano: "I, little brother Francis, want to follow the life and poverty of Our Most High Lord Jesus Christ and of his Most Holy Mother and to persevere in it until the end; and I beg you, my ladies, and I give you counsel, that you live in this most holy life and poverty always. And guard yourselves very much, lest by the doctrine or counsel of anyone you retreat from this in any manner forever."

Saint Clare, who was very close to Francis' way of thinking, wrote, "The Son of God has been made for us the Way, which our Blessed Father Francis, his true lover and imitator, has shown and taught us by word and example." We can add that charity is a force that never becomes a spectacle. If you perform charity, it is a gift for everyone, just as Francis was.[24]

Chapter 20
THE MENDICANTS

Throughout the twelfth century, many Christian laypeople demonstrated their own interpretation of poverty in various ways, seeing it as a fundamental characteristic of Christianity and with the conviction that they were being called to participate in the proclamation of the Gospel and the preaching of Christ's Word. At the same time, the third orders and confraternities of penitence displayed the same desire for spiritual education and profoundest religious life expressed by the laypeople. While these desires and studies may not have originated in the churches and monasteries, they existed in the faithful soul of a people who experienced a genuine need to follow Christ and to participate actively in the life of the Church even if they often did not have an adequate doctrinal education.

Peter Waldo, a rich merchant from Lyons, was one of the most significant of these figures. He sold all he had and followed the Lord by proclaiming the Gospel everywhere. Poverty and preaching became two genuine and essential needs for many laypeople, following their decision to observe the evangelical exhortations as precepts. They wanted to follow nakedly their naked God incarnated in Jesus.

The expression of this feeling underwent all kinds of developments; it was an impassioned issue in which maintaining a balance was always highly complicated. The choice of radical poverty resulted in anti-institutional or revolutionary movements. Preaching by people who often had no kind of training could often result in picturesque heresies or doctrines lacking balance which ended up being acceptable and followed by those who were fed up with the image that the clergy, friars, and episcopate offered. Innocent III decided to channel these anxieties and aspirations, present predominantly in France and Italy, by favoring and adapting certain proposals that would become reference points in ecclesiastical history.

The Cathars, the Waldensian "brothers" and "sisters," the Humiliates of Lombardy, the Speronists, and similar groups often sprang from this same desire for a demanding and perhaps overly reformist spirituality that was strongly present in the Christian population. It was partially absorbed or modified in an ecclesiastical sense by the nascent mendicant orders, the most significant of which were the Franciscans and Dominicans. Dante writes about their founders in *The Divine Comedy*: One, seraphic all / In fervency; for wisdom upon earth, / The other, splendor of cherubic light" (*Paradise* XI, 37–39).

In the twelfth century, there was a need to find an adequate response to people's new spiritual and social needs. This was particularly true in the cities that were springing up, thanks to a growing class of merchants who were free from the power of feudal lords and on the margins of the direct influence of the abbeys—which for centuries had marked the Christian life of the population—but open to the new preaching of the Waldensians, Patarines, and Cathars, all rebels against the Church. These doctrines and the obscure prophecies of Joachim of Fiore troubled the soul of the European people, who much preferred action and novelty. In this situation, what could the church offer the new merchant class who did not have time to go to the monasteries, had begun to read and write, and who instigated moral and religious discomfort for their lifestyle and the nature of their economic activities?

Dominic Guzmán (1170–1221), of Caleruega on the arid plateau of Castile, was struck by the poor and austere life of the Cathars and by their evangelical preaching, in contrast to the opulent life of the monasteries and the abstract preaching of the clergy. He

1. Anonymous, Saint John of Capistrano Preaches in the Square of Bamberg Cathedral. *Oil on panel, 1470–1475. Historisches Museum, Bamberg.*

believed that preaching should be based on Christ and on poverty: "We have renounced the century and we have given all that we own to the poor, following the advice of the Lord. We have decided to be poor and not worry about tomorrow, and we do not receive gold, silver, or anything similar, other than the clothes we wear and our daily bread."[25]

Aware of the canonical reform movement that had spread across Europe in the previous decades, Dominic founded the Order of the Friars Preachers with his first companions, deciding to live as paupers, owning nothing and resorting to charity in times of need. They refused to have fixed incomes or property. They did not want to be individually poor but institutionally rich, which was the case with monastic orders, nor did they want to isolate themselves in their monasteries. Instead, they decided to dedicate themselves to the people, particularly the abandoned and the indigent. Their churches had to be as simple as the first Cistercian churches.

The Franciscans and Dominicans created the third orders, one of the most successful innovations of those centuries. Laypeople who worried about their spiritual life were attracted to these orders as they felt they had something in common with the spirituality of the mendicants. Saint Francis had created the Franciscan Third Order, the "Tertiaries," the "brothers and sisters of penitence." Though remaining very much part of the world, they undertook the obligation of self-humiliation, reciting certain prayers, performing acts of mercy, and serving the poor and the infirm.

A Third Order of Saint Dominic also appeared. It was a way of entering the cities and infiltrating deeply into urban society. Thanks to the third orders, evangelical preaching became a tool capable of creating ferment and giving Christian shape to the emergent urban society. Thanks to them, the monasteries and convents were dedicated to curing souls with preaching and administering sacraments and spreading devotions, particularly that of the rosary. There is no doubt that value was given to poverty,

2. Francesco Rosselli (attr.), Tavola Strozzi. *Detail from the Church of San Domenico Maggiore in Naples. Oil on panel, 1472. Museo Nazionale San Martino, Naples.*
Thomas Aquinas entered the Dominican Order in Naples.

3. Façade of the Church of Santo Domingo of Oaxaca, Mexico, conceived as a large retable: above the portal, the statues of Saint Dominic Guzmán, founder of the Order of Preachers, and Saint Hippolytus, holding a church in his hand. The Dominicans, like the Franciscans, founded friaries all over the world.

but with the awareness that a valid spiritual statute had to be conceded to the new intellectual, juridical, economic, and artisan activities of the bourgeoisie. Merchants' profits were legitimized and consequently so were some forms of usury, creating a society in which work was no longer viewed as penitence but as a positive activity in which workers and intellectual and financial producers could find moral justification and social recognition.

Their sensitivity toward poverty and their relationship with the part of the nascent bourgeoisie that had welcomed them ensured that their apostolate was dedicated as much to emergent groups as to the multitudes of the exploited and marginalized victims of the new monetary economy, fallen nobles, prostitutes, and paupers that the city accommodated and produced at the same time. When faced with feudal power and arrogance, egotisms, hatred, and class differences, the Friars Minor opposed it with humility, charity, fraternity in Christ, and love for God and his creatures.

Despite this, there is no doubt that the mendicants placed themselves in an ambiguous position, having dedicated their apostolate to the citizens of the cities as a response to the new type of urban wealth. Yet there is also no doubt that they managed to obtain extraordinary results in the dynamics of religious and human life in the Middle Ages. On the one hand, the religious program of Francis of Assisi, a program the saint and his most faithful companions lived with intensity, was the same as the one that Jesus had proclaimed on the Mount of Beatitudes and implied a scale of values radically opposed to that of the world. This was in stark contrast to the society of the age, when the prosperous Italian cities put their economic interests first and the political and ecclesiastical powers limited their horizons to ambition and a thirst for earthly greatness. On the other hand, the Franciscans, timid but true disciples of Francis, acted as the critical conscience of a society, which often saw them as an incentive to religious life, an occasion for repentance, a program of reform, and commitment toward a more just society. In fact, we find the Church's traditional reaction when faced with new social and cultural situations embodied in the history of the mendicants: An initial rejection to dangers and negative aspects before gradual adaptation of the new aspirations, while amending them and making them conform more to the evangelical spirit. In this way, the use of money, remuneration for work, salaries for teachers, and profits for merchants was legitimized.

In the twelfth century, two other mendicant orders appeared: the Carmelites and the Hermits of Saint Augustine. A special and, in a sense, complementary relationship was established between these religious orders and the cities: While they were capable of understanding and responding to the need for religious renewal and to the moral disquiet of many citizens, the city also provided the setting, the economic support, and the very problem of the new economic and social situation. The city thus provided the needs and demands, while the religious orders responded with appropriate ideas and language. We find this complementary nature represented in Francisco Eiximenis' famous plan for an ideal city: The cathedral at the center of the city, and in each quarter a church and monastery of one of the four medieval orders.[26]

4. Ninth-century copy of Egeria's account of her pilgrimage to the Holy Land, the Itinerarium Egeriae. This fourth-century diary is extremely important due to its information about the journey, the places, and the liturgy of the Holy Land.

5. Drawing of an ampule (front and back) that pilgrims brought back from Jerusalem as a souvenir. Cathedral Museum and Treasury, Monza. On the back are the Cross and the resurrection; on the other side are the Apostles.

Chapter 21
PILGRIMS AND HOSTELS

"Though you have not seen him, you love him; and even though you do not see him now, you believe in him and are filled with an inexpressible and glorious joy" (1 Peter 1:1–8), writes the author of the First Letter of the Apostle Peter. Over the centuries, many people have ignored the letter of the Gospels, but they have still had an elevated, loving notion of Christ. It is likely that many discovered him in the good deeds of their neighbors, who confirmed the Good News they had heard in the churches, in the lives of saints, and in family traditions.

News about the new religion flew from one place to another in the world, thanks to itinerant messengers, soldiers who crossed the empire without hiding their faith, trades people or pilgrims who traveled to places sanctified by the lives or martyrdoms of famous Christians. The dioceses multiplied, and this saw the advent of "itinerant" bishops, nomads who carried the message to inhospitable places, far from the usual paths. These people had the strongest faith and devoted their lives to preaching where no Christian community existed. Syria, Mesopotamia, and the Arabian Peninsula were evangelized thanks to the nomadic tribes that had already been converted. Living in the most extreme austerity in the desert, monks and ascetics would preach spontaneously and offer hospitality to anyone who entered their monasteries, resulting in the conversion of countless members of the Bedouin tribes who traveled along the Eastern Syrian routes. The Roman streets also became channels of evangelization in a thousand different ways.

In fact, according to Christianity, each believer is an exile, a pilgrim, who is only temporarily on the earth and lives with the hope of reaching their true home in heaven. They live on the earth, but are inhabitants of heaven. The time in between is a pilgrimage along the paths of the world, an ascetic opportunity to be forgiven and acquire merits.

This continuous mobility, this tradition of traveling will always be linked to Christianity, thanks to pilgrimages to holy places, where the presence of divinity seems closer and more accessible. Helen, the mother of Emperor Constantine, went to Jerusalem to visit the places where the Savior had lived, marking the beginning of a devout practice that still survives today. Egeria, a woman from Galicia, traveled through the East with her companions, keeping a diary that has survived, in which she described the Christian traditions and liturgies celebrated in Jerusalem, Bethlehem, and other holy places. Later, over the centuries, millions of people traveled down roads, some longer than others, to visit sanctuaries, hermitages, or chapels, where they would visit graves, relics, or the images of key figures in the religious life of those regions.

In the Middle Ages, whether poor or rich, healthy or sick, young or old, they would set out toward sanctuaries to beg for help, atone their own sins, and give thanks for the aid they received. The entire West was crisscrossed with roads along which countless pilgrims would head to Jerusalem, Rome or Santiago, Aachen, Canterbury or Einsiedeln. They took with them not only their sorrow and pain, but also their culture, lifestyle, and understanding of reality. For these pilgrims, the people and objects they came across on their way could be a sign of Providence.

At the same time, driven by their love for God, Irish monks left the safety of their monasteries in order to live the ascetic ideal of abandoning their own land, and to spread the faith on an inhospitable continent. Great missionaries in Central and Northern Europe included Colombanus, Boniface,

PILGRIMS AND HOSTELS

1. The bridge on the River Arga in Puente la Reina, where the roads to Santiago de Compostela meet across the Pyrenees coming from France. In the Middle Ages, bridges were essential to facilitate the pilgrims' travels.

2. Hospital de San Nicolás de Puente Fitero, Itero del Castillo, Spain. This ancient pilgrim hostel along the road to Santiago has now been restored and the confraternity of Saint James of Perugia has opened it once again to pilgrims.

Willibrord, Killian, and Ansgar, to name but a few. Luxeuil (590), Fulda (744), Corbie (657), Echternach (708), St. Gall (750), and Corvey (822) were all important abbeys that they founded. These proved to be sources of the evangelization of populations and influenced Christianity and cultural diffusion considerably. A tangible result of this remarkable cultural fervor was to be seen in the libraries, where multitudes of manuscripts were copied, thus saving and preserving a good deal of Greek-Roman culture, the monks' writings, and chronicles of the times.

This culture and spirituality were also characterized by the saints of the places found along the four great French routes that converged in Puente la Reina in Spanish territory, and then continued along just one route until the threshold of the Portico of Glory in Compostela. With their lives and miracles, these saints captured the imagination of the people, announcing the incredible message of divine justice and eternal salvation with both creativity and strength. People saw these saints and ascetics as the visible living testimony of the future world, and of the best way of living the present. The pilgrims wandered from one sanctuary to another, visiting the relics of famous saints from the past, asking them for hope and forgiveness. It was there that the blind could see again; the deaf could hear again; the mute could speak again; the lame learned to walk again; those possessed by the devil were purified, and every kind of sickness was cured or relieved. These healings increased the faith and hope of this multitude of pilgrims, who were convinced that those saints had

the concrete mission of helping them in difficulty and hope, thanks to their merits and the intimacy of the prayers they could send to our Lord Jesus Christ. Near the sanctuaries along this route, hostels and hospitals were founded to welcome, refresh, and look after the pilgrims suffering from bad weather or physical infirmity. Santo Domingo de la Calzada and Saint Adelelmus of Burgos are two examples of such generous dedication to the pilgrims' needs, building new bridges, designing new roads, and improving both the hospitality and reception they could offer. The *Guide of the Santiago Pilgrim* describes these hostels as the "houses of God" where "the holy pilgrims could recover their strength, those in need of repose could rest, the ill would be comforted, the dead saved and the living protected."

Boniface VIII established and regulated this concern with purification and forgiveness, innate in humans and reaching fever pitch during the centennial years, when he organized the first jubilee or holy year in 1300, resulting in thousands of pilgrims traveling to Rome in search of something that would calm their anguished spirit. The pope did not make this decision on his own initiative, but as a response to the insistent request of pilgrims who arrived in the city, following in the footsteps of the ancients who claimed "every Christian that visits the sepulchers of the apostles during this centennial year will be forgiven their sins." The request was extended to all of Christianity, as a solution to the restiveness at a time of eschatological tension due to the influence of the ideas of the Cistercian monk Joachim of Fiore (ca. 1135–1202).

3. A pilgrim's feet are being healed. Relief on the Judgment Doorway of the Parma baptistery. Parma was situated along the Via Francigena, which went through Europe to Rome. It was a place of rest for the pilgrims.

4. Saint James and Christ Judge in Majesty. Detail of the Portico of the Glory, Saint James' Cathedral, Santiago de Compostela. Christ showing the glorious wounds, surrounded by the Evangelists' symbols and angels with the instruments of passion.

The promise of "complete and generous forgiveness" to anyone who had visited Saint Peter's tomb and the Lateran Cathedral during a fifteen-day period, after having confessed their sins, captivated and inspired Christian imagination and hope, and therefore increased the spiritual centrality of Rome. It was the most spectacular exercise of papal power since Urban II had granted the first indulgence when he initiated the Crusade. During an entire year, from one Christmas to another, anyone who had fulfilled the conditions laid down by the pope could benefit from the exceptional indulgence, for which the Church could draw on the boundless treasure of merits accumulated by Christ and all the other saints, and distribute it amongst the faithful.

This was a surprising but joyful move, and a forerunner of the hope of Christ the Savior and all the members of his Mystical Body. Nothing could stop the pilgrims: neither plagues nor wars nor the huge difficulties that many had suffered. Initially every fifty years and then every twenty-five, without fail they would set out to visit the apostles' tombs.

Once they reached Santiago de Compostela and entered the marvelous entrance of the cathedral, they encountered the heavenly glory of Christ, his apostles, the prophets, other apostles, and saints. Four extraordinary angels blowing trumpets in each corner, a clear reference to the four cardinal points, have the task of gathering the chosen so that they sing a new canticle. And we, the pilgrims of the earth, are among them.

Chapter 22
HOSPITAL ASSOCIATIONS

As early as 852, talking about confraternities that were usually of a corporate nature, Hincmar of Reims listed their activities: Collecting offers for the maintenance and lighting of the churches; encouraging forms of reciprocal help among their own members; taking care of deceased brothers' funerals; giving and collecting alms for the poor; and performing "many other deeds of compassion." During this period, these institutions already had a governing body and an extremely detailed structure. In the tenth century, associations of this kind and their objectives are mentioned often.

Times were hard, both in religious and secular life, and it was with great pain that laypeople felt the limits of their religious education and financial misery, and the poverty of an unjust society in which many were living in terrible conditions. These corporate confraternities were actually associations that offered reciprocal aid and concrete help among their members, with the aim of strengthening their rights and ability to respond to difficulties and limitations of diverse kinds. At the same time, they were also in charge of the organization and financing of religious activities, offering improved doctrinal education and courageously striving to help those among them who were worse off, and alleviating the poverty of all the others, which comprised nearly the entire population.

In the thirteenth century, the gradual development of the laity's own identity gained particular importance, because of the growth of a more complex social fabric following the model of the communes, arts and crafts associations, and university confraternities. However, this was also thanks to the fact that the Church had relied more heavily on its lay members during the harsh confrontations between the papacy and the empire. In the second half of the Middle Ages, the importance of the lay spiritual movements, in their variety and diversity, highlights the malaise of the more mature social classes. This was because they were more aware of their own value and independence, as well as of their influence on a society that wanted to be released from both the protection of the institutional Church and that of the Empire. They also showed the coherence of these people who had been taught the need to recreate the early apostolic community. In addition to preaching by example, they wanted to teach the doctrine with the word, at times with ardor, reviving the life of Christ with acts and institutions that wanted to alleviate the misery of so many Christians.

During the twelfth, thirteenth, and fourteenth centuries, the people were devastated by sickness and premature death, by insufficient means of subsistence, the desperation of being able to obtain forgiveness for their sins, the frailty of their bodies, and hunger and pain. In the church they found the hope for salvation, and in confraternities, for example, in the solidarity of Christians they discovered their needs could be alleviated. There was no organized health care or social services. But there was Christian love that offered a little security and fraternal proximity. These confraternities made it possible to experience solidarity and a sense of community, giving Christians the opportunity to unite and practice reciprocal love and group responsibility. With a church that was growing more and more clerical each day, confraternities offered a path for lay self-esteem and the performance of acts of generosity and solidarity, and became institutions that were able to deal effectively with poverty.[27]

Especially from the fourteenth century on, worries about death, personal salvation, and prayers

HOSPITAL ASSOCIATIONS

1. Interior of the late medieval Basilica of Santa Maria del Mar, Barcelona. This monumental building, which vies with the city cathedral, was a work of the fisherman's guild.

HOSPITAL ASSOCIATIONS

2. "Maestro of Observance" (attr.), Funeral of Saint Anthony. *Detail of the Altar of Anthony the Abbot, ca. 1440, from the Church of Sant'Agostino (?), Siena. National Gallery of Art, Washington. The work is part of a series of eight panels on the life of Anthony the Abbot; upon his death, he asked his disciples to bury him immediately in a secret place. By craftsmen from Siena, the work shows the particular attention that was paid to death and the accompaniment of the deceased; this was typical in the Middle Ages.*

HOSPITAL ASSOCIATIONS

3. Domenico di Bartolo. Fresco of the pellegrinaio of the hospital Santa Maria della Scala, Siena, 1444. Detail with the construction of the hospital, a fundamental event that involved the entire city.

Next page:
4. Gustave Courbet, Funeral at Ornans. Oil on canvas, 1849–1850. Musée d'Orsay, Paris. A painter of the Realist school, Courbet managed to transmit a sense of community in the religious rite.

4

for the deceased were present in all confraternities. Many joined in the hope that their prayers would be heard and they would therefore avoid the risk of dependence on the good will of their own heirs. These associations often offered a greater guarantee than the member's children or relations that their posthumous wishes would be carried out. In fact, the cult of the dead is as old as *Homo sapiens*. Funeral rites are immortalized in tombs and burials. They are testimony to the faith in an afterlife that made the living worry about the deceased's body and to express this with increasingly lavish religious symbolism. To all this Christianity added faith in Christ, the Alpha and Omega of the entire creation, and from the very beginning Christian charity made sure each body would be buried and prayers would be said. Now, for the first time in history, cremation and the dispersion of the ashes result in the complete disappearance of any immediate vestige of the deceased. Nevertheless, although contemporary society wants to eliminate death and act as if it did not exist, it remains a reference point that still accompanies us, making us all brothers and sisters. Taking his own religious, sympathetic sensitivity to extremes, this is why Lamennais asked to be buried in a common grave (1854) with the aim of "resting among the poor"; in other words, waiting for Judgment Day surrounded by those who had deserved the benevolence of God.

The importance of charitable work depended on the availability of means and the ability to collect alms without interruption. Until their revenues were confiscated by the various states in the nineteenth century, confraternities had a variety of assets: property in the country or towns and its respective revenue; cash revenue from annual dues; fines; alms; other assets that were dependent on either history or circumstance. As time went by, these needs required more structured and technically complicated forms if they were to be able to administrate the substantial property and agricultural assets they had acquired over the years thanks to donations and bequests.

Congregations were founded in the twentieth century, for example the Congregation of the Fraternity for Abandoned Old People, which looked after those who could not turn to their relatives. Today, now that the vocation for these religious congregations has decreased, lay people carry out this mission of love and compassion. In the face of so many acts of generous love that can be seen in this world, we can reply to Jacques Monod[28] and tell him that although we cannot see eternity, anybody who says no to injustice, anybody who forgoes their earnings and devotes their lives to improving their neighbor's life out of love, knows that God loves them and that they, in turn, love their brothers and sisters.

Today's religious congregations are inter-classist and cover all social fields; if effective, they are able to combine the official liturgy with mercy for people while their alms coffers are filled up to be redistributed amongst the needy. The most frequently offered sanctuaries obtain the same result, just as effectively.[29]

Chapter 23
LOSE YOUR FREEDOM, FREE YOUR NEIGHBOR

With the onset of Islamic invasions in Christian lands, Christians would frequently end up under their command, either as prisoners of war, exiles, or oppressed under their power. In these conditions, it was difficult if not impossible for them to practice their own faith, receive the sacraments, or say their prayers. This is why the Church remembered them with such sadness, was worried about them, and tried to free them: "Imprisonment is the most profound misery for humans because God created them in total freedom, and while they find themselves imprisoned under the power of the Saracens, their life could not be more wretched: They are not their own masters, they consume themselves in the deepest poverty" (Constitution of the Order of the Blessed Virgin Mary of Mercy).

The zeal and passion that existed in the Christian world during the crusades increased the concern for lands that had been lost and for the Christians who had fallen into Muslim hands. The "enemies of faith" fought with the arms of war and it was with those arms that Christians had to defend their own interests. The contradictions of Holy War were revealed: It was holy for the Muslims to spread and defend their faith by the sword; it was holy for Christians to bear the standard of the cross and uphold the presence of Jesus in the world. Christian feelings regarding the occupied lands and their imprisoned fellow Christians intensified.

We must remember that the danger to their faith did not only come from the actual constrictions or abuse they suffered. Above all, it came from the attraction some Christians might have felt for Islam, which was jealous of its own faith and socially compact, or from the temptation to acquire freedom and favors by accepting the religion of their keepers, leaders, or companions. The most defenseless were the women who lost any chance to practice their own faith when they entered a harem, and the children who quickly forgot their own background once they were adopted. Rumors abounded in Mediterranean ports about the harsh fate and dangers to the soul that prisoners in Africa were facing.

Juan de la Mata (1160–1213) and Felix of Valois (1127–1212) decided to demonstrate God's mercy and devote themselves to the liberation and ransom of these prisoners. They therefore founded the Trinitarians for the redemption of prisoners. Their first expedition to North Africa took place in 1199. They returned with 186 Christians they had freed from Berber dungeons. To obtain results like this, the Trinitarians used all the means they had, collecting alms by organizing volunteers who wandered throughout the kingdom, and offering to give up their own freedom if necessary, and remain in prison in the place of those they could not free in any other way.

They also founded "houses of mercy" where those who had been freed could stay, as they had nowhere else to go. They looked after the sick in the hospitals, while paying just as much attention to the souls and the missions of the infidels. They devoted their lives to the liberation of Christians in Algeria, Tunisia, Constantinople, and Egypt. They comforted those who had to stay, converted many renegades and apostates, and offered themselves as hostages in exchange for the freedom of others and, in many cases, sacrificed their own lives. On September 19, 1580, the author of *Don Quixote*, Miguel de Cervantes, was freed for 500 scudi.

Several years later, Peter Nolasco (1189–1256) founded the Order of Our Lady of Mercy for the Redemption of Captives (the Mercedarians),

LOSE YOUR FREEDOM, FREE YOUR NEIGHBOR

1. *Arab medieval military vessels fought supremacy on the Mediterranean with great effectiveness against the fleets of the Crusaders. Cantigas de Santa María, n. 95, F139D (thirteenth century). Real Biblioteca del Monasterio de El Escorial.*

LOSE YOUR FREEDOM, FREE YOUR NEIGHBOR

2. The Mount of Joy, where arriving pilgrims would first see the walls of Jerusalem. Very often, the pilgrims would arrive from North Africa where they risked being taken prisoner by the Arabs.

3. Symbol of the Mercedarian order.

4. Symbol of the Trinitarian order.

5

6

5. Cloister of Mercy in Mexico City, reconstructed in 1634. Following the discovery of the New World, the Mercedarians went to Central and South America to help those who were worse off, and dedicate themselves to education and teaching.

6. Cloister of Mercy in Quito, Ecuador.

initially established in Barcelona by an association of laypeople with the aim of saving and liberating imprisoned Christians who were in danger of abandoning their Christian faith. The raison d'être of its members' vocation and commitment is summarized in just a few lines: "The work of liberating the prisoners is for the edification of the kingdom of God; it is an authentic service to God's people, defending the faith amongst the oppressed, carried out with a spirit of perfect charity in the likeness of Christ our Savior." In 1218 it became a mendicant order.

The Mercedarians eventually adopted a fourth vow, promising to expose themselves to the dangers of the sea, enemies' arrows, and to accept imprisonment, torture, and even death if required. As early as 1291, they had already declared they were willing to put into practice what Jesus says in the Gospel according to John: "No one has greater love than this, to lay down one's life for one's friends. The fourth vow is to remain hostage in the land of the Moors, should it be necessary to free any Christian prisoner; when we are afraid that [this Christian] might deny their faith, we are obliged under the punishment of mortal sin to free them and stay at their side until the order has freed us, which is a sign of great perfection of giving one's life to one's neighbor…."[30]

After years of suppression due to political and social conditions, since the end of the eighteenth century, the Mercedarians have devoted their attention to the penitential mission, working in prisons with the inmates, a work that corresponds to their fourth vow.

Today, prisons still house a wide variety of criminals, with different degrees of culpability and possibility of release. The mission in prisons is to assist the inmates and their families, and to support those who are released, helping them become reintegrated in society by finding a house, school, and suitable employment. Assisted by their specific training and devotion, these religious and lay associates are able to reawaken a sense of hope and personal dignity in these inmates. Sensitivity toward the problems of prisons is growing in dioceses, and the number of volunteers working in parishes and religious institutions is multiplying. These people dedicate their time and ability to communicate to prison work, using signs and symbols of justice, truth, and love as a testimony of the Gospel they are proclaiming. Christian communities are growing more aware of the problem of incarceration and are aware that a materialistic society distances itself so that prisons are far from the Christian community. These volunteers are aware of the need to offer opportunities for reintegration to those who have broken the rules of society for personal or social reasons. Let us remember that among them are Christian lawyers who are working in this specific field, and the countless people who look after the houses where young people stay when they leave prison, helping them find a suitable space to start a social life and foster relationships at such a delicate moment in their lives.

Chapter 24
HELPING THE SICK

We have been told that we have to love our neighbor like ourselves, but we should add that if we really want to understand our neighbor, we ourselves have to be able to experience the state they are in. Knowing they are infirm, a sick person is more aware of the anguish felt by those suffering in the same way. Because of their illness, the sick belong to the world of the poor and of those who suffer the anguish of uncertainty, pain, and a lack of protection.

Between the peak of the Renaissance and the beginning of the Reformation, the Portuguese John of God, or Juan de Dios (1495–1550), experienced with the greatest lucidity the testimony of Christian solidarity and liberty, in a period marked by religious wars and divisions in the West. Born in Évora, he fought for Charles V against the French at Fontarabia, and against the Turks. After leaving military service, he devoted himself to herding sheep in Seville and worked in Ceuta. In 1537, while in Granada, he heard Saint John of Ávila preaching and felt completely transformed when he heard his sermon on the Beatitudes in Luke 6:20–26, particularly the blessedness of the poor. Profoundly transformed, he felt he was a terrible sinner and began walking the streets bitterly lamenting his own sins. People thought he was mad, and he was imprisoned with the mentally ill, where he was mistreated.

John of God decided to devote his entire life, "following naked the naked Jesus Christ and making oneself poor for Him who, being the wealth of all his creatures, became poor for us to show us the path of humility."[31] John of God was considered mad the very moment he understood the true nature of God's love, when he recognized his own sins and vehemently asked for forgiveness, just as Jesus had been mistaken for a madman and had been taken back home (Mark 3:21). He made himself similar to Christ, followed in his footsteps, performed simple acts of charity by giving the needy consolation and alms, and nothing else was important to him.

Aware from experience how the sick were treated, in particular the mentally ill or incurables, John of God, "seeing the lunatics who were with him be punished, said: 'Jesus Christ let me out in time and grant me the grace to have a hospital where I can look after all the poor abandoned people or those without intellect, and serve them as I desire.'" With the help of several people he managed to rent a house, equipped it with the bare essentials and, when he saw so many poor people lying in the streets, naked, full of sores, and sick, "began to give beds to the poor people he found throughout the city." For him the hospital was a holy place, the house of God, open to all the poor without any distinction: "The city of Granada is large and very cold, especially now in winter…Because the house is open to everyone, it takes in all manner of sick people. There are people with useless limbs, the maimed, the lepers, the dumb, the insane, paralytics, and some who are suffering from cancer. Others are afflicted with senility, and there are many children, as well as the innumerable travelers and pilgrims who arrive here" (Cartas y Escritos 18–19; 48–50). He comforted them, looked after them, and gave them clothes, cloaks, tunics, shirts, shoes, and socks.

His identification with human suffering was to mark his entire life, his actions, and his work. This is why the work done by John's hospital was universal and not limited to any particular social, cultural, or religious sector. Anyone who was in need or had been abandoned had a right to be there.[32]

During the twenty-first century, these Brothers

1. *Filarete's design for a hospital in the ideal city. His design was actually used for the construction of Ospedale Maggiore in Milan in 1456. At that time, hospitals were a problem, but nothing could be done without the congregations and orders who assumed responsibility for them.*

2. *The Tiber Island and Fatebenefratelli Hospital, detail of the perspective plan of Rome by Antonio Tempesta, 1593, the 1606 copy of which is preserved in the Vatican Apostolic Library. This was one of the great initiatives by the Order of Hospitaliers.*

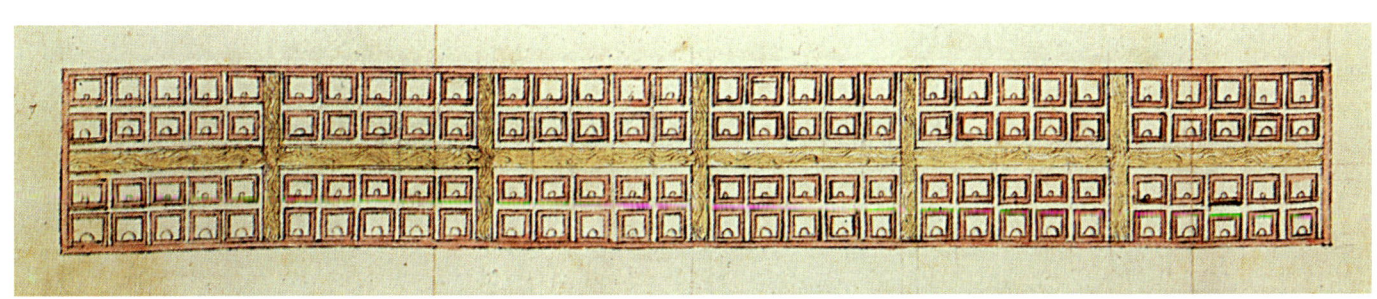

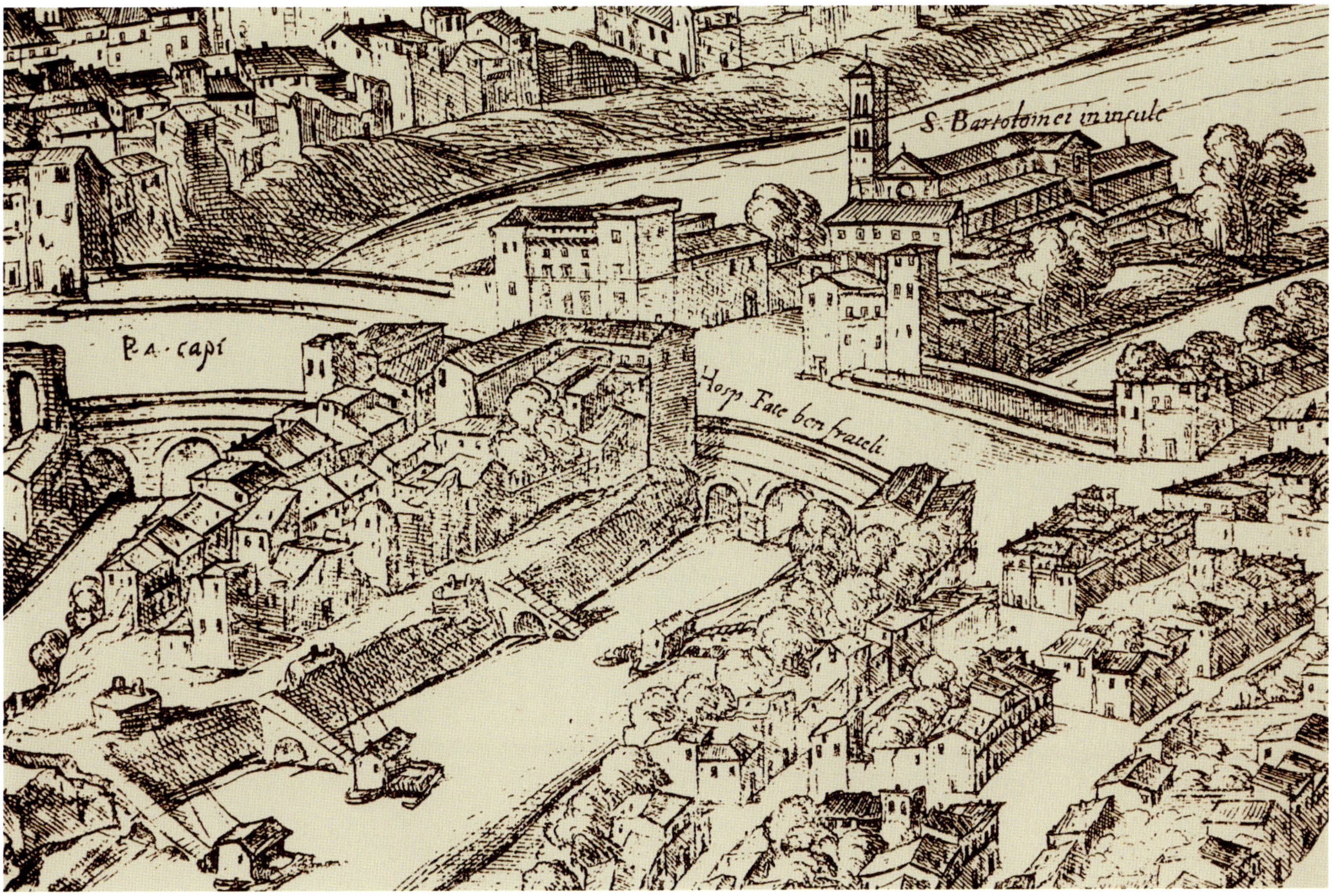

HELPING THE SICK

3. Aerial view of the Tiber Island.

Hospitallers have preserved their founder's charisma in the hospitals and clinics that are open to the homeless, as an expression of the extent of its generosity; the terminally ill during the last stages of their sickness when they would receive palliative treatment; patients with AIDS; drug addicts; immigrants, the elderly, and people who were either infirm or suffering from chronic disabilities. They therefore continued to practice the Gospel of mercy in the face of poverty, sickness, and suffering.[33]

Several years later, we have the example of Camillus de Lellis, who suffered nearly all his life from the pain and worry caused by an incurable sore on his leg. He witnessed the terrible conditions of nearly all the Roman hospitals that had very little means and where the staff lacked either vocation or the wish to endure the wretchedness of the sick they were meant to look after. It was extremely difficult to expect professionalism from those who were unprepared, and it was impossible to expect charity unless it came from the love for God and was inspired by our Lord.

At a certain point in his life, on February 2, 1575, repenting his youthful misdeeds, he converted, and discovered in the depths of his soul Christ's identification with the sick. "The poor sick people are God's eyes and heart, and what we do for these unfortunate people we are doing for God himself," he wrote to his religious brothers; he acted accordingly for his entire life. He quickly realized that too often the behavior of those working with the sick had nothing to do with love, but only with their low wages and boredom, and therefore did not meet even the most basic standards. As a result he decided to gather together merciful men who were moved by the sight of a brother or sister in pain, ready to devote themselves to the poorest of the poor and to those who could no longer rely on their own strength.

Saint Camillus is tangible proof that charity does not consist in words and theories but in facts, deeds, and devoted people. The expression "charity as action" appears dozens of times in his first Rules—so that life is distilled to charity without interruption, and generous devotion to those who are crying out of wretchedness, and those who keep nothing for themselves. These deeds and the care for the sick have to be carried out "with the affection a loving mother feels when her only child is sick." This beautiful expression, used for the first time by the Brothers Hospitallers of Saint John of God in Jerusalem, compares the continuous, generous love of a mother who asks for nothing in return, to the love of God. Saint Vincent de Paul uses the same expression when talking to the Daughters of Charity: "Your main concern has to be that of serving these poor sick people with tenderness and warmth, commiserating with their ills, listening to their complaints like a good mother; because they see you as a wet-nurse and as a person God has sent to help them."

The only protagonist is the person who is sick; he or she deserves total priority: "What concerns these religious helpers most must be the problems of the sick, being present where there is pain, plague, and misery." Summoned by the military authorities, in Naples five brothers were sent to Spanish ships with soldiers aboard in quarantine, suffering from typhus. They obeyed "knowing that they were surely heading toward certain death out of love for God, and giving thanks to Holy Obedience for having deemed them worthy of such." In 1590, plague devastated the city of Rome, claiming 30,000 lives. Those helping the sick multiplied and were present in hospitals, private homes, and on the streets, working with charity, humility, meekness, and compassion. Twenty-five young sisters and brothers lost their lives on this occasion. Reading the chronicles of this disaster and others, we remember Jesus' words: "No one has greater love than this, to lay down one's life for one's friends" (John 15:13).

For thirty years, Saint Camillus spent most of his time in the Holy Spirit Hospital in Sassia, a medieval complex that Sixtus IV had rebuilt in a magnificent Renaissance style. Today we can still admire the huge gallery that is 120 meters long, 20 meters wide and 30 meters high. This was where there were rows and rows of beds for the sick. In the middle under an octagonal dome is an altar and the beautiful ciborium by Palladio. This is an example of extraordinary esthetical expression of the Gospel, with Christ surrounded by three hundred sick people, Christ at the center of human suffering. This was probably not the most suitable site to place the

4. Pierre Subleyras, Camillo de Lellis Rescuing the Sick in Ospedale di Santo Spirito. *Oil on canvas, eighteenth century. Museo di Roma.*

5–6. *The central octagonal tower and impressive Sistine ward of the south wing of Ospedale di Santo Spirito in Saxia, Rome.*

Next page:
7. *Interior cloister of the "Ca' Granda" Hospital in Milan, designed by Filarete. The Camillians founded a house in Milan after those in Rome and Naples.*

altar and distribute the sacraments, but there is no doubt that this arrangement was a splendid symbol of the practice of charity: From Christ present in the Eucharist, to Christ present with the sick, sick people that Camillus always treated as if they were his lord and master, as did Vincent de Paul later did with the poor.

We can also find these religious in prison infirmaries, where they would help the prisoners with their needs and comfort them. In fact, Christians have always worked in prisons, particularly because that was where they found brothers and sisters who had been accused of belonging to an inferior class of society; later, however, they also worked there because they were aware that being close to any kind of sinner pleased our Heavenly Father. They did not visit and help them because they ignored their malice and sins, but for the very opposite reason: because they knew that Christ had come to justify the sinners, and his disciples therefore had to try and convert the hearts of those who very often could not be blamed for having been led astray.

Saint Camillus' motto was "More charity in your hands," and his first biographer wrote that, just as monks praised the Lord with their song and voice, so did the hands that helped the sick, performing acts of mercy for one's neighbor. In other words, for Camillians, their Divine Office was their help and vigilance in hospitals and with the dying. There is no doubt they meditated because they constantly saw and loved Christ in the sick, and it was to them that they devoted all their care and time. God was also praised in the same way by the many lay volunteers who helped in this order and the religious hospitals founded by Saint Benedict Menni, both with pastoral work and looking after the sick in their many hospitals.

During the last years of his generalship, there was a terrible dispute between the Saint Camillus and many of his brothers regarding whether the religious members should take on the tasks and management of the hospitals themselves. However, the reasons of the two positions aside, this is an example of a reality that is constantly present in the history of the Church, and one we have already seen in the life of Saint Francis. If we focus completely on the sick, are we not damaging, complicating, and restricting the order's life? Would it not be more logical to pay more importance to the life of its members rather than the needs of the sick? Should the work for the poor, sick people not be subordinate to the organization, prayer, and education of the members? This was the principle Saint Bonaventure saw in the Franciscans, and it was the one that the Camillians who succeeded their founder followed. However, surely neither Francis, John of God, nor Camillus led their lives according to the rules of common sense in balancing the spiritual life and active charity.[34]

Chapter 25
TEACHING THE POOR

Some people who have dedicated their lives to God are compelled to teach. Submerged in the worries caused by the profound human suffering that we find in every society, these generous spirits have helped by founding hospitals, kindergartens, shelters, reformatories, and other charitable institutions. However, as late as the nineteenth century there were very few institutions devoted to education, probably because it was considered less urgent than people's primary needs.

In the sixteenth century, a third of children received no kind of religious education whatsoever, while others received just the most basic teaching. Despite ecclesiastical precepts, even catechism was taught irregularly. In fact, very often faith was not accompanied by personal religious concern or the desire for a better education. Nevertheless, in all ages and in all dioceses, we can find people who felt the need to receive or to teach a sounder doctrinal education.

There were catechism schools that were very popular in the parishes, as well as several municipal public schools that offered lessons in reading and writing, grammar and catechism, but the students had to pay the teacher. This meant that the poor who could not pay were automatically sentenced to inactivity and ignorance. Saint Joseph Calasanz (1557–1648), a Spanish priest of strong character and profound spirituality, was keenly aware of the problem of illiteracy and the vices of those who grew up on the streets; this was why he decided to devote his life to them. "After having visited the sick and poor in Rome, it was with great sadness that I understood that nearly all poor children fell victim to vice since their fathers could not afford to send them to school."[35]

Calasanz decided to found a school that was open to any poor children who wanted to attend; it was completely free and only for them. This was how

Previous page:
1. *Church and Institute of Joseph Calasanz in Peralta de la Sal, Spain, the saint's birthplace.*

2. *Colegio Calasancio, Bogotá, Colombia.*

the free public primary and middle school originated (1597). Driven by charity and the love for God, the Order of Poor Clerics Regular of the Mother of God of the Pious Schools (Piarists) was then founded to provide teachers for these poor children. "The prefect must receive the poor with great charity, even if they have no shoes, are dressed in rags or have no cloak, since it was primarily for them that our institute was founded."[36]

In 1626, Calasanz explained the nature of his work in a memorandum to the cardinals of the Holy Office: "The objective of the Institute of the Pious Schools is to teach children, in particular the poor, many of whom do not go to school or learn any trade and become dissolute and indolent and therefore much more prone to gambling, all owing to their fathers' negligence....To cut such an evil that is so harmful to society at its very root, the Fathers of the Pious Schools are willing to take on the laborious task of teaching them out of charity." The fact the schools were free of charge and only for the poor made him famous, and he was soon recognized in all the cities where the Fathers set up these schools, all of which had well-organized classes, programs, schedules, and moral, religious, and social education.

Aimed particularly at the poorest of the poor, this education was an effective means to devise and apply solutions to the many social problems that existed at the beginning of the modern age.

This concern about child education continued during the seventeenth century and increased as time went by. Parish priests and clerics all over demanded the opportunity for a humane, Christian education for the poorest members of the parishes, but in reality there were not enough sufficiently prepared

3–4. Two contrasting images: On the one hand, the urban space (4) has been transformed into a Baroque "theater scene"; on the other, we can see the extreme poverty of those living in the city (3), as well of those living in the poor areas on the outskirts.
3. French peasants in the seventeenth century (drawing by A. Baldanzi).
4. Andrea Pozzo, Perspectiva Pictorum et Architectorum, *vol. I, Rome 1693, fig. 71.*

teachers for the task. Jesuits, Barnabites, Oratorians, Ursulines, and countless other congregations set about organizing classes and founding schools. The first of the "little schools" for poor children was opened in Lyons, for primary education. In Rouen, Nicolas Barré (1621–1686) founded the Sisters of the Infant Jesus, offering poor children free lessons. Many others established similar schools in different cities. In 1680, Jean-Baptiste de La Salle (1651–1719), founded the Brothers of the Christian Schools, who vow to devote themselves to the education of poor children and to live as religious brothers in poverty and devotion.

Before, a teacher taught individual students, one at a time. The Christian Brothers pioneered the classroom method in which lessons were given to an entire class: Each student followed the lesson in their book, and was questioned in turn. This is the method used in modern primary education. The Brothers of Christian Schools could take on no other ministry; they would only be Christian teachers, devoted to the education of children. Obviously, this education was aimed at the children of parents of the most humble origins and no expectations, but as a result of the education they received some went on to become part of the ruling class. Doubtless this was revolutionary in the sense that it broke the monopoly on education held by the aristocracy and important middle-class families. It also helped consolidate the future of the Church as it resulted in generations of laypeople who had received a sound catechesis, as well as a good education and knowledge of modern culture. These Christians then gradually began to take an active part in ecclesiastical associations and activities.

For them, as for Saint Joseph Calasanz's Piarists or

the Marists (1863), for Rose Venerini (1656–1728) or Lucy Filippini (1672–1732), teaching was a true ministry that consecrated the brothers or sisters to the Church and to young people. During the nineteenth and twentieth centuries, countless female and male congregations founded schools and colleges where forms of Christian life were taught together with the sciences and literature of the time. The most famous founder and pedagogue of this period was probably Don Bosco. His work focused on helping poor children who had been abandoned in the cities, or who had come to Turin from the countryside—children who were used to living in danger and exposed to all the risks on the streets. Don Bosco guaranteed their personal growth thanks to a better education. We should remember that he worried that if the public schools run by governments ignored religious values, the social fabric would start to crumble. From that moment on, Don Bosco was convinced that the problem of education was linked increasingly to that of the regeneration of society and civilization of the people. The Church was able to preserve its presence in contemporary society, thanks to the education of generations of young people without any means, who went on to participate in the progress of society. Don Bosco wrote to his disciples: "Do you want me to suggest a relatively easy, highly advantageous job that produces great results? Well, work on the good education of the young, especially the poorest and most neglected, who are the most numerous, and you will rightly be giving Glory to God, procuring the good of religion, saving countless souls and cooperating to great effect with the reform and

5. *The Consolata Sanctuary in Turin has always been a reference point for the city. It was very close to the hearts of the Confraternity of Saint Vincent and the Little House of Divine Providence founded by Saint Joseph Cottolengo. Don Bosco's boys had particularly close ties to the sanctuary, and they prayed there fervently when Don Bosco was seriously ill.*

6. Restructuring plan for the working class district in Mulhouse, France, 1852. Following the Industrial Revolution, administrators and entrepreneurs were more concerned about the factories and the supply of labor. If it had not been for the intervention of countless religious confraternities and the laypeople associated with them, the education of the poor would have fallen by the wayside.

well-being of civil society; because reason, history and experience have shown that religious and civil society will be good or bad depending on the good or bad youth that surround us."[37]

In reality, all young people need an integrated education. Civil authorities often tend to monopolize education, but Christians know that the presence of religious values and the evangelical message are indispensable, catechesis aside, if their children are to receive an integrated education. The anti-Christianity of Enlightenment authors and the anti-clericalism of the political regime simply confirmed to Christians the need for their own educational centers. For example, the Marianists (William Joseph Chaminade), the Religious of the Sacred Heart (Madeleine Sophie Barat), the Marist Fathers (Jean-Claude Colin), the Clerics of Saint Viator (Louis-Marie Querbes), the Sisters of Saint Anne (Maria Rafols), the Company of Saint Teresa of Jesus (Saint Henry de Ossó), the Teresian Association (Pedro Poveda), and countless other congregations, groups, and lay institutes all had the objective of educating the young, both scientifically and religiously. Important universities were also founded that suffered as a result of government policies, but they managed to survive thanks to the prestige acquired by the quality of their teaching. Some examples are the Catholic University of the Sacred Heart in Milan, the Catholic Institutes in Lyons, Lille, and Paris, and the Universities of Comillas (Madrid) and Deusto (Bilbao). In the United States, the Catholic Church maintains a significant presence, especially thanks to its parish schools and countless universities.[38]

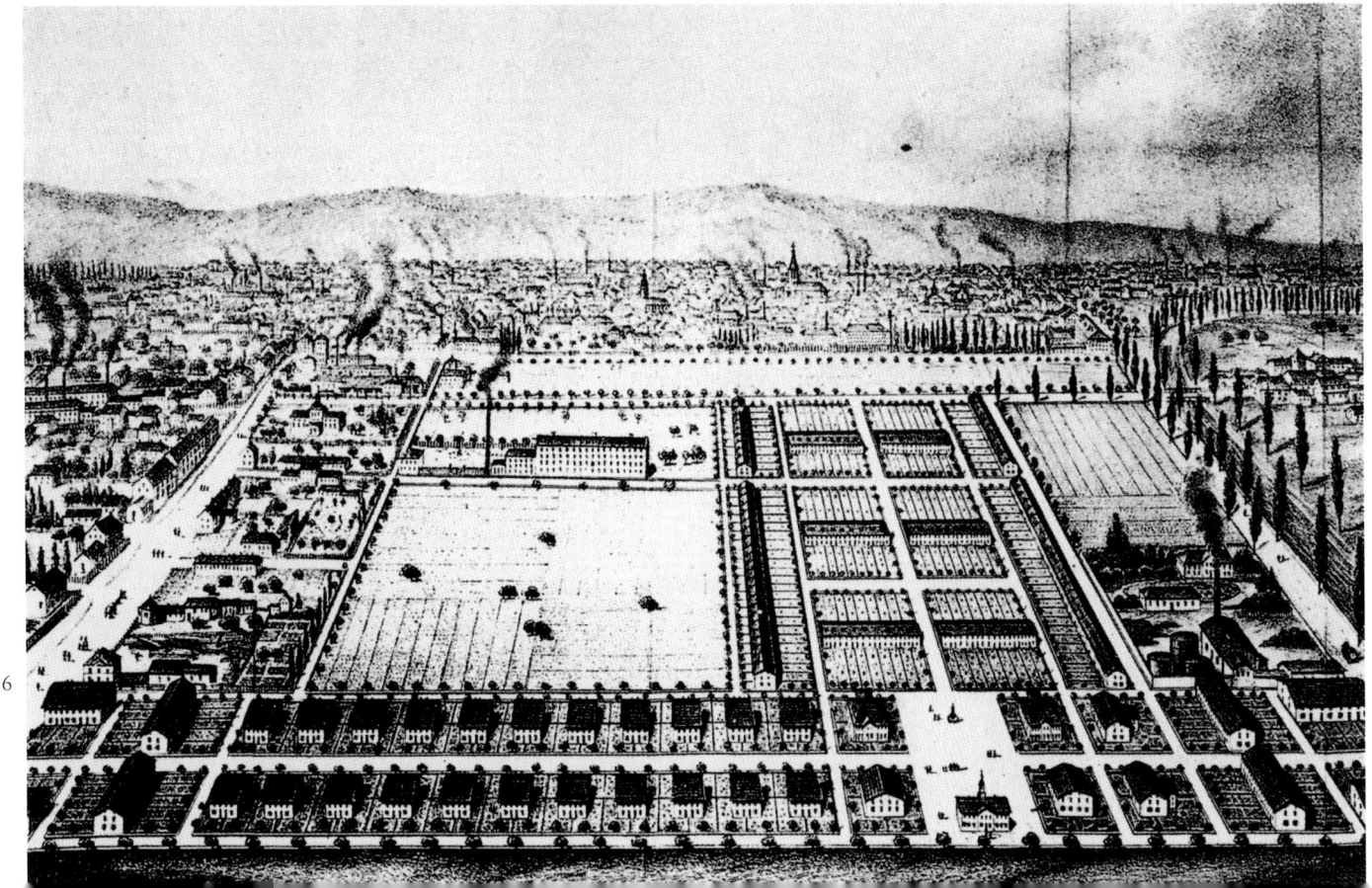

Chapter 26
TEACHING THE IGNORANT

If we do not know God, if we do not live according to Christ's teachings, if we are not reborn but cling to the ways of the old man, we are poor. We are poor if we continue to be subjected to a world of violence, hate, egoism, and injustice, without knowing the Good News of God's care for us and brotherhood among people.

At one time, Christians in cities had easier access to a more thorough religious education, good priests, and well-prepared religious men and women, but there was large-scale misery and ignorance in rural society. Everybody was aware of this, although not everyone was sensitive or convinced enough to see the need to preach this in the world, spiritually educating the people, supporting rural parishes, and responding to the hidden hunger for God's Word. These people believed instinctively, "without probing, but without being able to explain the reasons for their faith," as Paul suggests.

Saint Vincent de Paul organized an order of priests (the Congregation of the Mission) with the aim of going to villages that lacked religious assistance, where they would stay for at least two weeks, preaching, teaching, and hearing confessions, always for free. The Christian population thus was able to witness something that struck a chord with them: Priests who lived in poverty, but who preached the Word passionately to ignorant people who were capable of listening with interest and willingness to change. According to the approval for the new congregation, signed by Urban VIII (1633), the missionaries' raison d'être was the salvation of the poor peasants who lived in the poorest villages, houses, and neighborhoods. They were to teach God's commandments to the ignorant, instruct them in the rudiments of the faith, administer the Eucharist, and talk familiarly with the people in terms they could understand. These

missionaries had to act as if the people listening to them were pagans with an ardent desire to know the Lord, spurred on by Christ's commandment: "Go into all the world and proclaim the good news" (Mark 16:15).

The most striking sermons were about the seriousness of sin, the existence of hell, and the consequences of a lack of repentance, as well as the need to convert, to transform one's life, and to obtain hope and peace thanks to the purification of the spirit generated by the devotion to the Virgin Mary, the Eucharist, and the prospect of reaching heaven. At the basis of this preaching, we find the fundamental themes of the missions: God's mercy and salvation, confession and reconciliation, the gravity of disbelief, Judgment Day, the need to give back what we have taken, and the repudiation of vengeance. Another fundamental aspect of the missions was teaching catechism: The missionaries were convinced that a soul could not know Christ or his doctrine if it did not know the generosity of God, or believe, hope, or love as the Gospel asks.

This method of preaching in a direct, simple, and familiar way far from theological complications or formal language was practiced frequently in the history of Christianity. Louis-Marie de Montfort in the French provinces, Capuchins and Jesuits in Protestant regions, and the different missionary congregations in general, were aware of the urgency to preach to the illiterate simply and accessibly, explaining the catechism in informal meetings in a conversational and personal way. The Franciscans used painted catechisms to teach the illiterate locals, and popular European preachers used the altarpiece and stained glass windows, music and theatre, and imagination and creative passion to impress listeners and to show the love and justice of the triune God.

The missionaries were equally concerned with the lack of bread, always scarce in large areas. They worried about the hunger of people imprisoned by poverty and without hope. This is why Vincent de Paul made sure that every mission ended with the creation of a charitable confraternity, which completed and confirmed the spiritual results of the missions. In the nineteenth century, Frédéric Ozanam created the Society of Saint Vincent de Paul, which spread to numerous countries, composed of laypeople who visited the poor, stayed by their side, taught them the rudiments of religion, provided their basic needs, and spoke to them about the love of God.

Earlier, in the eighteenth century, Alphonsus de Liguori founded another religious congregation, the Redemptorists, with the same aim: To evangelize the abandoned in the Neapolitan countryside, ignorant of the gospel and often also of the most elementary morality. The popular missions became

1. Saint Vincent eats with the poor. Popular image.

2. Saint Vincent rescues an orphan. Modern mosaic. Provincial House of the Daughters of Charity, Cagliari.

3. Frédéric Ozanam wrote for the newspaper L'Ère nouvelle, which was inspired by Christianity. The paper used to transmit Christian teachings and fought for social justice and human rights.

one of the most successful pastoral methods of the last few centuries, although we cannot ignore the fact that, concentrating on an intense examination of conscience, and of the presence of Christ and his salvific action for just a few days, the effects could soon dissipate. However, it is always true that, for those who felt their hearts touched by the Word and by the life of Jesus, this encounter often turned into a decisive opportunity for personal reform and renewal.

Starting in the mid-nineteenth century, the Missionary Sons of the Immaculate Heart of Mary (Claretians) continued this work and would devote much of their activity to the popular missions. The missions, which lasted three or four weeks, were aimed at converting sinners and ended with a Eucharist. Their program combined preaching eternal truths in the sermons with explanations of the commandments in their moral preaching, in which they denounced vices such as gambling, unsuitable literature, and alcohol abuse. They were also concerned with tracing a program of perfection, in which they proposed rules for living well and for salvation, which the good Christian was supposed to observe every day, every week, every month, and every year, for all time. The nineteenth-century missionaries' style was certainly theatrical. They wanted to shake people up with a wave of feeling, evoked by describing recent disasters and the threat of future misfortunes. The results could be admirable, but were often short lived. Despite this, on many occasions, believers became aware that being Catholic meant becoming aware and assuming the risk of obligations and behaviors that often meant going against the grain, abandoning past habits, and acting responsibly, in accordance with what they believed. It was a means of creating a more responsible lay community.

In the nineteenth century, many Christians had the flame of faith within them, in other words, the Christian who believes in Jesus Christ with simplicity and accepts Church teaching but cannot explain why they believe or exactly what it is they believe in. This situation certainly was not ideal and was dangerous at the time when attacks on Christianity were increasing and spreading thanks

4. Edgar Degas, A Cotton Market in New Orleans. *Oil on canvas, 1873. Musée des Beaux-Arts, Pau, France. Large colonial businesses dominated the world, setting an agenda that diverted attention from religious questions.*

5. Holy water font with image of the Sacred Heart. Chiesa dell'Egiziaca, Pizzofalcone, Naples.

to advances in communication that reached everywhere, disturbing and confusing many believers who had never questioned their faith. In these cases, the popular missions became an important support, explaining clearly the requirements of the religion they believed in.

By the early twentieth century, the progressive exclusion of believers in the more secular countries led to Christians having a more considered and aware, a more internalized, less routine religion, purified of outside interests. Manifestations of religiosity gradually became more personal and warm, more focused on the figure of Christ, also thanks to the popularity of devotion to the Sacred Heart. Pius X renewed the emphasis in the liturgy on the Eucharist, encouraged frequent reception of communion, and lowered the age of first communion from twelve to seven. These changes led to more regular confessions and a clearer understanding of the need to demonstrate the requirements of the Gospel in daily life with decision and conviction.

At the same time, the number of catechists grew in parishes and suburban neighborhoods; university students organized Sunday schools in the poorer neighborhoods, while the Conferences of Vincent de Paul and other associations induced more sympathetic Christians to visit and help the neediest families and individuals.[39]

During these years of mass migrations, Christians in parishes and apostolic organizations taught other immigrants the language of their new country, as well as other subjects that could help them find a job or provide career options for those already working. This was not just an act of charity, but also a way of creating ties between people belonging to different worlds, of integrating into the community those who felt uprooted, of achieving esteem and reciprocal understanding, and a way of creating and strengthening the community of believers.

Chapter 27
CHRIST IN THE PRISONS

From the beginning, accused of atheism or of treason against the emperor, Christians soon got to know the inside of prisons and forced labor. From the very beginning they organized visits and aid to those who were being punished.

Throughout Christian history, all did not have the same rights and responsibilities. Sentences were often unfair, based not so much on the crime but the social class of the accused. Roman law considered prisons not as places of permanent punishment but temporary detention centers while waiting judgment. However, given the complexity of some legal procedures, detention could go on indefinitely. The courts did not condemn people to prison but to death, slavery on the galleys, corporal punishment, or exile.

The presumption of innocence did not exist and secrecy increased the insecurity of the accused. We frequently find examples of courts using torture to obtain confessions, which were sometimes false, and wardens accepting bribes. In many cities, Ramon Llull (ca. 1232–ca. 1315) created the office of public defender for the poor, who were often taken to court unjustly. This was a sign of a changed mentality toward the unfortunate.

Given this situation, from the first centuries of ecclesiastical history we find various attempts by Christian organizations to alleviate the lives of prisoners, which differed depending on the place and the circumstances, with the constant aim of treating them like beloved children of the Father and members of the community of believers. In nineteenth-century France, the Brothers of the Sacred Heart fought actively against abuses in prisons. Vincent de Paul spurred his missionaries to work both in the prisons and among the galley slaves, that they loved, "not in word or speech, but in truth and action" (1 John 3:18). We can concur with Bernanos that the greatest misfortune is the acceptance, not endurance, of injustice. Accepting injustice degrades the soul. It destroys morale, opens us to evil, and perverts relationships. Religious sensitivity and the awareness of the evangelical counsels lead us to a more explicit recognition of human dignity and rights. This was the path toward a greater consideration of the pastoral of prisoners.

The questions of punishment, justice, and the condition of prisoners (who often languished in inhumane conditions) led to the desire to transform prisoners from objects into subjects, to ensure that prisons were humane, going beyond the hope of repairing the disorder caused by the crime. Those who have dedicated themselves to this peculiar mission have been concerned not only with re-establishing justice, but also rescuing the human subject who had done wrong.

Only the Church can bring about a fundamental, global, and definitive rethinking, returning to its roots, remembering God's universal, real, and effective paternity and the universal brotherhood of his children. It must remain aware of the original sin present in all humans, but also of the fact that we are saved in Christ. This presupposes that an essential conversion takes place in the same Church, abandoning not the words but the practices of teaching, organization, and government that have marked its history for too long. Inquisitions, excommunications, and other canonical or moral punishments, castes and classes present in the communities, and first- and third-class Christians are anti-evangelical distinctions. Our Church, if it converts from within, has the power that comes from the Spirit and the doctrinal authority to condemn the injustice present in many parts of society. This

CHRIST IN THE PRISONS

1. Simon Vouet (1590–1649) or his school, Saint Vincent de Paul (1581–1660). Maison des Lazaristes, Paris. The saint was an advisor to Queen Anne of Austria, to whom this portrait belonged. He founded the Congregation of the Mission, also known as the Lazarists or Vincentians in 1625, and, with Louise de Marillac, the Daughters of Charity in 1633. He is depicted here at the end of his life. His simple demeanor and lively and benevolent eyes give him a kindly air.

2. Arrangement of slave quarters on a slave ship. From an eighteenth-century engraving. Musée des Arts Africains et d'Océanie, Paris. The ship was designed to contain as many slaves as possible. Crowding the slaves in physically prevented them from revolting.

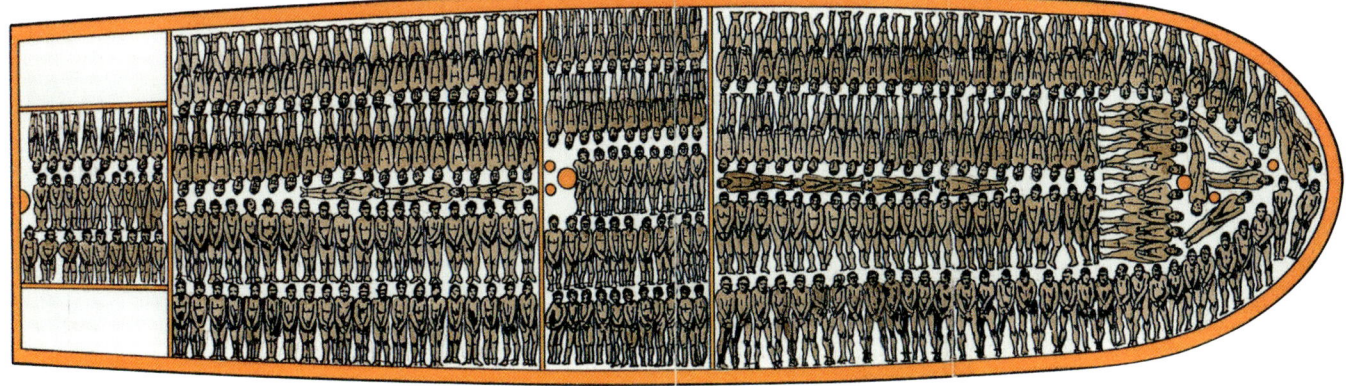

3. "Le Nuove," prison complex in Turin. Two Daughters of Charity in the prison nursery, with children of female inmates.

is evoked in the prayer said over the offerings on the feast of Saint Vincent de Paul: "O God, who enabled Saint Vincent to imitate what he celebrated in the divine mysteries," which can also be valid for those who manage to be consistent in their lives with what they are celebrating.

Many Christians over the centuries have been aware of the injustice afflicting the innocent who find themselves imprisoned, unprepared, and unprotected. At the same time, we could not expect the guilty who were manipulated by those in political or economic power, to be prepared to give. These Christians dedicated much of their lives to humanizing prisons; helping prisoners in their conditions and teaching them their rights, while at the same time explaining the gravity of their offense. All Christians are aware of being sinners before God, and begin the celebration of the Eucharist with an act of contrition. The behavior of these Christians was neither disingenuous nor anti-establishment on principle, nor did they participate in enlightened ideological optimism, but instead remained aware of the fact that the existing social organization was not the best possible and that justice could certainly be improved. This is the basis for their hope in a better, more just, and sympathetic world. For the Church it is one of the most difficult and disinterested works, but Christians have to be aware that the suffering of prisoners, the defense of a person's dignity, and the safeguarding of rights cannot be ignored by the followers of Jesus Christ. Religious support in prisons is delicate but irreplaceable. It has to be accompanied by acceptance of the prisoner as person and by a commitment toward the prisoners and their families. The primary interest is for the person and then for their faith. Only those who accept, listen, and identify with the prisoners' situation have the credibility to invite them to transcend their situation and experience it according to their faith.

Chapter 28
THE SIGNS OF THE TIMES

The Christian community shares the weaknesses and strengths of all humanity. There are not many geniuses, saints, or leaders among its members; mediocrity and inconsistency, egotism and violence abound. The characters of the Old Testament and of Christian history frequently show human frailties and abandon God without thought, in spite of benefits received. These are more common than are obedient and faithful followers. As a result, we have wars, oppression, ill-gotten gains, the exploitation of the weak, the arrogance of power both within and outside the Church. But these things are mere shadows: they have not managed to obliterate charity from the earth. Actually, in human hearts, in these "clay jars," our love for God and for our brothers and sisters never stops growing and bearing fruit. I do not think I am wrong when I say that in our changing history, love predominates over faithlessness and egotism. In every age where sin abounds, mercy, generosity, and solidarity outweigh it.

In order to understand the "signs of the times," we must see that the history of salvation and the history of the world are interwoven. Yves Congar wrote, "One of the gravest shortcomings of the training of the clergy during the nineteenth century and even at the beginning of the twentieth century is the ignorance of history and the lack of a historical sense. To this shortcoming we can add insufficient biblical knowledge and a conceptual-juridical presentation of the Church. For the same reason, the sense of eschatology is lacking. Specifically Christian historical sensibility attributes a meaning and an aim not only to individual existence, but also to the union of humanity and the world." The word of God is not a monologue but a conversation.

Awareness of the signs of the times means following the footsteps of the living presence of God in human history and discerning them in the midst of routine. It means identifying the ten just ones in the midst of evil, because these will attract God's blessing and kindness. Apparently, like human history, the history of the Church does not seem admirable or promising, and yet, as soon as we empathize with the love and goodness present in many places and in many humble and simple people, we spontaneously proclaim Francis' *Canticle of the Sun* and become enthusiastic about the many indications that God's love has been poured into our hearts.

The French Revolution, with its hate and persecution, appeared to have ended Catholicism in France. After more than a thousand years of a rich and creative religious life, it seemed that the noonday devils had taken over French society and culture, destroying its traditional social organization and eroding the religion that was identified with the history and culture of the country.

However, it was not all confusion and destruction. Many Christians kept their faith, hidden and silent, but also faithful and active. Some of them gave their lives peacefully; others opposed the regime with courage, both in the Vendée and elsewhere. Among them were the Carmelite nuns guillotined in Paris. At times of confusion and abandonment, the Church was at its best, with the majority of its children showing their unshakable belief in their Lord.

The following decades were confused, painful, and full of contradictions. The rash persecution by governments caused some Catholics to lack appreciation of the new values of liberty and democracy. They did not comprehend the social consequences

THE SIGNS OF THE TIMES

1. The Declaration of the Rights of Man *(1789)*.
Oil on canvas, late eighteenth century. Musée Carnavalet, Paris. Although the image with the divine eye at the top is not Christian, it is hard not to understand these aspirations expressed here. Nevertheless, it took a long time for the church to acknowledge them.

THE SIGNS OF THE TIMES

2. Massachusetts State House, designed by Charles Bulfinch, Boston, 1795–1798. A symbol of democracy, for a long time it was the largest public building in the United States. The cupola was gilded in 1874. We would have to wait a long time before a pope (Francis) would declare that there is no democracy without justice.

3. Eugène Delacroix, Liberty Leading the People. *Oil on canvas, 1830. The Louvre, Paris. Liberty leads the people in a revolt against oppression and injustice. In fact, it would be the rich bourgeoisie to bring the "citizen-king" Louis Philippe d'Orléans to power in France after the Paris insurrection of 1830.*

of the new system; they did not realize that nothing could recreate the past. Trapped by their desire not to lose power and influence, and distracted by their conviction that the changes ahead were the result of sin and evil, the majority of the hierarchy did not understand the inevitability or positive aspects of social and cultural change. Cardinal Consalvi, priests such as Antonio Rosmini and James Balmes, as well as laymen Hugues Lamennais and Frédéric Ozanam, were aware of the need to accept the good and Christian roots of the changes, but nobody listened to them. It was not until the Second Vatican Council that the church demonstrated its ability to create guidelines for integrating Christian values with modern culture.

On the other hand, the workers, isolated in rural areas or the most impoverished parts of cities, areas that seemed to be abandoned by the Church, were despised by the industrial bourgeoisie. The drama of the Church in the nineteenth century was that of the contrast between religion and the middle and working classes. There were many causes and factors that escape us, but we cannot forget how difficult it was for most of the hierarchy to understand the nature of a society eager for democracy and liberty, a difficulty that in some ways exists even today—above all in Latin countries, from which many in the hierarchy come.[40]

Catholic sensitivity and the generosity of the new religious congregations highlighted concern for the new poor and for the wounds inflicted by the industrial economy: the abandonment of the sick and the elderly, the exploitation of child labor, and prostitution. Personal generosity and organized charity were certainly not absent, but their practitioners probably lacked the foresight needed to oppose institutionalized injustice and to defend the worker and insist on dignified living conditions.

The colonial policy of some European countries, drafted at the Conference of Berlin (1885), responded to the participating countries' need for economic growth and to the difficulty of keeping up with more advanced countries. Christians found an opportunity to evangelize formerly closed nations and were able to organize a surprising multifaceted presence: catechism classes, hospitals, schools, and universities. Today we understand that history, our ties with the past, and patriotic feeling, made it difficult for some to understand that times had changed and that it was wrong to take over territories without considering the rights of the inhabitants to maintain their own personalities and values. The presence of Christian institutions was very positive in many ways, not just for evangelization, but also for educating and raising populations that had suffered with no capacity for development. Nevertheless, the original sin of colonialism consisted in European arrogance and in the extortion of some rulers who did not respect the rights of the natives, even if there were voices raised in protest.

Throughout the twentieth century, there was much development in the role of laypeople in the life of the Church and in the promotion of women in society. However, an excessively clerical Church that was often incapable of understanding the signs of the times, placed obstacles in the way of both these developments, provoking discontent and irritation among its lay members, who were obviously in the majority. A society such as the Church can hardly accept such profound differences in the twenty-first century. In effect, the inability to understand what is right and the urgency of the signs that present themselves often stop us from responding adequately to the many challenges we have to face. We think of Vincent de Paul's initiative in the sixteenth century, when he asked a group of women to create a religious community that was restricted to the convent and did not limit itself to liturgical prayer or educating the young. The saint himself was aware of his audacity: "For eight hundred years or so, women have had no public role in the Church; in the past there were some called deaconesses. About the time of Charlemagne, however, by a discreet working of Divine Providence, this practice came to an end; persons of your sex were deprived of any role and haven't had any since then. And now that same Providence is turning today to some of you." However, despite his reputation, Vincent was unable to achieve what he wanted.

In reality, it is possible to respond in various ways to the signs of the times but unfortunately, the

4. *Caricature of Bismarck putting the Kulturkampf into practice. Staatsbibliothek, Berlin. The chancellor, stamping on freedom of opinion, pulls the rope to fell the Roman Church. A doubtful Satan watches him and asks how long it will take to demolish it. "Three or four years," replies Bismarck. "Well," replies the devil, "I've been trying for eighteen centuries and I still haven't managed!"*

5. *Winslow Homer,* Bell Time. *Engraving, 1868. The work depicts workers leaving a factory in Massachusetts. Working conditions changed how people lived. The labor movement organizes the defense of workers; Christian congregations fight social hardship, poverty, lack of education, and for the needs of the poorest.*

responses are not always adequate. Christians believe that the Gospel offers the fundamental rules for choosing well and, although to many it can seem simplistic, there is no doubt that fraternal love continues to be the starting point. It is always unacceptable to try to resolve problems at the expense of the dignity, freedom, and rights of others; the smallest and most defenseless have to be considered first at all times. The history of the last two centuries teaches us that it is impossible to know and understand the signs of the times without considering justice, solidarity, and the love of God.

Chapter 29
NINETEENTH-CENTURY RELIGIOUS FOUNDATIONS: RESPONSES TO POVERTY

In the nineteenth and twentieth centuries, after the social and political upheavals created by the French Revolution and by the rise of more democratic political systems in the west, and after the social change due to industrialization and the resulting social changes in Europe and the United States, we see an increase of new religious congregations, ready to respond to the new challenges posed by the industrial, social, and techno-scientific revolutions.

The industrial expansion enriched many, but it also created much poverty, resulting in ills such as infant mortality, insufficient sanitary infrastructure in the new neighborhoods, the exploitation of women and children forced to work long hours for little pay, and impoverished young women turning to prostitution. Cholera epidemics and the persistence of smallpox caught the civil authorities unprepared, leading to many deaths. These were the challenges facing religious hospitals that were often on the frontline.

These new religious institutions, which multiplied in towns and cities, were founded by religious who dedicated their lives to the needy through their presence and charitable actions. They did not just want to be at the service of others, but also in communion with them. They were particularly dedicated to children and the elderly, traditionally the two most exposed and weak social groups, to the sick, particularly the mentally ill, and to those left to their own fate in an environment that was hardly conducive to solidarity. Many of these congregations were created to teach, while others were founded to work in African missions.

The prevalence of institutions founded by women is notable.[41] No field was closed to their charitable presence. They could be found in schools, where they offered children and youths basic literacy, trade schools, day-care centers, dispensaries, shelters, kindergartens, home care for the most neglected, and hospitals. Religious sisters lived out their vocation among the most fragile and vulnerable in society. In France and Italy, over 400 religious congregations were founded, along with 150 in Spain. It is amazing to think that over a thousand new female congregations sprang up in Europe, providing resources in the majority of countries and cities of Western Europe.

As the nineteenth century gradually came to a close, the number of religious congregations dedicated to teaching grew, while those in healthcare remained stable or decreased. By 1861, hospitals, shelters, and other healthcare or social centers accounted for just 15 percent of religious activity in France, while primary or vocational teaching was 67 percent (with the exception of Spain, where healthcare services remained quite high). This inequality of resources was mostly due to the Church's desire to counter the Enlightenment and anti-clerical influences dominant in the period, which influenced those who would govern society in the decades to come. In some cases, this led to an increase of services for the ruling classes. From a strategic point of view, the reasons for this seem reasonable, even if the evangelical spirit did not always seem to head in the same direction.

Was this creative and generous action a response to unjust situations and structures? Effectively, it was a valuable response to the ills caused by a lack of social controls provided by a capitalism greedy for gain, but it did not try to change the structures. I do not think that we could have expected the clergy or religious of those times to contribute toward changing the political and social organization.

NINETEENTH-CENTURY RELIGIOUS FOUNDATIONS: RESPONSES TO POVERTY

1. With the Industrial Revolution, the urban landscape changed; factories dominated parts of cities. Here a German coking factory is depicted in the mid-nineteenth century (tempera by G. Bacchin).

2. Jeff Katz, The Potato Famine. Engraving, ca. 1846. In the countryside, dire poverty developed due to epidemics and other factors. In less than a decade, the famine that ravaged Ireland between 1845 and 1849 led to a million and a half deaths while the same number of Irish people were forced to emigrate.

3. Don Orione greets the people during a festival. Luigi Orione was born in 1872 in Alessandria, Piedmont. He founded various organizations devoted to the care of children, orphans, and the disabled that can be found all over the world. The Orione family was reunited in the Piccola Opera della Divina Provvidenza (Little Work of Divine Providence), the name that Don Orione gave to his congregation. Luigi Orione was canonized in 2004.

However, it is disconcerting to think of the passivity of many laypeople who were sincerely Christian and endowed with important responsibilities in politics and in society. A few decades later, both seminarians and priests began to talk about the urgent need to immerse themselves in the masses. Their ideal was to integrate themselves with suffering humanity, at the risk of losing themselves in a world for which they were ill prepared. They lived with the hope of embodying these people, of being like them. Many priests abandoned their parishes to live in more impoverished neighborhoods, to share the life of their brothers and sisters. They wanted to live the priesthood in the very heart of the Church of the poor. Unfortunately, two world wars and Marxist ideology made this impossible.

Many workers sent their children to religious schools, but they never set foot in church because they thought that the Christians who attended services were too far from their situation and from their needs. They admired the Christians who helped them, but refused the institution, which they felt was too identified with the things and the people they abhorred. Charity was often simply considered almsgiving, but we should not forget that from the nineteenth century on, it had to be accompanied by the requirement to give one's own to everyone, and the evangelical spirit recalls that "one's own" depends on individual needs and requirements. In any case, we should recall the many laypeople who thanks to their own research, their own legal proposals, and their own experience in the factories, proposed more just laws regarding work and social security.[42]

It took the Second Vatican Council to create an authentic conversion of hearts, not in the sense of a greater generosity, but in the greater understanding of the need to live side by side with the poorest, to go among them, and to understand the choice of poverty as the capacity for sharing one's own life with those of the needy. Two bishops in Brazil, Hélder Câmara and Pedro Casaldáliga, became spokespeople for the rights of the less well off in various countries, as did many other priests, religious, bishops, and laypeople.[43]

In any case, in places where the Church collapses, does the condition of the poor, the elderly, and the sick improve or does it also collapse? If the Church does not transmit the love of God, who will? Who will transmit the love of the Son of God incarnate? There will be, and there are, many Christians who are unfaithful to the Divine mandate, but in many others the urgency of Christ remains to baptize those who seem to have not been invited to the table due to their miserable life; to visit illiterate children or families who live in squalor in hovels, or mothers who cannot breastfeed their children; and to accompany the marginalized elderly and other lonely people of all ages who find consolation and hope in the Christian community.

Chapter 30
THE CATHOLIC WORKER MOVEMENT

The Catholic Worker movement was founded in 1933 by the Catholic intellectual and activist Peter Maurin and by Dorothy Day, a left-wing journalist and writer who converted to Catholicism. On May Day of that year, Dorothy and some youths who supported her went to Union Square in New York, and started selling the first edition of the weekly *The Catholic Worker* for one cent, a faithful exposition of the ideology of the movement, which was eventually sold all over the country and is still sold at the same price today. It proclaimed a human and social revolution that sprang from the timeless quality of the human spirit and not from the conflicts of a world in evolution.

With her conversion, Dorothy Day, a radical American, transformed her personal repudiation of injustice into a constant mission of helping the disinherited. Together with Peter Maurin she established "houses of hospitality" in numerous cities in Canada and the United States. These homes focused on helping and guiding people who found themselves on the margins of civilized society toward a fuller human life. These houses were situated in poor neighborhoods and accommodated blacks and

1. Masthead of the weekly The Catholic Worker, *designed by Ade Bethune.*

2. The artist Ade Bethune, Dorothy Day, Dorothy Weston, the French philosopher Jacques Maritain, and Peter Maurin, 1934 (Marquette University Archives, Milwaukee, Wisconsin).

3. Peter Maurin opposite the headquarters of The Catholic Worker *on Mott Street, New York (Marquette University Archives).*

whites, fishermen, dockworkers, mariners, families with children, the unemployed, the sick, and those unable to work. It was not a question of merely giving food and clothing, but also of offering a roof, a warm and friendly environment, and a joyous testimony of Christian life.

"When one loves, there is at that time a correlation between the spiritual and the material...All sacrifice, all suffering is easy for the sake of love." This was the cornerstone of the Catholic Worker movement, which helped to free people from the tyranny of the senses and to start living under the spirit and with the spirit. They chose non-violence, always demonstrating a personalized conception of life, denouncing the dehumanizing aspects of the two phenomena of the age, nationalism and capitalism, refusing the spread of the dehumanizing characteristics of the state according to the model depicted in George Orwell's *1984*.

Once when talking to some university students she said, "When I was your age and was at the University of Illinois, women couldn't vote and the poor could fall back on nothing but the charity of the rich. I remember as a girl asking my mother why— why things weren't better for people, why a few owned so much, and many had little or nothing. She kept on telling me that 'there's no accounting for injustice, it just is.' I guess I've spent my life trying to 'account' for it, and trying to change things, just a little—and that is what I believe people like me ought to try to do: We've been given a leg up in the world, so why not try to help others get a bit of a break, too!" The members of the movement dreamt of a Church that was not a refuge from the cruelty of people, or an institution of power that tried to maintain its privileges, but instead a place of lively encounter between God and humanity, of immersion in the world, similar to the one created by Jesus centuries ago. Dorothy wrote in an article published in 1936: "Let us be honest, let us say that fundamentally, the stand we are taking is not on the ground of wages and hours and conditions of labor, but on the fundamental truth that men should be treated not as chattels, but as human beings, as 'temples of the Holy Ghost.'"

"All the way to Heaven is Heaven," wrote Saint Catherine of Siena, and Dorothy Day frequently cited this phrase, searching for inspiration in its profound meaning. By living for charity and distancing ourselves from violence, we try to impose a purpose on the world. The members of the movement maintained a pacifist attitude against the winds and rising tide and this stance cost them many readers: "We are still pacifists. Our manifesto is the Sermon on the Mount, which means that we will try to be peacemakers. Speaking for many of our conscientious objectors, we will not participate in armed warfare or in making munitions, or by buying government bonds to prosecute the war, or in urging others to these efforts" (January 1942).

Dorothy Day was arrested on numerous occasions for her demonstrations, in which she participated whenever she thought it was right. She maintained an intense intellectual and spiritual life, wrote books and articles defending her ideas, and was consistent in her beliefs. She found the answer to her great questions in the life of an itinerant preacher who died on the Cross alongside two thieves two thousand years ago. She found inspiration in the poor of the twentieth century, similar to those that Jesus loved. She chose to spend her life with them, helping them and learning from them. Sometimes she talked of her great loves: Her love of literature and writing, her love of Jesus and his Church, her love of the prophets whom she read constantly in her tattered Bible, and her love of the common people with empty stomachs that she tried to fill and disoriented lives that she tried to put back on track.

It is not possible to understand this immensely creative and generous movement that opened its arms to those who sought help, human warmth, and guidance, without considering its community spirit and the characteristics of a social, religious, cultural, and political movement, which for de-

4. *Dorothy Day (Marquette University Archives).*

5. *Dorothy Day and the original staff of The Catholic Worker, William Callahan and Margaret Polk, ca. 1936 (Marquette University Archives).*

6. *The staff of The Catholic Worker on the steps of the house on Charles Street in New York (Marquette University Archives).*

7. *Dorothy Day and the original staff of The Catholic Worker (courtesy of Henry Beck).*

THE CATHOLIC WORKER MOVEMENT

8–9. *Mott Street, New York. As well as being the headquarters of the paper, it was the house of hospitality for the disinherited and for seasonal workers. The poor stood in line for the soup kitchen (Marquette University Archives).*

Opposite:
1. *Still from Robert Bresson's film,* Diary of a Country Priest, *based on Georges Bernanos' novel. The scene depicts the dialogue between the priest and an older colleague.*

cades has attracted numerous troubled and generous people, and helped generations of the needy in myriad ways.[44]

Jesus was the founder of a community movement and this has been the cornerstone of Christian history. In the course of two thousand years, groups of Christians have come together to be present in the world, to walk together, to develop projects that improve human life, to accompany the weakest, and to face evil in all its guises. It is touching to realize that at any time, in any place, men and women have come together with willingness and imagination in order to create a happier, more united humanity that is closer to God and his creatures, in projects that embrace all the manifestations of human life, from the cradle to the grave, in an open spirit that embraces both hemispheres and all continents.

Our love for God and for our brothers and sisters is a constant stimulus in society. It spurs us on, suggests, and animates. At times, disturbed by the violence and egoism present in our world, we forget the great utopias that continuously mobilize human beings: The utopia of being children of God, of being brothers and sisters, of creating a world together, of overcoming calamities, hate, misery, obstacles, fears, and doubts.

These unusual people, illuminated by an idea or a love, are capable of giving their own life to follow a calling, they are generous to the extreme, and they enlighten, animate, and enthuse those of us who often have no project, no hope, no help, and no consolation. It is not easy to imagine life without saints, people who love God and who care for human beings.

Chapter 31
SAINTS AHEAD OF THEIR TIMES

The history of the Church is one of progress, change, creativity, and constant adaptation to different mentalities and cultures, but it is also one of personal and institutional conflicts. These conflicts, their motivation, their very nature, show us different things. On the one hand, it shows how it is understood and how love is practiced among its members, but on the other, it shows us the dominant unrest of intolerance and fear that exists where freedom of spirit and fraternity should rule.

In this context we would like to reflect on the difficult Christians: The non-conformists, the reformers, those who were ahead of their times, but also saints, who acted within orthodoxy and the ecclesiastical community. The Dean of Blangermont said to the country curate in Bernanos' novel,[45] "Let God save us from the reformers!" To which the curate replies, "Lord Dean, many saints were reformers." "Then let God save us from the saints as well!" Indeed, quite a large number of saints made life difficult for their superiors, for the hierarchy, and even for the religious orders they had founded.

The stories of those who suffered or were outcasts for defending ideas that were eventually accepted and were to have a positive influence on Church life are actually quite troubling. Just think of how Savonarola might have struggled with his conscience before denouncing Alexander VI, who was often an unworthy pope. Could he have remained silent in his stubborn search for a Church that was purer and more evangelical than the one represented by Alexander, his family, and the Curia? This Dominican's fight is an example of a problem that is central to modern Catholicism: What is the correct relationship between office, hierarchy, and individual, between the Church and individual conscience?

Gregory VII, who nobody would have dreamt of accusing of instituting rash innovations, said, "Christ did not say: 'I am the tradition' but 'I am the truth.' A tradition, no matter how ancient and widespread, must always withdraw when faced with the truth." In a Church that has always been typified in history, the purification and distinction of what is actually a later addition to the essential heart of the faith is a pressing matter. Over the centuries, most conflicts and ecclesiastical excommunications were caused by marginal issues concerning things that were routine, formalistic, and traditionalistic; in other words, by the radically human part of the Church, which was often doubted out of love, out of compassion for someone who was suffering undeservedly, or out of compassion for someone who had left the church community after having been treated unjustly.

The history of the Church offers us an array of people who were remarkable for a thousand different reasons. Some were before their times, championing principles or theories that eventually prevailed but were

met initially with incomprehension and widespread refusal. Some agreed with the most active or creative movements while the Church remained anchored in its past and traditions. Others attacked privileges they thought were unjust or simply anachronistic, incurring the wrath of those who wanted to preserve them, as Cardinal Consalvi remarked two centuries ago, "Nobody is more against change than those who have something to lose because of it." It is not easy for a society composed of so many different members to be in perfect harmony, but where possible, we should live together in charity, understanding, and reciprocal respect. Often, fraternal co-existence among Christians has been hindered, causing unnecessary pain to people and institutions, by the spirited defense of truth—or what we believe to be the truth—without taking into consideration the fact that someone else believes a different truth; this could be because of the authoritarian or intolerant character of someone who believes they have greater knowledge and authority than the rest of the community, or because of the arrogance of power. I believe it was Bernanos who wrote that the most difficult thing is not suffering for the Church, but because of the Church, because of people without prospects, people who are intolerant, or people who have an excessive opinion of their own responsibilities and skills and, above all, because of people who feel no charity. These people are unaware of the fact that first we must look for love, and only then can we look for morals and rules.

Let us look at some of the people who lived in similar situations. Thomas Aquinas had to fight on various fronts because of his innovative theological beliefs. In 1270, driven by envy and confused by the simplicity with which he upended the modes of thought they had established and defended out of convenience, the Archbishop of Paris and the teachers of theology tried to cause his downfall in his dispute with John Peckham. The newly converted John Henry Newman was spurned by the most conservative because he defended the independence of personal consciousness. Another example is Bartolomé de Las Casas, who was and remains a controversial figure, because he criticized the harm caused to the natives by the colonists' selfishness and greed. Unlike Montesinos, he was not assassinated but he had to leave his diocese and was ostracized. Others who suffered a similar fate include

2. Benozzo Gozzoli, Triumph of Thomas of Aquinas. Fresco, 1470–1475. The Louvre, Paris. The saint is portrayed between Plato and Aristotle, and is blessed by Christ. A pope, bishops, and monks are watching the scene. Averroës is depicted at the saint's feet.

Lamennais, Rosmini, Yves Congar, Henri de Lubac, Pedro Arrupe, and Hélder Câmara.[46] It was nearly always a question of a divergence of opinions between different schools, people who identified their own opinions with the revelation or truth, revealing the scarce respect they had for the latter. This was a common occurrence in certain ecclesiastical circles.

Many Christians who had made innovative contributions faced opposition from people who did not want to hear anything new. Congar, and other innovators like him, were aware that in the reformism of the years 1940–1950, ecclesiastical authority was not questioned, and that it was possible to find forms of evangelization that were better suited to a state of affairs that no longer corresponded to that of Christianity, and not even to that of a world that was used to respecting religion; in other words, better suited to an all-out pagan, selfish, and laic world. These "awkward" Christians were looking for more communal, missionary forms of Church, with parishes, schools, and deeds that were more suited to existing situations, a change in the ministry organization and a more fluid relationship between the laity and the hierarchy, including a better understanding of laypeople's function in the Church. These pioneers, people of great religious zeal and intellect, faced immense suspicion and rejection, and endured interior isolation.

In the past, saints suffered at the hands of church authorities: Saint John of Ávila, Cardinal Morone, Saint John of the Cross, Saint Ignatius of Loyola, Saint Joseph Calasanz, Saint Louis-Marie Grignion de Montfort, and countless others, and not for objective reasons but because of their persecutors' pride, intolerance, and ignorance. Saint Basil was accused of heresy before Pope Damasus, Saint Cyril of Jerusalem was sentenced to death as a heretic and deposed by a council of forty bishops, Saint Athanasius was accused of witchcraft, and Saint John Chrysostom of immoral habits. As we can see, Christian communities are not always places of communion and reconciliation.

We should also remember that the founders of religious orders often were banished by their own disciples. These are the great "difficult" Christians: for example, Saint Francis because of his evangelical radicalism, William Joseph Chaminade because of his simple honesty, or Saint Rafaela of the Sacred Heart simply because she clashed with her successor's interests. At times, these founders also had to fight against the Church authorities because their intuitions were incompatible with rules and traditions. Thanks to their constancy and faith in God, they were eventually recognized and gained approval. Often it was the simple people who recognized the religious and human value of these new foundations and supported them enthusiastically.

I do not know why minorities, the wretched, the weak, and the insignificant arouse such fear and anguish, sowing uncertainty and alarm in the majority or in those who govern and exercise power. History offers us a wealth of seemingly small figures who made the most powerful hesitate or even managed to defeat them, like David and Goliath: John XXIII, Mar-

3. Unlike Thomas, who was vindicated, Reverend Jean-Marie de Lamennais, depicted here in a portrait by Paulin Guérin, 1831, had his 1834 condemnation upheld. He advocated the separation of church and state as well as freedom of conscience, both considered against church teaching at the time.

tin Luther King, Hélder Câmara, Teresa of Calcutta, Brother Roger of Taizé, or Nelson Mandela are the "Davids" of the recent past who have inspired countless people, and shown how the fragility of some people is a source of life, a source of future, and utopia for humankind. The God who came down to pitch his tent among the weakest continues to take the form in the fragility of people. He died on the cross while they often suffered persecutions and abandonment, but they still continue to be a source of inspiration for many people.

Of course, there have been periods of harmony, conciliation, and dialogue as well, and for its followers the Church has been the beautiful bride they have lived with, in joy and spiritual consolation. Some have been able to create enriching experiences; for example, Chiara Lubich (1920–2008), founder of the Focolare Movement, whose members are men, women, laypeople, single, celibate, married, Christians, and followers of different religions—even those who professed no particular religion—but were attracted by the ideal of a united world. Its spirituality focuses on Jesus' new commandment: "Love one another as I have loved you"; "that they may all be one" (John 15:12 and 17:21). This led to listening, fraternity, benevolence, and the loving understanding of other people's reasons, and dialogue as a testimony of Christian behavior. Chiara Lubich worked incessantly for the union of the Church, for ecumenical dialogue and fraternity among peoples, who are all the transcendental fruit of the love for God and for our brothers and sisters; it is these results that show the sincerity or falseness of many Christians who overuse the words *love* and *charity*.

The Church should always show the unity of divine people in its own life. The fact that they are all one constitutes, or should constitute, ecclesiastical longing. The mission of the pope, bishops, and Christians has to be the center of communion in their respective fields. This is the only way to achieve what the Second Vatican Council says: "The messianic people, although it does not actually include all men, and at times may look like a small flock, is nonetheless a lasting and sure seed of unity, hope, and salvation for the whole human race. Established by Christ as a communion of life, charity, and truth, it is also used by Him as an instrument for the redemption of all, and is sent forth into the whole world as the light of the world and the salt of the earth (cf. Mt 5:13–16)" (*Lumen Gentium* 9). Being incapable of creating unity in the dioceses and Church is one of the worst sins a bishop could commit because this is his main mission. Unity does not consist in uniformity or blind obedience, and even less in what one individual thinks and decides in each church, but in fraternity, understanding, and mercy, in love and reciprocal pardon.

4. Chiara Lubich.

Opposite:
1. Cardinal Giacomo Lercaro conversing at the time of the Second Vatican Council.

Chapter 32
THE MYSTERY OF CHRIST IN THE POOR

Preparations for discussions at the Second Vatican Council followed the same procedure as previous councils. Theologians and bishops met in advance to draft an outline of what were considered the most important issues, from both theological and pastoral perspectives. The word *poor* did not occur particularly often. We do know that in the first months, a pastoral attitude and climate gradually developed, along with a desire for renewal. The discussion groups tried to present the various issues in accordance with the hopes and problems they were experiencing at that time.

One group of around fifty bishops from Latin America and Asia wanted the council to tackle the more pressing human difficulties and worries, in particular regarding the poor and those suffering from hunger and destitution, as they were well aware that the problem of poverty had significant theological implications. Before the sessions began, a group of workers gave these bishops a document in which they asked them to voice the hopes of the workers' world, the world of the small and the poor, during the council meeting; in other words, they were asking them to consider the relationship of love that unites the Church with the poor, identified in Jesus, so that anyone who turned to the Church would recognize in it Jesus of Nazareth. The bishops were well aware that if they did not succeed in tackling the subject with courage, they would have neglected one of the most important human and evangelical issues.

Meetings parallel to those of the council meetings were held, and it was here that bishops from diverse countries insisted on the need for the Church to set out on a path of evangelical reform and self-understanding, with poverty as the central issue. The starting point was to be the spontaneous decision to do without any personal wealth, luxury cars, prestigious homes, and excessively expensive episcopal accoutrements, replacing them with simpler, less expensive ones. However, this was no easy undertaking. They were convinced that the bishops would not be able to talk of a poor Christ unless they themselves lived in poverty. Christ had said that his kingdom was not of this world, but our weaknesses have transformed his Church into an empire and it is not easy to get rid of so much anti-Evangelical baggage.

The most important result the group achieved was probably the speech that was made on December 7, 1962, by Cardinal Lercaro, Archbishop of Bologna, in the council hall. Before the bishops, Lercaro proposed the "Church of the poor," an expression taken from the teachings of John XXIII, as the prevalent theme of the council ecclesiology: "This is the hour of the poor, of the millions of poor people all over the world, this is the hour of the mystery of the Mother

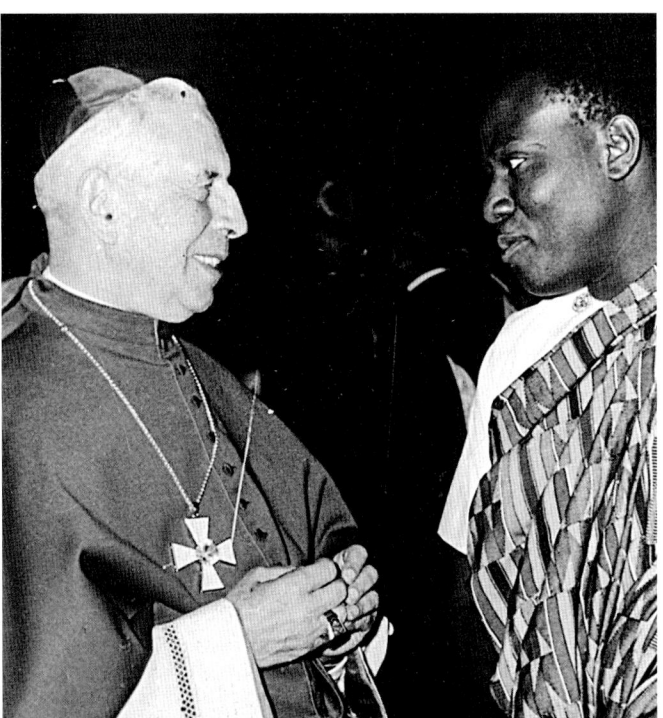

Church of the poor, this is the hour of the mystery of Christ, above all in the poor."

Lercaro was not satisfied with this subject being elucidated in yet another document, as just one of many issues to be studied. On the contrary, he wanted it to be seen as the only "subject of the entire Second Vatican Council," "the essential element, the point of clarification and coherence of all the arguments that have been dealt with so far, and of all the work we will have to carry out." The Cardinal believed that the broadest and most decisive horizon of the Church should be that of the poor, and the pastoral attention to their needs and wishes. He insisted that this was urgent because the problem of poverty was distressing and inescapable, so much so that he believed the council was taking place at the "hour of the poor."[47]

This situation meant the bishops and theologians needed to study the evangelical doctrine on poverty in depth, as it was an "essential aspect of the mystery of Christ." Lercaro requested clarification regarding the profound "ontological" connection that existed between the presence of Christ in the poor and his presence in two other realities of the mystery of Christ in the Church: the Eucharist and the hierarchy. Finally, he indicated several necessary consequences of this new consideration of poverty in the life of the Church: The reduction of the use of material means in ecclesiastical organization; the adoption of a new lifestyle and attitude by the ecclesiastical authorities that was to be less pompous and more austere; faithfulness of the religious orders to poverty, not only individually speaking but also in communities; abandonment of customs and traditions, rites and symbols, patrimonial structures and relics of the past that not only did not create anything, but were also a source of scandal; and a profound commitment to give oneself to everyone but—following the example of Christ—preferably to the poor.[48]

John XXIII had already put forward the subject of the "Church of the poor" in his speech on September 11, 1962, one month before the opening of the council: "Confronted with the underdeveloped countries, the Church presents itself as it is and wishes to be, as the Church of all, and particularly the Church of the poor." We must not forget that Christian spirituality considered poverty not only a relinquishment

2. *Pope John XXIII announces the Second Vatican Council. The "Church of the Poor" is already mentioned in his preparatory address to the Council.*

of assets and worldly goods, but also as a gesture of friendship and fraternity toward the less fortunate. This means overcoming any existing barrier, with the aim of showing friendship and closeness to our neighbors. Poverty itself is the highest wall of separation. However, we cannot ignore the different ways in which theologians considered poverty both before and after the Second Vatican Council. We will certainly find thoughts and nuances that were inconceivable beforehand. For example, in his first encyclical, John Paul II invited the bishops to help him discover the path toward lost poverty. It would also be both very useful and enlightening to take into account the progressive reactions of bishops and churchmen after the Council. The Spirit of the Lord is certainly present here as well, in the slow, complex evolution after the Council.

We have to admit that many things have changed beneath the ecclesiastical shield since then: Paul VI sold the tiara given to him by Milan and gave the money to the poor. Just before the end of the Council, the same pope gave each of the bishops a commemorative medal. On one side was a crucifix before which the pope was placing the tiara, while from heaven an angel was giving him the miter and Gospel. This is the message of the Church of the poor: it no longer wants to be the sovereign of the ways of the world, but wants to be evangelical and missionary. Ever since then, no pope has worn the tiara, since it actually only represents political sovereignty and terrestrial power. Other customs that have been abandoned include the gestatorial chairs, the Roman patriciate, the papal court, and most of the Vatican military corps. The cardinals are no longer considered princes and no longer wear ermine cloaks with trains; a considerable number have also relinquished their palaces and rings with precious stones, although some of them still appear to be nostalgic for the past.

In particular, it seems that these churchmen now have a better understanding of the need to live in institutional poverty; in fact, together with many other bishops, some have decided to live and work in the poorer neighborhoods, alongside those most in need. The Christian community has to keep watch over this attitude to ensure that the new generations continue along the same path.

3. The first session of the Second Vatican Council, in which the "Church of the Poor" was to be discussed.

THE MYSTERY OF CHRIST IN THE POOR

No matter what, however, ecclesiology has been enriched by the concept of the people of God. These people are made up of the poor who see the promises God made to human beings over the course of history come true in their own lives. It is made up of men and women who need to be saved. The Church has revived this concept to show that it is an integral part of human history, it is aspiring to the kingdom that is about to come, and is fulfilling Isaiah's prophecy: "The blind receive their sight, the lame walk, the lepers are cleansed, the deaf hear, the dead are raised, and the poor have good news brought to them" (Matthew 11:5). This concept of people makes it possible to affirm that God's children all share the same dignity. This is the intuition of those most affected by poverty when they say: "At least when we pray in Church we see there is equality. God loves the rich and the poor in the same way."

Several years later at the Medellín conference (1968), those gathered said that "the Latin-American episcopacy could not remain indifferent to the terrible social injustices that existed and still exist in Latin America, forcing most of our people into painful poverty, and in many cases inhumane misery. A muted outcry is coming from millions of people who are asking their pastors for a liberation that will come from nowhere else" (Medellín, 14, 1–2). The conferences of the Latin American episcopacy that followed in Puebla (1979), Santo Domingo (1992), and Aparecida (2007) maintained this close analysis of the situation and communal and personal needs. Unfortunately, most Christians know very little about such realities and documents.

4–5. *Paul VI in Medellín, Colombia, for the 1968 Conference of Latin-American Bishops.*

Chapter 33
HÉLDER CÂMARA AND ÓSCAR ARNULFO ROMERO

A historian of the Second Vatican Council described Archbishop Hélder Câmara as "someone who seeks the impossible." He spoke without restraint. He was convinced that it was impossible to proclaim and bear testimony to the Gospel while surrounded by gilded Baroque ornaments, candelabras, and tapestries. All he cared about was what Jesus asked, not the dust of the centuries that covers so many churches and ecclesiastical institutions.

When they sent him a questionnaire with fifty questions from Rome, he replied that they did not take into consideration the most serious and fundamental questions of the time, such as the excessive population growth in Latin America, or the underdevelopment of two-thirds of humanity. He felt that there is one question the Church should ask itself frequently: Are the things that were important to Jesus important to us? The Lord criticized severely all those who, forgetting love—in other words, forgetting God's very behavior—concentrated on trivia, useless rites, and superficial traditions, and he denounced these "transgressors" mercilessly. "Indeed, an hour is coming when those who kill you will think that by doing so they are offering worship to God. And they will do this because they have not known the Father or me" (John 16:2–3). At times the whip of intolerance has been used in Christian communities, by those usurping power and displaying an attitude that we will certainly not find in the Gospel and that has very little to do with Jesus' teachings. Nevertheless, there have always been people who were willing to sit in the back row, who have forgiven seventy times seven, have turned the other cheek, and have built the kingdom of God with humility, with the tranquil strength and conviction that it is God who sows and reaps.

Hélder Câmara firmly believed that only if we accept the consequences of the identification of Christ with the poor will we be able to act in the way Jesus asks us to in his description of Judgment Day: Fighting courageously for peace, love, and justice without paying attention to the worries of this earth, which are always connected to personal interests; exercising power only as a service; and the Church as the antithesis of imperiousness, manipulation, and imposition.

"It is impossible to be Christians if you are not on the side of the poor," he repeated to those who approached him. "You cannot achieve peace without practicing justice, and today justice implies economic and cultural development. Political independence has to be accompanied by financial independence, and if it is lacking it is the Great Powers that subdue the nations. It is dishonest to speak of freedom to two thirds of humanity who cannot understand the meaning of the word." It is neither honest nor coherent, we could add, to expect freedom from people who have not been given the economic conditions they need for freedom.

He dreamt of a poor and servile Church, as an institution and as a communal example of faithfulness to Jesus: "The bishops of Latin America should free themselves of the lands of the Church and transfer them with intelligence to the poor; they should openly support structural reforms without exception; they should encourage anti-violence movements until they exercise a democratic pressure that helps overcome the inertia and egoism of the economic powers; they should encourage development by trying to guarantee a humane, Christian meaning to protect the human dimension in investments and prepare people for development with educational programs that transform the subhuman masses into peoples."[49]

On one occasion, free of any constraints, as an inhabitant of a continent of poverty and ignorance who wanted to express his judgment on the compli-

1–4. Hélder Câmara (1) and Óscar Romero (4) next to an aerial photograph of Mexico City (photo A. Stabin) and ruins of a neighborhood in Cochabamba, Bolivia, in the 1980s (photo C. Lavayén). Development in Latin America exploded, leading to the abandonment of some areas and the growth of slums.

cated network that had disfigured and benumbed the Church over the years, he stated, "Yesterday they asked me what I would do first, if I were Pope. I began by reminding them that being Pope was not at all easy. It's really difficult. Even being archbishop is difficult. I don't know what I'd be able to do. But I know what I would like to do. I would take office in the middle of Saint Peter's Square. I would tell the people and the world, following Paul VI who gave away his tiara because he didn't want to be and never again wanted to be a king in this world, at that moment, my conscience would make me tell the countries that had accredited ambassadors in the Holy See that, although the Pope wants to maintain good personal relationships with all countries, there is no longer any reason for there to be ambassadors in the Vatican, or nuncios in governments…I would say the same thing, with great delicacy and weighing my words so I didn't hurt anyone, to the Roman patriciate. I would also communicate my decision to transform the Vatican into a simple museum and library, entrusted to an international institution that was committed to preserving these organs in the service of culture (the rent would be used for the poor). A mania for poverty!… Until the Church is a servant like Christ, until it stops offering the world the scandal of a strong, powerful Church that lets itself be served, I think it is essential to do all of this immediately, on the first day. Do you realize what revolution would take place?…A reform of the Roman curia would be next. Depending on to what degree the collegiality and attitude toward the bishops ceases to be one of mistrust and surveillance, the curia could be simplified greatly…The costs would be much less: Without if or buts; without having to run the Vatican (the small guards would remain to guard the Museum, the Library, the Cathedral, the costs of which would be covered by the tenant institution); with the actual decentralization of the Church government, the Pope would have nothing to do with the assets that cause such outrage. The Pope's prestige might suffer drastically. But is prestige essential? What is essential is that the identification between Christ and his direct, immediate representative on earth is easier for people. What is essential is that humanity does not see the Church as another kingdom, another empire…."[50]

Is this vision utopian, something that can never come true? In any case, it highlights the importance of Jesus' words: "But you are not to be like that," do not act the same way the world does, do not identify yourselves with the world. As an institution, as a religious community, you also have an obligation toward yourselves to act as individual Christians following Jesus. Even the institutions have to give testimony, and act as the instruments of love for God, and of the beatitudes pronounced by the Lord.

On March 24, 1980, the Archbishop of San Salvador, Óscar Arnulfo Romero, was assassinated before the high altar of the cathedral for having been a staunch defender of the peasants and poor people in El Salvador, where injustice meted out by a handful of bullies meant that anyone who was against their projects was in imminent danger. He was neither the first nor the last. Before him, the Jesuit Rutilio Grande (1977) had been tortured and assassinated; he had founded dozens of grassroots ecclesiastical communities where peasants and believers from the Americas could evaluate their everyday life with their beliefs, with other priests, catechists, and followers. Romero never defended violence but he was aware of the social and, in a certain sense, the revolutionary importance of Christian love: "The Church has always condemned violence as a means in itself or when it is misused against human rights, or used as the only means to defend and affirm a human right. We cannot do evil to achieve good. A soldier is not obliged to obey an order that goes against the law of God. An immoral law need not be respected. The Church must not remain silent in the face of such abomination. Reforms are useless if they are accompanied by bloodshed. In the name of God and the resigned people, I beg you, I command you: Put an end to the repression!" Whenever he could, he spoke with total freedom about the consequences of the Word of God on human actions and its importance in the situation in El Salvador.

In a sermon he gave on December 3, 1978, he said, "The Church is close to any man who puts forward just claims in an unjust context, and who works for the kingdom of God. The kingdom of God is nearer the border zone of the Church, and so the Church appreciates everything that is in accord with its fight to establish the kingdom of God. A Church that only

Next page:
1. The Dominican father, Jacques Loew, toiled in the docks of the port of Marseille and founded the Mission Ouvrière Saints-Pierre-et-Paul, a small community of worker priests.

tries to make sure it remains pure and uncontaminated would not be a Church in the service of God and men."
Both Câmara and Romero spoke and warned about the Church's responsibility regarding the development of the people. The speeches the Brazilian archbishop gave in several European cities often courageously cited the moral responsibility of the Europeans in countless unjust situations in the Third World. Together, Hélder Câmara and Óscar Arnulfo Romero drafted the final Puebla document, in particular paragraph four in chapter two, entitled *Evangelization, Liberation and Human Promotion* in which we can read: "There are two complementary and inseparable elements: Liberation from all forms of sin, from personal and social sin, from everything that lacerates humans and society and the source of which lies in egoism, in the mystery of injustice; and liberation from the progressive growth in being, thanks to the communion with God and men, which culminates in the perfect celestial communion when God will be in everyone and there will be no more tears. This is a liberation that is being fulfilled in history, that of our people and our own, embracing the different dimensions of existence: Social, political, economic, cultural, and the whole of their relationships. In all of this the transformative richness of the Gospel must spread, with its own, specific contribution that has to be protected."

A few years after Archbishop Romero's death, Don Pino Puglisi and Don Giuseppe Diana were assassinated in the South of Italy, one of them outside his own house, the other in the sacristy, both with a clear warning: "You, man of God, celebrate your Mass, but don't get involved with the poor and politics." This was an old warning: They had already used it with Christ.
Five centuries earlier, in 1511, the Dominican Antonio de Montesinos gave a Christmas sermon in the settlements of Santo Domingo where he voiced the thoughts of some of the Dominicans present in those lands, "You all find yourselves in mortal sin, you will live and die in this state because of the cruelty and tyranny with which you treat these innocent peoples. Tell us with what right, in virtue of what justice, do you keep the South American Indians in this cruel, horrible slavery. Who authorized you to wage these detestable wars against people who are living quietly and pacifically in their own villages, and to exterminate an infinite number of them with unheard of murders?…Are they perhaps not men, without either soul or reason? Perhaps you are not obliged to love them as you love yourselves?" Together with Montesino, Las Casas, and Francisco de Vitoria, many others defended the human rights of all the inhabitants of the American colonies, but all too often egoism and ambition bore more weight than the evangelical commandments.[51]

Chapter 34
THE WORKER PRIESTS

In 1943 Henri Godin and Yvan Daniel wrote the book *La France, pays de mission?*[52] a description of de-Christianization in France and an impassioned call for the country's re-evangelization. As this was reproduced in other traditionally Christian countries in the following years, how did this situation come about? With the advent of the Enlightenment, religious criticism, attacking the Church, deism, and radical rationalism that refuted transcendency became fashionable. Nearly all intellectuals and the bourgeoisie abandoned religious practice. The culture of the Enlightenment was characterized by its indifferent attitude to religion and an anthropology that ignored transcendency. Darwin's theory and modern theology appeared to have turned their backs on Christian tradition.

Even more painful, however, was the fact that the Church was also abandoned by the working class. The new poor and destitute, cramped in soulless slums devoid of quality of life, the new product of an egoistic mindset that exploited workers who had no protection from the state because neither the necessary laws nor family rights existed. In France, as in Great Britain and Germany, which were the most industrialized countries, this new social class had replaced the traditional faith and church attendance with the new socialist theories and the People's Houses; the disconcerting result of this was that the Church simultaneously lost the middle class and the socialist workers.

After countless futile attempts to draw closer to and help people who were without rights or beliefs, in 1943 Cardinal Suhard, Archbishop of Paris, founded the Mission of France. This was an attempt to interpret the new situation and announce Christ with a renewed voice and with newly found energy. It led to the idea that priests should personally experience the conditions of the working class. It was in these years that a considerable number of priests abandoned their parishes to go and live in the poorer neighborhoods, so they could be closer to their brothers and sisters. They wanted to be among those who were suffering, together with the poor, putting into practice Jesus' words: "And the poor have good news brought to them" (Luke 7:22). They wanted to experience their priesthood in the very heart of the Church of the poor.[53]

Similar initiatives by other priests multiplied surprisingly quickly although not always with success; at times they were accused of being more militant than concerned with evangelization, and more workers than priests, although their generosity and goodwill was never questioned. In Marseilles, Father Jacques Loew and other Dominican friars worked in the port docks as longshoremen. Loew, however, was so struck by the circumstances surrounding Cardinal Mindszenty's trial that he refused to sign the petitions the Communists circulated for peace and against the atomic bomb. It was there that the Little Broth-

2. Father Joseph Wresinski fought for the homeless in France. Here he is in 1968, while a slum near Paris was bulldozed (photo L. Prat).

3. Father Wresinski delivering his famous lecture, "Defeating Poverty," at the Sorbonne in 1983. Today, the organization he founded, ATD Fourth World, continues his work throughout the world.

Opposite:
4. Auto assembly line in the 1960s (illustration by G. Bacchin).

ers of Jesus showed it was possible to be contemplative while working in the most arduous and difficult places, and living in the most wretched conditions. Workers' fraternities were established in different places and had three key characteristics: Repeating the secret life of Jesus in Nazareth, practicing a heartfelt and profound Eucharistic life, and demonstrating evangelical love with their own lives. The priests of Prado, the Voluntary Workers for the Rights of the Poorest Man, the ATD Fourth World Movement, and numerous other similar initiatives were a gathering point in all countries for many young people who were tormented by the estrangement of the hierarchy from the people and abandonment of the Church by many who had been Christians in the past. Gilbert Cesbron gave an evocative description of these settings in his novel *Saints in Hell*.[54]

This experience of worker-priests is a beautiful page in the life of the contemporary Church. With its perplexities and vagaries, distressed by the massive desertion of the workers and the number of those who had joined social movements that united the weakest and most wretched in society, it was this Church that tried to incarnate itself among the poor and those who had strayed from it, driven by the desire to share the life of countless brothers and sisters, looking after their problems and difficulties, and therefore following in Jesus' footsteps. Although this took place in France, following a very well-thought-out plan, similar initiatives had been started elsewhere, albeit localized and on a smaller scale. In a way, it was a matter of "rubbing shoulders with the barbarians," an action that meant overcoming the ecclesiastical and cultural barriers that separated the Church from the non-Christian world, the working world in particular.

This choice was so revolutionary and innovative compared to traditional practice that, from the very start, it met with misunderstanding and prejudice, in particular regarding its attempt to reconcile life as a priest with working in a factory or the like. But did not the environment of these places, the workers' lifestyle, and the effort of manual labor contaminate priestly obligations and spirit? Giovanni Battista Montini (later Pope Paul VI) did not think so when, in 1948 at the Congress of Catholic Graduates he said the following while celebrating Mass, "While, on the other hand, it is necessary to sympathize with others in total friendship to construct common good, not to alienate oneself from forms of everyday life, and to go to everyone as some priests did in France when they put on their overalls to go and work in the port with the workers to be closer to them"; although his opinion might have been slightly different five years later. In 1953–1954, Rome suppressed the movement without seeking or offering alternatives, in a climate of controversy that involved all French society. In *Le Figaro*, François Mauriac said he hoped for a concordat that would allow the State to protect the freedom

of the French clergy from Roman rule. It was thanks to Cardinal Liénart, Bishop of Lille, that the French Mission was allowed to continue in the form of a *prelatura nullius*, with a more centralized organization. There were various reasons for the crisis but only one of them proved to be decisive: The traditional definition of priesthood and how it is practiced. Those in charge in the Holy See were unable to overcome a mentality that many regarded as rigid and incomplete, and had decided that the priesthood as defined in the Council of Trent was not just one of the many possible priestly models, but the only one. They were unable to accept the need to place the problems in their historical context and to reason not only from a dogmatic point of view, but also from history. In reality, this was a conflict between two views of the world, two different ways of conceiving society and the Christian community, and of the definition of de-Christianization.

In the third session of the Second Vatican Council, a group of bishops asked Paul VI to authorize each bishop to allow his priests to maintain professional jobs as well as their pastoral duties. The aim of this was to make it easier for the faithful and those who had become alienated to discover the face of a Church that was poor and a servant. After the Council there was no lack of priest workers in some dioceses but subsequent ecclesiastical evolution seems to have made this interest vanish in seminaries and among the clergy. This was a situation we could describe using the words of the poet Charles Péguy, "They have clean hands, because they no longer have hands."

Chapter 35
WILLINGNESS TO LISTEN

"Lord, hear our prayer," is a supplication we repeat in liturgy and in our personal prayers, convinced that God, our Father, is always listening to our requests and our needs. "Listen to the cries of your people," the prophets would wail at moments of anguish. "Ask, and it will be given you; search, and you will find; knock, and the door will be opened for you. For everyone who asks receives, and everyone who searches finds, and for everyone who knocks, the door shall be opened," Jesus had told his disciples (Matthew 7:7). During the course of Christian history, bishops have listened to believers in the sacrament of penance, acting as God's ear and listening to endless anguish and human secrets. At a moment of meditation and intimacy, Christians open up to a listener who is a mediator, a healer, and merciful.

In Caritas, many volunteers go to the homes of the elderly and sick to keep them company, so they have someone to talk to, showing them they are not alone, in a world that seems to be interconnected but is often so inhospitable that its inhabitants isolate themselves in their homes, not even trusting their next door neighbors. The worst misfortune for many people is being aware that they are considered worthless, and that their own sufferings are ignored or underestimated. "The worst thing is the contempt or difference of one's neighbors."[55] The organization of Christians in parishes, in communities of faith and life, tends to encourage greater reciprocal knowledge and confidence although the current decline of parish feeling and the religious individualism of many believers make these communities fade away until they actually disappear. Over the last few years, we have given a new meaning and value to war, conflicts of identity, religious differences, and economic and social disparity, so that we now find we are part of a world that is more dangerous and more full of conflicts, not only at a local and national level, but also at a continental and global one. We have to learn to live in unity. The way to do so successfully is to encourage dialogue with people on the street, the dialogue of religions, and the dialogue between different cultures. We have to get to know each other better and be more receptive because we are full of reciprocal reservations, distrust, and prejudice. On the other hand, there is also a considerable secularization of values and relations, a new materialism that isolates the religious principles of transcendence and fraternity. What attracts attention in our western society is young people's ignorance of their cultural and religious roots, the meaning of the art they see in museums, and the origins of festivities and traditions. Now more than ever before it is necessary to revive the Christian identity so that it is possible for Christians themselves to have a dialogue that enriches them. Interest in the unity of Christians does not mean irenics or indifference, but a realization of the absurdity that is represented by many Christians who care more about some ecclesiastic tradition that is of no importance than Jesus' commandment to be united. The words of Christ regarding the need to be united in the Gospel according to John constitute an unavoidable commandment for his disciples. In this sense, hate among Christians has been one of the most serious sins against the Spirit, while a spirit that sincerely believes in ecumenism is a sign of obedience to the Lord's commandment.

In fact, dialogue with God and with one's brothers and sisters constituted the heart of Christian communities. The liturgy of Mass includes a dialogue between the priest and God, between the priest and the assembly, between the assembly and God, and among the faithful with the sign of peace. The reciprocal greeting among those who attend Mass in one of the last rites before communion constitutes an exchange of

WILLINGNESS TO LISTEN

1. Otto Dix, La Guerra. Triptych, tempera on board, 1929–1932. Gemäldegalerie Neue Meister, Dresden. Imitating the famous Renaissance triptychs showing the major themes of faith, Dix paradoxically depicts the destruction of war in a medium usually used for objects of veneration.

faith and hope, affection and complicity between the participants in the fundamental rite of the Christian religion, and a demonstration of the fact that they feel they are fraternal members and are spiritually part of the same human community.

The parish bells would summon and inform, and the faithful would listen, draw their own conclusions, and go. The bells were the community clock, the announcement that God was with them, and an invitation to remember him in everyday life. For centuries, the parish was a meeting place, where one could get to know people, converse, and celebrate with the whole neighborhood.

Every love is reciprocal listening, worrying about the other person, believing one has the same dignity and the same rights. Early Christianity did not abolish slavery, but the brothers would listen to one another and sit at the same table; they would pray together and eat the same bread. Parishes became the village social center. The Church has asked itself many times how

2. *Sano di Pietro.* Saint Bernadine Preaching in the Campo of Siena. *Tempera on board, 1440–1450. Museo dell'Opera del Duomo, Siena. Saint Bernardine preached against usury and for solidarity with the poor. He instituted the* monte de pieta, *charities that offered low-interest loans to the poor.*

3. *Noël Hallé (1711–1781),* Saint Francis de Sales Gives Saint Jane de Chantal the Rule of the Order of the Visitation. *Oil on canvas, eighteenth century. Church of Saint-Louis-en-l'Ile, Paris. The Rule of the Visitation nuns was innovative in that the religious women were to assist the poor outside the cloister. However, it was soon changed to conform to the Council of Trent's decrees that strengthened the strictness of cloister law.*

4. Volunteers from the Community of Sant'Egidio. Not only do they offer material assistance to the poor, they also provide companionship.

it can continue to be the Church of the poor, how it can listen to them, open itself up to them, understand their language, love them, and confide in their evangelical capacity since they are poor, so that at any given moment it is able to discover the joyful liberty of poverty that has been adopted by choice. Nowadays, we are able to walk into a crowded elevator in our apartment house without saying hello; we can travel one hundred kilometers by train or plane without speaking to the person next to us; we can take part in religious gatherings or vigils and pray with devotion, but we do not feel we are close to anyone around us. Today, many who receive Holy Communion do not feel they can exchange the sign of peace with their own brothers and sisters. They feel they are members of an ethereal Church, but not the brother or sister of the person next to them, especially if they are not dressed in a way they deem suitable. In an assembly of people who call the same God "Father," this is a contradiction.

If we listen to those around us, we will end up creating a community of brothers and sisters, just like Charles de Foucauld's Little Brothers of Jesus. Listening to nature and to those he met along the way was Francis of Assisi's secret. Bernardine of Siena listened to the desperation of those who had fallen into the trap of usury and founded the Mounts of Piety. Listening, defending the natives of all kinds, and being close to them was the glory and charisma of priests during various colonial eras. Listening to the anguish and needs of those around them was the task of Catholic Action and many other apostolic organizations; Bartolomé de Las Casas listened to the cries of injustice oppressing the natives and promised to fight for them. John Vianney, the cure of Ars, would listen day and night to the distress of those who confessed to him and was able to calm them thanks to the forgiveness of Christ. Hélder Câmara would listen to his diocesan communities and asked the Council for an authentic conversion of the Church and greater closeness to those in need, listening and building bridges, and discovering new ways of serving better, as did John of God and Camillus de Lellis. Listening to encourage knowledge and confidence, risking destruction and hostility, is what the Community of Sant'Egidio does in its dialogue with the other religions. Listening so that anguish is replaced by confidence and the possibility of salvation was how the Trinitarians and the Order of the Blessed Virgin Mary of Mercy did in their work in Mediterranean ports. And finally, the Second Vatican Council listened and interpreted the signs of modern times and suggested answers for Christians. All of

WILLINGNESS TO LISTEN

these tried to cure, free, defend, accompany, and save their brothers and sisters, but above all, they strived to keep up human relations, to listen to invocations and suggestions, and to keep people company in their solitude. First, we need friends, and only then do we need doctors and priests.

Listening demands and expresses the need for contrition and forgiveness. A Church or priesthood that offers forgiveness in the sacrament but not in life, that reconciles in the sacrament but is unable to make peace with the world, with people, with the anguish and bewilderment of human beings, is a prisoner of its own weakness. Real forgiveness presupposes the freedom to love, and this is very difficult. If we are to love, we have to give ourselves, while if we are to forgive, we only need a little generosity. The Inquisition, excommunications, and the never-ending recollection of demons indicates a disconcerting miscomprehension of the fact that the Lord came to save us and not to condemn us. The intransigence and intolerance that are so widespread in the life of Christianity and the diffidence of so many theoreticians of charity, lead us to suspect that very often people are listening to us less than they should.

The willingness to listen presupposes purifying doses of humility, comprehension, and the ability to fathom the personal situations of those who have opened themselves up to us, baring their own intimacy in the hope they will be understood and reborn. The peasant missions dreamt of by Alphonsus de Liguori and Vincent de Paul target this ability for solidarity and proximity. In the nineteenth century, the men and women who founded congregations for the elderly, the abandoned, the sick, and the homeless children wanted to regenerate the weak, derelict fabric of society, revive a mistreated justice in peoples who had been unjustly organized by egotism and brutality.

It is at home in the family that one has to listen with the greatest attention and joy to God our Father, and to listen to each other with respect and affection. The family is the ideal place to sense the importance of shared love, not only with those near to us but also with those around us. It is here, during the development of our own personality that we are shown how the love of God who created us must make us respect his creatures. This small domestic church must be a space of comprehension of the human family, of the ties that unite us, and of our reciprocal responsibilities. Years ago, the sacred history that was taught in these early years was intimately connected to the life of Christ. Our minds opened themselves to our Christian roots and to the understanding of our place in the world, a world that we have been given so that we can improve it and make it more human.

WILLINGNESS TO LISTEN

5. The Visitation. Detail of fresco in the apse of Saint-Martin in Nohant-Vicq, Indre, France, early twelfth century. The face of Mary meets the face of Elizabeth. The intensity and joy of the impending motherhood of the two is strongly expressed. The Incarnation enters history through a family.

6. The Kiss of Joachim and Ann. Fresco, Notre-Dame in Pouzauges-le-Vieux, Vendée, France, early twelfth century. The Holy Family was preceded by Mary's family. Her parents, Ann and Joachim waited twenty years to conceive a child. Their faith was the context in which Mary prepared for her destiny: to be the mother of Jesus.

Chapter 36
SILENT COMPANIONS: CHARLES DE FOUCAULD'S LITTLE BROTHERS AND SISTERS OF JESUS

Sermons in the Sahara is a work by Charles de Foucauld. Despite being one of the most fascinating characters of recent times, full of projects, concerns, and feelings, he died without a single disciple.[56] On December 1, 1916, he was assassinated in the desert of Tamanrasset with a shot to the head, kneeling in his front doorway, his hands tied behind his back. His body was found in a ditch; he was holding a small monstrance that he carried with him. It was a death he had described some time earlier: "Think that you are to die a martyr, stripped of everything, stretched out on the ground, naked, unrecognizable, covered with blood and wounds, violently and painfully killed, and desire that it be today!" His spiritual children have initiated forms of religious life that open up new ways of presenting the Christian faith in a pluralistic and secularized world. The intermediary between Foucauld and his spiritual descendants was René Voillaume, a fascinating character who was immersed in the writings and spirit of that solitary man assassinated in the Algerian desert, and who was capable of translating Father Charles' insights into groups of spirituality and action.[57]

It is not a monastic order (they do not withdraw from the world); it is not a mendicant order; it is not one of regular clerics (they want to live off their work, like the poor); it is not a modern congregation (they do not pursue an "active" life in the sense of a work of mercy or apostolate); and neither is it a secular institute, but

1. The hermitage of Charles de Foucauld on the plateau of Assekrem, 80 kilometers from Tamanrasset, in southern Algeria.

2. The Hoggar Mountains, Algeria. Many of the openings in the rocks have ancient cave paintings.

SILENT COMPANIONS: CHARLES DE FOUCAULD'S LITTLE BROTHERS AND SISTERS OF JESUS

SILENT COMPANIONS: CHARLES DE FOUCAULD'S LITTLE BROTHERS AND SISTERS OF JESUS

a fraternity of brothers and priests who work and live a contemplative life together on equal terms. They do not try to preach a Christian life to their brothers and sisters from the pulpit, or through catechesis or teaching, but through friendship and love by living alongside their brothers and sisters. By following the example of their founder, they are convinced that if we want to follow Jesus and search for God's face, we cannot place ourselves outside the world, but we have to "go to Nazareth," where the people are. We should not distance ourselves from people, but approach them and merge with them. When he was ordained, Charles de Foucauld was aware that he had to dedicate his life and priesthood to the most neglected, and his followers have done the same.

Their spirituality consists in letting themselves be loved by God and searching for his face in prayer, in everyday life, and in the faces of those they live alongside, following in the footsteps of Brother Charles, who said that we should "see a brother in every human being," and live among the poor and the marginalized, living like them without preaching or evangelizing, but simply loving them. Total equality between the brothers and priests was clearly established from the very start—an equality that presupposes a unique religious and doctrinal training for everyone and a

3. *Charles de Foucauld in Algeria, 1912.*

4. *This picture from 1902 shows Charles de Foucauld with slaves he has just ransomed.*

5. Interior of Charles de Foucauld's hermitage on the plateau of Assekrem in Algeria.

6. René Voillaume (1905–2003), founder of the Little Brothers of Jesus, photographed in 1999 sitting on the well in the courtyard of the house in Nazareth, with other members of the brotherhood.

breach of the exclusive relationship between priesthood and responsibility.

Thanks to the slow and continuous evolution of their desire to respond to the needs of the people, they soon became convinced that the long hours devoted to work impose a different rhythm to the prayer they had been practicing in the monastic fraternity in the desert. Their whole life and Eucharistic spirituality acquired a new and intense Samaritan dimension by sharing the everyday anxieties and sufferings of the poor. It is an intensely personal Eucharistic celebration, linked to life, struggle, and hope.

They do not hide what they are, but participate with simplicity and normalcy in the lives and problems of their neighbors. The confidences of their workmates and neighbors, the injustices they suffer, their weaknesses, and their immense needs stimulate the brothers' hearts, minds, and energies and bring them even closer to God; but they also discover that their companions try to listen to the reasons for their faith, their hope, and their lifestyle, in a reciprocal sharing. One of the brothers wrote to me, "I talk about God a lot. Without Him I wouldn't know how to express myself, I wouldn't know how to be a confidante, I wouldn't know how to be a friend." It is another way of evangelizing.

The contemplative nature of their religious life has been clear since the very beginning, with the Eucharist as its heart and soul. It is in the Eucharist that the brothers find the source of their love for others, leading them to live completely and happily at the service of their brothers and sisters, and to sharing their daily troubles and concerns, just as Father Foucauld did. These constant contacts help the brothers to conserve the sense of the people's suffering, everyday problems, and worries in their contemplative life. Thanks to a life lived in poverty and in daily work, they share the fate of the workers and find in this personal experience the secret of their devotion and a stimulus for their prayer.

In the fraternities, work is considered a way of participating in the life of the people, of making concrete their vote of poverty. Voillaume wrote in *Seeds of the Desert*, "It is not merely a spirit of poverty, which is compatible with any activity or any work; it is being poor among the poor, a worker among workers, small among the small of this world, and it is a choice that contains terrible requirements. It is a call from Jesus to Father de Foucauld and to us. Everything pushes us toward it." Work is a pivot that helps the brothers find a place in society and be seen as being like many others. It places them in a neighborhood, in the union. They are workers who try to be present in their neighborhoods, helping, assisting, and keeping company.

Magdeleine of Jesus, founder of the Little Sisters of Jesus, exhorted the disciples to become part "of the same family, the same environment, the same country as those you want to save; you will take on their language, their customs, and even their mentality, however different they are from your own. You have to become one of them....Like Jesus during his life on earth, make yourself all things to all people: An Arab in the midst of Arabs, a nomad among nomads, a worker among working people, but above all be human among your brothers and sisters. Do not think that living among people will hinder your life of union with God. Do not set up barriers between the world and yourself; do not think that as a religious you have a special dignity to safeguard."[58] We find the houses of the Little Sisters in the roughest, most abandoned and peripheral neighborhoods while they pick grapes or work in the fields of Lisboa, or clean the floors of city workshops or subways.

It is a new conception of religious life, which is not necessarily more generous but is certainly more integrated in the daily life of society, closer to the joys and sorrows of the workers and the person on the street: "You are not asked, in the name of religious modesty, to live with eyes cast down, but to open them to see up close the miseries and beauty of human life and of the entire universe." The ideal is Father Foucauld's: "I live the Gospel, in absolute poverty, abandoning myself to the utterly abandoned...and, above all, in the fullness of love." They do not want to practice conventional poverty, but the poverty of the poor.

7. *A well in the desert. Drawing from Charles de Foucauld's notebook, 1885. Two symbols representing the monastic dimension: the desert to withdraw to, and water (the well), which gives life.*

Chapter 37
MOTHER TERESA AND THE MISSIONARIES OF CHARITY

By the second half of the twentieth century, Mother Teresa had become a person who was admired, followed, and visited by ministers, cardinals, and bishops, not because of her wisdom or her power, but because she was considered one of the greatest sources of spiritual energy in a world painfully lacking values and transcendence.

When she was very young, she sensed her religious vocation. Her congregation sent her to India where, after her novitiate and profession of vows, she started teaching middle-class children. She soon became aware of the shocking poverty in which much of the population of Calcutta lived, and she felt an extraordinary inspiration deep inside her that led her to devote the rest of her life to alleviating the conditions of the poor, "the poorest of the poor," and guiding them toward God. She felt called to leave her original community and to found a new one, embracing a lifestyle that made her identical to the poorest of the poor, living, suffering, and loving with them and like them. She tried to instill in those people a sense of self-respect, teaching them that God loved them.

Young people soon began to join her. They were willing to live with her in the manner of the poor of India, eating only rice and salt, until someone explained to them that if they continued to eat so frugally they would end up catching tuberculosis, which afflicted the poor population they were trying to help. How could they work for others if they did not eat properly? Mother Teresa accepted the advice and decided that the sisters' food should be simple, without delicacies, but sufficient for someone who had to work hard all day.

Every morning, while they worked in the slums, the dispensaries, and the homes for the dying and for children, the sisters—whose mission centered on curing their brothers and sisters with love—were aware that what supported them internally was the strength of Christ, who they had received in the Eucharist. This strength enabled them to carry out their tasks with the happiness that the Holy Spirit spreads in the hearts of those who belong to Him and who serve Him with total dedication. Were they pleasant tasks? Not always, but they performed them with faith, moved by the words of the Lord, who after washing the disciples' feet promised them that they would be happy if they did the same.

Wherever they go, the Missionaries of Charity open schools for the poorest slum children: Sunday schools for teaching the young ones to pray, and professional schools that teach others how to cook and engage in various professions in order to earn a living; they open numerous dispensaries and prepare young men and women for marriage and family life. They clothe the naked, distribute medicines to the sick, and build housing for abandoned children, for the elderly, and for the mentally ill; they do the cleaning, thus setting an example to the poor, encouraging them to work and not be idle. In some places, they have established hospitals capable of accommodating hundreds of people and hostels for abandoned women. Poor people feel their constant presence, they begin personal relationships, and they view them as their own.

The first major work of the missionaries was the Home for the Dying Destitutes in Kalighat, housing numerous dying people who had been abandoned on the streets. One of them confessed to Mother Teresa, who was caring for him while he was dying, "Thank you, mother! I have lived on the street like an animal; thanks to your loving care, I will die like an angel." Teresa treated them like people and

MOTHER TERESA AND THE MISSIONARIES OF CHARITY

2. William Congdon, Bombay, 20. *Oil on panel, 1973, detail. Groups of "larva men" on the sidewalk of the Indian metropolis. For the American painter Congdon, the streets of India were sites of the radically impoverished human condition.*

taught them to be like people, even in death, taking them off the streets. Toward the end of her life, she revealed that around 45,000 people had died under that roof. Later she founded the City of Peace, a colony and rehabilitation center for lepers. They were not just offered cures, tranquility, and medicine, but also hope: hope and faith in the eternal goodness of God. The young, educated sisters knelt down before the sick, washed their wounds, smiled, and encouraged them, never losing their patience or cheerfulness. Although these people are strangers, the sisters are like kin to them, reflecting God's love with simplicity.

A great admirer of Saint Francis, Mother Teresa reminded her sisters that the saint was not ashamed of asking for the poor and receiving leftovers, which he shared among them. In the same way, the sisters were not to be ashamed of begging for the poor, even if this represented a form of poverty looked down on in the modern world.

She always spurred on her sisters gently, "Be happy, God loves you, particularly when the work you do in his name is hard." She urged them to imitate Saint Francis' perfect happiness, his total abandon in God, and his filial faith in the Father who created us that he might love us. In fact, every day the sisters recite Saint Francis' prayer: "Lord, make me an instrument of Your peace." This prayer sums up the spirit of Mother Teresa and her work: My happiness depends on the happiness of others and on the love of God. We are his instruments, "a pencil in God's hand" to write what he wants and decides on the heart of human beings. One day, in the Home for the Dying Destitutes in Kalighat, a visitor was admiring the peace that reigned. Mother Teresa told him it was due to the presence of God. God was always present and active with his love.

Many Christians in history have managed to combine their concern for a more just and united, fraternal and open world with the intense filial feeling they receive

1. Mother Teresa in the Khaligat Home for the Dying Destitutes in Calcutta.

3. *William Congdon*, Crucifixion, 64. *Oil and ashes on panel, 1973.*

4. William Congdon, India, 4—Calcutta Station, 1. *Oil on board, 1975.*

Congdon, who came from a wealthy Providence, Rhode Island, family, served in the Second World War driving an ambulance on the Italian front. After the war, he settled in New York to paint, going to the Bowery, a neighborhood that at the time was full of homeless people. He met Dorothy Day and the Catholic Workers, and painted the most destitute areas of New York, a sort of preparation for India, which he visited in the 1950s. In the 1970s, he met Mother Teresa, who reminded him of Dorothy Day, but what is more important is what is expressed in his paintings. Crucifixion, 64 *is a "larva man": Congdon sees Christ in the figure of the meekest and most impoverished.* Calcutta Station, *with the bodies lying on the ground, is a sort of apocalyptic construction of human privation.*

MOTHER TERESA AND THE MISSIONARIES OF CHARITY

5. A smiling Mother Teresa of Calcutta, wearing the habit of the Congregation of the Missionaries of Charity, which she founded.

6. A group of Missionaries of Charity during the Eucharistic Congress in Charlotte, North Carolina, in 2005.

from an ever-present God. We recall the names of Catherine Labouré, Elizabeth Ann Seton, Frédéric Ozanam, Joseph Benedict Cottolengo, Luigi Orione, and many other great saints, founders, and generous protectors of society who fill our Christian history. As often happens, they are less concerned with words, formulas, and concepts than with feelings and coherence, dedication and acceptance of the great commandment of love. It is always about discovering the presence of God, who inspires and attracts through his way of being and acting. His children thus serve him spontaneously when helping others, when assisting them, defending them, and protecting them, curing the wounds and sufferings of the pained brothers and sisters of Christ. The realization that the sacred is present in life reinforces their respect and love for God.

Chapter 38
EMMAUS AND POST–WORLD WAR II COMMUNITIES

Concern for sick, abandoned, homeless brothers and sisters with no future, the suffering of those who live with us, and the needs of those we do not know personally, but we know exist, continue to challenge our goodness and our sincerity. In our believing communities, the number of people, initiatives, and institutions that have been established with the aim of improving the lot of many peoples subjected to a constantly growing misery throughout the five continents has multiplied.

There are numerous people in our world who refuse to accept poverty and injustice, and who feel akin to the poor. They fight exclusion and dedicate their lives to defending human rights, even if it means risking their own lives.

Abbé Pierre (1912–2007) was aware of the sufferings of his neighbors from an early age, because his father put him into contact with the most disinherited. This encounter would change his life. After having discovered Saint Francis of Assisi and having decided to become a Capuchin friar, he renounced his inheritance and distributed it among various charities. He soon started housing in his own home people who had lived on the streets in the utmost poverty, and when he sought a means of supporting them he turned them into scavengers, going through the garbage collecting items that were still usable. By 1949, he had founded Emmaus. Work, community life, and helping the neediest are the traits we can find in this small group of pioneers that would make up the essence of the movement. In 1952, he publicized the lack of housing for the poor in France, and he worked on building the first apartment houses with his coworkers, thus forcing the government to recognize the seriousness of the situation. Abbé Pierre's group was constantly working toward having no more homeless people sleeping on the streets. After his radio appeal, he garnered an incomparable amount of solidarity, "the insurrection of goodness," which forced the French parliament to approve a law for the construction of welfare housing. Thanks to Abbé Pierre, nobody can claim that providing accommodations for the poor is not the duty of the state. His abilities and his charisma "of serving first those who suffer the most" led him to undertake a universal battle that would benefit many isolated men and tramps.

His movement spread to five continents, becoming a world crusade against poverty and in favor of peace. He visited many nations, defending with words and deeds those who had no voice. He established innumerable communities, inspired by the same principle for all: "Poverty judges the world," accusing those who not only did not mobilize themselves, but who also looked the other way and ignored reality. He was the backbone of the movement, but he could count on thousands of volunteers who were dedicated body and soul to obtaining more humane and just conditions for the abandoned people of this world.

In his lifetime, he denounced all forms of injustice, he fought against hunger in the world, and he indefatigably animated the actions of the Emmaus communities. He transformed himself into a spur against the indifference of those who had the capacities and the means to solve many of the problems that existed among the weakest and the most marginalized of society. In 1974, after the oil crisis, he protested against the new forms of poverty on behalf of the new poor: "Deplorable rich, who accumulate gold and jewels in bank safes! They are thieves, because goods and fortunes should be shared at times of crisis. We must help those who are on the point of dying; we must help them by creating vital businesses in which they can find work and a salary. We need the voices of the men and women who have no voice to stop the powerful from sleeping." He could not accept that in the twenty-first century, in a wealthy country like France, in a country in which three million could afford second homes, but the same number lacked decent accommodations, millions of people were living below the poverty line; he urged the young not to feel impotent against such suffering and to act courageously because inaction was considered a crime against our humanity.[59]

The Dominican Henri Burin des Roziers has been a lawyer for the landless in Brazil for thirty years. He was the first lawyer to take an important landowner to court for killing a peasant who could not fulfill his financial obligations. Aggregated to the Pastoral Commission for Land, and in the service of the rural workers of Brazil and the peasants' cause, working alongside other missionaries and some laypeople, he decided to defend the peasants in court. He was aware that this was how not only the people subjugated and enslaved by large landowners, but also a good part of the political and police class, could escape a desperate and clearly unjust social situation. He felt the need to search for a legal route to resolve the agrarian problem and to highlight the contradictions existing between the law and reality. This commitment by most of the Brazilian Church attacked the foundations and destabilized the climate of terror and silence that had been imposed with force. From its very beginning, this generous and courageous effort led to the birth of new social movements, encouraged the trade-union formation

1. Abbé Pierre at Neuilly-Plaisance (1954–1956) in front of a truck: "Emmaus, ragmen, builders."

2. Photo from a Koldo Chamorro report on a community founded in Mato Grosso, Brazil, by the Claretian Pedro Casaldáliga, currently Bishop Emeritus of São Félix do Araguaia. A protestor against the evils of economic liberalism, Casaldáliga has supported this community, which houses some of the world's poorest children.

3. The Jesuit Pierre Ceyrac (1914–2012), an extraordinary figure similar to Jules Monchanin, who was totally dedicated to charity. In 1936 he was a missionary in Madras (Chennai) in India. He became head of a large student movement, opening self-run farms in Manamadurai for the poorest. Between 1980 and 1993, he worked in the Cambodian refugee camps in Thailand. This photo was taken in one of those camps.

of workers, affirming that there is no real life without dignity. He defended the pluralism of ideas and the ecumenical nature of the movement that from the very beginning had supported the struggle of the disinherited of the earth. He celebrated the faith and announced the hope, with a lot of pain and anxiety, and with a great deal of enthusiasm and solidarity.

In 1992, when Father des Roziers was added to the secret list of those who were to be assassinated, the Master General of the Dominicans, Timothy Radcliffe, sent him an open letter in which he wrote: "Have faith, your brothers from all over the world are with you. We feel very proud of what you do to protect the rights of the peasants; it is a great work of justice and a true Dominican preaching the Gospel."[60]

In the most industrialized European countries after 1968, the issue of the third world migration raised its head: the problem of immigrants and the absence of rights for those arriving from a foreign land. Numerous priests and laypeople defended the rights of the immigrants, opposing the obstacles placed by businesses and public administrations. Using judicial and economic tools, and with thousands of helpers, the Caritas groups of each country dedicated huge efforts to the task of welcoming immigrants and making their lives easier. They warned that every nation would become a bunker of fear and diffidence, and they supported welcoming attitudes, which rejected the instinctive fear of the new "invaders," doing everything possible to welcome them and integrate them, despite the undeniable difficulties present in such

4. In 2008, Sœur Emmanuelle (1908–2008), was voted "Woman of France" by Elle. *She wanted to devote her life to the poorest: she achieved this at the age of fifty-four, when she was sent to Egypt, where she would live with the ragmen of Cairo's shantytown. It was here that she understood that poverty, if not extreme, is wealth. An international movement sprang from this idea.*

complex and pluralistic societies, in which non-conformists and violent activists abound. It is not an easy task, but all the parishes are involved, and Caritas deals courageously and creatively with one of the most complex challenges of hope in the last few decades.

This welcoming attitude is present in various guises, depending on the different situations in our society today. One of the most worrying problems is that of the prostitution of African women and children. In a sense, we are facing a new version of the slave trade that existed at the beginning of the modern era, a global traffic that takes place under the eyes of all nations and has become a market that enriches individuals and organizations at the cost of the weak. It is the industrialization of the sex trade. The increase in social inequalities and the impoverishment of numerous populations, which predominantly affects women and children, causes emigration, favors human trafficking, and encourages prostitution. The groups that control the sex trade are violent, and it is not possible for parish or diocesan organizations to deal with the entire problem. We should not forget the religious congregations that have been established to deal with it, the many organizations specifically dedicated to helping those who suffer this kind of slavery, or the Caritas programs. In each case, general pressure from Christians on governments and international institutions is imposed, and so far, they have been the only ones capable of successfully taking on this type of organized criminality.[61]

4

Chapter 39
CARITAS INTERNATIONALIS

In 2011, Caritas Internationalis, the ecclesiastical organization composed of 165 national Caritas, and a subsidiary of the different episcopal conferences working in close connection with the Apostolic See, was without doubt one of the most prestigious institutions in society thanks to its humanitarian and charitable work and the reliability of its documents. Caritas aims to annul or mitigate the effects that cause the most destitute to suffer, as well as inculcating respect for human dignity. It searches ceaselessly for remedies to cure all ills and it is involved in a committed and generous fight for justice. In the words of John XXIII, "Organizing Catholic charity using the appropriate technical means and starting with the needs of the entire world, you take the immediate presence of the Church to places of suffering in the world. You thus efficiently adapt the charity to the needs of the truly poor people today, and you know how to effectively use the aid that Catholics offer to ease human miseries to alleviate their pains" (Fifth Caritas Internationalis general assembly, 1960).

The Caritas members are aware of the need to link economic growth and development to social policies regarding the distribution of goods and services, thus making it feasible for everyone to have access to the basic levels of well-being needed to guarantee human dignity. They strive to maintain their presence in the less fortunate social settings through assistance, publicity, community action, training, education, and the practice of universal solidarity. This starts with Caritas creating connections and interactions between the most powerful and generous churches and those of the third world.

Charitable action seeks to help vulnerable people, in other words, poor families and those with social integration problems: children from immigrant groups and ethnic minorities; disabled children; and those who live in single-parent families or in depressed neighborhoods. For young people it offers training and educational courses, the promotion of youth volunteerism, support for those in situations of conflict, and community action. They work with women burdened with family duties, with insufficient economic means, with little support from their family or social network, and with suffering from bad health; they work with women who suffer violence, and who work in the sex trade. They keep the elderly company, they maintain conditions of hygiene, health, and shelter, they promote the development of self-esteem, they maintain cooperation and close coordination with the social and health services, and they create day centers. Currently, one of their most important activities concerns immigrants, and includes their arrival, temporary accommodation, legal advice, training, and co-development.[62] Working with disabled people presupposes an integral attention to the person and their environment, with a special attention paid to the family environment.

These are just some of the Caritas activities, which are obviously more numerous in needy countries, particularly when there are serious economic crises. To carry out their mission and their Samaritan vocation, the parish Caritas groups are involved in a continuous process of getting closer to the poor and the excluded, with the aim of discerning the real needs of the poorest and discovering the most appropriate way to respond to them. The financing that Caritas relies on fundamentally comes from specific campaigns, diocesan organization, and individual donations, although other private and sometimes public funding is available, depending on the country.

The presence and intense cooperation between various national Caritas with the more unfortunate countries of Asia, Africa, and the Americas includes questions of health and education, the promotion of women's rights, the construction of infrastructure, emergency prevention and reconstruction, environmental action in the Amazon, Bolivia, and the Caribbean, community participation, the fulfillment of basic social needs, and work in rural zones to promote development. They also work on pacification and understanding in the Balkans, development programs in Chechnya, long-standing support plans in Albania, work with the elderly in Armenia, training for workers and specialists in Serbia, Ukraine, and Mauritania, and programs in the fight against human trafficking in Ukraine. These are just some examples of the innumerable works and cooperative actions in almost every country in the third world.

I will now mention four initiatives undertaken in the first months of 2011. Haiti still suffers enormously from the consequences of the earthquake in 2009: Among the numerous projects carried out on the island, the North American Caritas has almost completed the construction of the bridge linking the island of Saint-Jean-du-Sud to various villages. It is the only communication route existing between the inhabitants of the island and the mainland, the only hope that 35,000 people have for leading a normal life. The same inhabitants who will benefit from the bridge have also worked on its construction, and with this salary, they have been able to support their families.

In Samoa and Tonga, the Australia and New Zealand Caritas have been the main collaborators on the islands' laborious reconstruction after the tsunami in 2009. Projects include: Food, clothing, restarting schools, and reconstruction of the damaged dwellings. During the first weeks, the inhabitants were offered psychological help to deal with the consequences of the enormous stress they had suffered.

In Peru, with the active participation of Spain's Caritas, the local Caritas is concerned with health, child nutrition, potable water, health services, basic hygiene, and projects to ensure that the local populations can support themselves with their own work.

1

1. *Summer 2012. Syrian refugees flee the civil war, arriving in Jordan. Jordanian Caritas provides them with means of subsistence, including clothes and blankets prepared by the Central Mennonite Committee for Syrian refugees in Zarqa, Jordan.*

2. *June 2012, South Sudan. In Agok, Caritas organized schools for thousands of students who had fled the violence on the border between Sudan and South Sudan; considerable numbers of qualified teachers were recruited to work in these schools.*

3. *Promotional picture for the Indian Caritas' Food for All campaign, December 2013.*

All of this occurs among the Andean populations living in unstable conditions that are exacerbated by earthquakes and climate change.

In Egypt, Caritas' fundamental objectives are nutrition and culture in the desert areas surrounding Cairo, Alexandria, and Giza. The complex intervention foresees the cooperation of forty-five NGOs and international agencies such as UNESCO, coordinated by Caritas. Twenty thousand students aged between eighteen and forty-five receive aid. Recently, they added a program with the aim of providing rural communities with libraries and better educational structures. The Jesuit Gabriel Nabil explains that teaching reading, writing, and arithmetic is fundamental in these areas.

Caritas Internationalis is a tangible demonstration of the solidarity and concerns of believers when faced with situations of conflict and emergency around the world. It is a further demonstration of the Church's interest in promoting the common good, and a sign of the love of Christians for their brothers and sisters of all races and conditions.

Chapter 40
JESUS AND PAIN

The mystery of Jesus begins with the realization that he was excluded; that he led a life lacking stability, and that he died discredited, disregarded, humiliated, and executed between two thieves. Pascal describes him with his total radicalism: "Of thirty-three years, He lives thirty without appearing. For three years He passes as an impostor, the priests and chief people reject Him. Finally, He dies, betrayed by one of his own disciples, denied by another, and abandoned by all" (*Pensées* 636 B 792). He was and is the cornerstone of the world and of the Church, but he made the poor the protagonists and lifeblood of his most important affirmations and of the life of his Church.

"They are like sheep without a shepherd": Jesus thus described those who followed him, an expression that indicates concern, compassion, and the desire to alleviate their condition. In the course of his work, Jesus showed that he was close to the people, interested in their lives, involved in finding solutions to their problems, in broadening their horizons, ready to offer them concrete answers to their worries.

All the pages of the Gospel transmit this determination of the Lord to mitigate or suppress pain: His sympathy for a mother who had lost her daughter, his empathy for the Roman centurion who interceded on behalf of his slave, the cure of the hemorrhaging woman, his concern for the starving multitude that followed him, his immediate response to the supplication of the man we know as the good thief: "Truly I tell you, today you will be with me in Paradise" (Luke 23:43).

In the life of Christians, we find all the manifestations of the character, generosity, and egotism of the human spirit, but it is difficult to find in the history of humankind so many expressions of love and dedication toward others as there have been in the Christian communities. Innumerable spaces of communion have arisen in the shelter of our faith in Jesus, examples of simple or sublime generosity performed by anonymous people or groups of volunteers who offer what they have, their time and their eagerness, with the aim of eliminating poverty.[63]

Human pain has myriad causes and festers in different ways, embracing all aspects of life: The sick, the abandoned, orphans, those who have separated or miscarried, those without decorum, who doubt God, the blind, those who suffer injustice or endure prejudice. The gas chambers of Nazi Germany, the genocides in Cambodia and Rwanda, the murder of Jesuits and of Bishop Romero in El Salvador, the Communist gulags, the poverty brought about by unfettered capitalism, and other crimes and injustices that are constantly perpetrated in the world, represent Christ's permanent pain, the angst of God provoked by human history. In effect, sometimes the grace, goodness, and power of God find themselves so submerged by the ocean of evil and pain that God seems to be crucified yet again in a blind and perverse world; yet there is no doubt that despite everything this painful situation has been faced courageously by Christians over the centuries. Christ is the Alpha and the Omega of the universe, the creator and the final destination of human beings. Every pain resounds in him as if it were his, every love present in the world ultimately pours forth from him, who at the end of history will present himself as the victorious Messiah.

The ten just men have always been in the Church, and they have kept Christ's presence alive through the succession of martyrs and those who have followed him. There have always been people who have become combatants on behalf of the excluded

1. Curing of the bleeding woman. Wall painting, catacomb of saints Peter and Marcellinus, Rome. "Jesus went throughout Galilee... curing every disease and every sickness among the people" (Matthew 4:23). This scene is full of symbolic and expressive power. The painting is at the center of a large lunette of an entombment recess. Jesus appears in it as a "healer," and all that is required is to have faith in him.

of this world, people armed with love, hope, and knowledge to fight ignorance, hunger, and exclusion. Certainly the sin of egoism and exploitation is still present, but grace has never completely died. Mercy, the need to share with others, identifying ourselves with others, allowing those who suffer to enter our lives, transforming this suffering into hope, is always the result of a conversion, and the merciful continue to be beatified in this world, and are the seed of every new creation.

The believer does not have to think that their generosity represents an extraordinary personal virtue, but on the contrary, they have to remain convinced that their ideas, their thoughts, and their actions do not belong to them, but are part of their faith in Christ. Although many Christians manage to practice a demanding Christianity in their personal life without worrying about identifying with those who are poor and despised, it is essential to announce and recognize that this individualism without soli-

2. Raising of the daughter of Jairus. Sarcophagus, marble (detail), early fifth century. Musée départemental Arles antique, Arles. The ultimate is the resurrection, to which everyone is summoned through Jesus.

darity does not consider an essential element in the preaching of Jesus: Its community spirit. Jesus did not just remind us of the rights of all humans due to them being children of God, but he placed the love and awareness of universal fraternity at the basis of his preaching. He wanted to create the contagion of love, because love opposes whatever impedes, obstructs, and hinders the essence of his message. For him, human rights are based on love and, taking a step further, he affirms that the poor can understand better than anyone its meaning: "At that time Jesus said, 'I thank you, Father, Lord of heaven and earth, because you have hidden these things from the wise and the intelligent and have revealed them to infants" (Matthew 11:25).

It was this thought that transformed the patrician Jerome Emiliani (1485–1537). Handsome, cultured, prodigious, and a valiant and courageous soldier after defending the freedom of Venice with all his might, he dedicated his life and his fortune

JESUS AND PAIN

to caring for orphans, convinced that the best way to find God was to look for him among the disinherited. Thanks to him, the Somaschi congregation was founded, which continued the apostolate with numerous centers of charity.[64] Today we can say that the houses of Cottolengo or Don Orione and many other religious congregations of other groups of good people are the shining demonstration of the fact that there have been, and there are, many people who devote their lives to defending the weakest because they understand that the more they love, the more they live.

In defending them, they are close to Jesus. Blaise Pascal wrote that "Jesus will be in agony until the end of the world," and many subsequent writers, such as Bernanos or Julien Green, have expressed in their works the conviction that human suffering is always in relation to the suffering of Jesus Christ.[65] When the Church is poor and accepts those who have nothing; when it lovingly serves all human beings, in particular those who most need serving; when it welcomes those who have been abandoned by everyone, its strength lies in its vulnerability. When it is capable of loving and acting only on behalf of humanity, of all humanity equally, people will see themselves in it, in the same way that the cripples, the invalids, and the blind recognized themselves in Jesus because he responded to their hopes. Only in this way can the Church become a community of believers in Christ, who they hear and who they consider their Lord. Only in this way will what they repeat on their lips coincide with what they think and force them to act. The angels of mercy have always been present in human history, in simple and ignorant people, in saints and sinners, in those who hope in God despite the apparent absurdity of their existence. Everybody allows the love of God for the world to transpire in some way. Believing, hoping, and loving, despite pain and death, is the victory demonstrated by all the saints that have been in the world, and all of those who, despite their solitude, their confusion, their pettiness, and their contradictions, despite their doubts and their sins, have confided in the Lord.

3. Herri met de Bles (ca. 1500–1560), Way to Calvary, *detail with a fallen Christ and the peasants on their way to market. Oil on panel, 1530s. Gemäldegalerie der Akademie der Bildenden Künste, Vienna. This sixteenth-century Flemish painter's ideas were akin to those of Erasmus of Rotterdam. Here, Jesus' Calvary is painted as an "episode" amid the normalcy of everyday life.*

1. *Saint Peter's and the Vatican Palaces, viewed from the center of the square.*

Chapter 41
POPE FRANCIS: "BUT YOU ARE NOT TO BE LIKE THAT"

2. Sala Ducale in the Papal Apartments, Vatican City. The stucco with putti supporting a screen was based on Bernini's Baroque design for the restoration of the rooms.

This wide-ranging history of charity depicts the enduring aspiration of many Christians to be faithful to Jesus' mandate to consider ourselves brothers and sisters, to love one another, and not to allow any child of God our Father to be marginalized, mistreated, or forgotten.

However, we are aware of our weaknesses and our innate inconsistencies. In fact, our history is often a clear demonstration of collective inconsistency. We speak in one way in our religious documents and from the daily pulpit, but in life we frequently act in a contradictory fashion. As well as numerous examples of love, commitment, and generosity, of sublime acts and lives of silent commitment to others, we discover a routine of selfishness, oppression, and a lack of consideration. Once again, we are clay vases containing the Spirit. The Psalms recognize this state of affairs when they state, "The LORD has compassion for those who fear him. For he knows how we were made; he remembers that we are dust" (Psalm 103:13–14).

What is most striking is the fact that traditionally our organizations and forms of authority and government maintain certain lavish practices that are distant from the people. The very fact that the pope is still a head of state with all the paraphernalia that goes with it seems distorting and hardly exemplary. Cardinals are viewed as the princes of the Church, and bishops and parish priests have occasionally assumed elitist ways of life and command. The ongoing, centuries-old tradition means that we have a pope and bishops who live in incredible palaces or mansions, are transported in luxurious vehicles, carried in gestatorial chairs, and accompanied by an entourage of monsignors, servants, and guards. Their personal life might be simple and austere, but the image they transmit is one of living in a world that is hardly compatible with the evangelical spirit.

The same thing happens in religious congregations. The members have often lived lives of austerity and rigor, but the image that abbeys and convents have conveyed is one of grandiosity and power. This explains why in popular revolts, starting with the French Revolution, religious men and women have been mistreated for belonging to the rich and powerful classes.

On the other hand, we come across the enormous cultural and artistic riches that the Church owns. It is true that in the exercise of its pastoral work, the Church has accumulated and transmitted an important wealth of culture over the centuries. These extraordinary works of art, ideas, and manifestations of the power of other epochs have been created and faithfully preserved in ecclesiastical environments. In each of them, we can find the influence that the religious spirit has had in all aspects of life. However, it is easy to see the contaminating effect of human pride and the longing for power in religious environments and spaces that we hoped would be capable of overcoming the temptations of power in order to follow the Master, in his company, simply, and in poverty.

At a time when many Christians are disconcerted and lack hope, Francis has come as a surprise: a pope who has come from a distant land, an exotic figure for a Christianity that remains European and Western. The new pope has taken the name of Francis, a name incompatible with pomp, pride, aloofness, human power, and glory. No pope has ever dared to assume this name, aware of the commitment that it would signify. They could not name themselves after the "poor man" of Assisi while living in a palace, traveling in limousines, with a court of functionaries, servants, gentlemen in dinner jackets, and submissive bishops.

In reality it is very hard to accept that someone would call himself the vicar of Christ, the Christ who died on the cross after a life of pure abandonment and hope in the Father, while simultaneously living surrounded by such theatrics. Indeed, this contradiction is demonstrated not only in the pope, but also in the lives of many Christians who call themselves disciples of Christ while they live alongside their naked, hungry, and excluded brothers and sisters. At any rate, there is no doubt that the large gap between theoretical formulations and obstinate reality in Rome continually widens.

Shortly after his election, meeting with the journalists who had come from all over the world to witness the conclave, the new pope said to them, "How I would like a poor Church for the poor!" Obviously, many popes have spoken of poverty in various ways, but I am sure that nobody has so

openly and determinedly pronounced this desire and conviction, which in reality was a prerequisite for the traditional model of the Church. The Church's preaching has to reach the "'existential periphery'...; be shepherds with the 'smell of your sheep,'" which means: you have to live and be with the poor before theorizing about them; you have to feel and act like shepherds before approaching them. A few days later, and with the same meaning, he stated, "The Church has to escape its 'ideological narcissism.'"

In fact, this simplicity, humility, and accessibility respond to his conviction that all power is service and that the poor are the nucleus of his raison d'être, as well as of Christian life. He turns to humanity every day, urging us to keep in mind the dignity and the needs of the most indigent, the weakest, and the least important. He reminds believers that in Jesus' message the poor are the priority. In each homily, his simple words express a weighty message: We cannot talk about poverty in the abstract, without having personal experience of it. He asked the accredited diplomats to the Vatican to ask their governments to control the economy and protect the weak from an exploitation that does not consider individuals. "Money has to serve, not govern." What is striking about his words regarding the poor is that he speaks from the heart, and we therefore feel personally drawn to the subject. He had and has the necessary freedom to question conventional categories found in politics and in the Church. He has challenged the Marxist elements of liberation theology, and he never ceases to challenge rampant capitalism. He deplores a relativism that empties faith of its meaning and rebuffs the fundamentalism of those who abhor change or who want to turn back the clock.

His proximity to human beings does not reduce the seriousness of their needs. In Argentina, he attacked unbridled corruption with determination and without regard. Corruption, he stated, destroys and makes slaves of people, it makes us lose the decency that protects truth, it destroys hope and friendship, and it only recognizes complicity. "Even in Christian communities there are climbers," said the Pope, "who consciously or unconsciously think they can climb over or under the fence, but they are

3. Pope Francis waves to the crowd in St. Peter's Square.

4. Saint Francis in Cimabue's fresco Majesty. *Assisi, Lower Church.*

thieves and robbers. Why? Because they steal the glory from Jesus, they want their own glory....A religion is a bit like a shop, no? I give the glory to you, and you give it to me. But these didn't enter via the right gate. The gate is Jesus and those who do not enter via this gate are in error." In his speech to the young pontifical diplomats, he asked that they try to be "free of ambitions or personal aims, which can cause the Church great harm....No careerism, please." He will be unyielding against the abuse of children and he will not have a Vatican bank unless it is transparent, nor will he stand for a clergy that has been numbed by its own trappings. One reasons for the nomination of Pope Francis as person of the year is the fact that, thanks to him, the perception that much of the world had regarding the Church has changed. Undoubtedly this new perception of the Church that has arisen since his election is striking and important from both religious-pastoral and cultural viewpoints.

A few years ago, *Time* defined the Catholic Church as the largest multinational corporation in existence, in terms of its organization, structure, and branches. Although this was not an inaccurate description, it did not actually consider the Church's raison d'être and specificity. But recently, the increasingly negative media coverage has underlined some serious problems in the Church in various parts of the world: Marcial Maciel and his Legionnaires of Christ, the Vatican Bank, the theft of documents from Pope Benedict XVI's apartment, and messages that seem far from the reality of many who suffer daily. All of this has been a serious blow to the credibility of an institution whose principal quality is precisely its credibility.

For our part, we should bear in mind the poverty suffered by many Catholics compared with the thoughtlessness, doctrinal closure, and intellectual arrogance of some of the clergy; a poverty that has grown in recent years, when the pluralism of ideas and the secularization of society should have led to quite a different attitude, more humble, more welcoming, and with more dialogue. Many Catholics have placed themselves on the sidelines of the Church, opting for *à la carte* Christianity.

The arrival of Pope Francis appears to have broken the ill-omened spell, disconcerting and provoking unease in more than a few, and sympathy and widespread hope in innumerable people from all walks of life. In putting a photo of Pope Francis on its cover last year, *Time* refers to a new perception of the Church and I am sure that this is the reason why many magazines chose Pope Francis as their person of the year.

When trying to explain this new perception, I would like to compare the experience of two recent popes who tried to break inertia, comfort, and egotism, and who tried to give more importance to the Gospel than to the too-human historical traditions that have prevailed in our history. I am referring to John XXIII and to Francis.

As soon as John XXIII (1958–1963) began his pontificate, Christians were fascinated by the new pope's attitude. His reign produced such a significant ecclesiastical change that it appeared as if all the seemingly admirable past, since the pontificate of the aristocratic Pius XII, was in fact anachronistic and decadent. He spoke of the need to overcome antiquated customs and traditions and strove to clean centuries of dust the Church had accumulated. He diminished his own importance and tried to get closer to his fellow human beings, discarding the disdainful mask that many wear when they want to become human idols.

It is surprising to note how, with just the naturalness and humanity of his behavior, this pope shattered the status quo and became the beloved pope who was close to Catholics and the faithful of different religions. He proposed a way of behaving, of creating a fraternal community, and of feeling like one of its members. Occasionally I have thought that the key to this change was Pope John's conviction that every person and all humanity is worthy of respect and love, even when living in error, or belonging to a different religion, or to none at all. Thus, without much fuss or deliberation, he crushed the nineteenth-century deceit that had impeded the acceptance of freedom of conscience based on the principle that only truth has rights and not error, defining error as anything not taught by the Church.

The character and the methods of the new pope have caught us off guard; they offer another concept of the Church, not so much for the principles they stand for, but for the priorities, the way of living in the world, and of translating the Gospel. To understand our surprise, we should reflect on the contradictions in our lives. On the one hand, we are aware that the Christian world experiences a sort of schizophrenia, which does not appear deadly because we have lived with it for centuries. Its God-made-man dies on the cross and has no place to rest his head; it gives us the Samaritan and the father of the prodigal son as models; it states that it is practically impossible for a rich person to enter God's kingdom; it tells us that those who we marginalize, exclude, and impoverish unscrupulously will sit at his right hand; it tells us to pardon seventy times seven; to use the beatitudes as a life model; it asks us only to call God our Father and to consider ourselves brothers and sisters; it advises us not to seek positions of power because only the last will be the first.

We preach these mandates and many other equally important ones with conviction and authority, but our organization and our way of relating with each other, both in Church and in society, run on separate parallel tracks. The Vatican as an artistic complex can consider itself a glorious work of human culture, but as a reference point of the Christ who had nowhere to rest his head, it is an embarrassment. The Roman curia and the Church's system of government can be offered as an example in the history of power and law in the West, but I very much doubt whether they abide by Christ's mandate "But you are not to be like that" (cf. Luke 22:26): that is, do not act as the world acts. Bishops wear miters, but their way of governing depends on their broadness of mind and, above all, on their spirit. Unfortunately, there is no doubt that too often history demonstrates that they consider themselves to have been crowned as princes, rather than as representatives of he who came not to be served but to serve.

I know that this schizophrenia is part of all human history—one only need look at the world of politics—and yet we should expect more consistency. In reality, what is surprising and encouraging is the fact that Pope Francis, audacious and courageous in his exigencies and in his lifestyle, asks us to return to the sources of identity and existentiality of humankind. He indicates that the Church has to go outside of itself and toward the peripheries, avoiding the danger of a theological narcissism that distances it from the world by sealing Jesus Christ within its walls. On the contrary, changes and reforms have to be based on an evangelizing Church that goes outside and not on an elite Church that lives inside itself and for itself. He said that he wants to extricate himself from positions, material privileges, and policies to achieve an apostolic way of life, a life that for many has ended in martyrdom, focusing his existence and words on the love and mercy of God.

Pope Francis encourages us to love both poverty and the poor and excluded in the world, to reject the mentality of princes and patrons, not to be ambitious or look for promotions, to watch over our brothers and sisters, and to care for hope as if it were a precious commodity. Above all, he asks all of us to exercise a type of authority that is deeply rooted in the capacity to serve. The great thing is that he is not asking us to do anything new. All of this can be found in the Gospel, and in numerous acts of courage and joy performed by the Fathers of the Second Vatican Council. We have the impression that Pope Francis, just like the Second Vatican Council before him, aims to invert the priorities that have often dominated the Church, abandoning the constant reference to ecclesiastical institutions, and to their authority and efficiency, as the center and measure of our faith and of the Church. Instead, it appears that he wants to convert the Christian community into a place of communion and welcome. Rethinking and changing the priorities also implies recognizing the value of conscience, of faith, and of the signs of the times as supreme ecclesiastical criteria. Ordinary people around the world like this new attitude and it explains why Francis is considered one of us, as a Roman taxi driver said a few days after the pope's election.

Why did Jesus scandalize his contemporaries? He ate with sinners, performed miracles on the Sabbath, and he spoke about God with great confidence. He did not mix the sacred and the profane. In abandoning the throne, in reducing distances, in sitting on the same bench as the faithful, in continuing to live in the guest house rather than the papal apartments, and in mingling with his brothers and sisters, not only does Francis not diminish his prestige or his authority, but he puts things in their place and reminds us with simplicity how Jesus behaved. Christ was the same in the creation of the universe and in the incarnation or crowning with thorns, and yet we often linger over that which best suits our tastes.

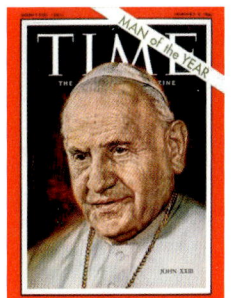

5. Cover of Time, *1962, in which Pope John XXIII was named "Man of the Year."*

6. Cover of Time, *2013. Pope Francis as "Man of the Year."*

Obviously, he is not considering changing God or the doctrines that tradition has bequeathed us, but of purifying the ways of understanding, conceiving, and experiencing the transcendence and presence of God in our souls. Perhaps he has found the greatest difficulty in this: Being born again—in other words, converting. We often give greater importance to how rather than to what, to the faucet rather than the water, to routine rather than to life. Pope Francis has indicated that we only need to confide in Jesus rather than in superstitions, in ourselves, or in our self-sufficiency.

Jesus referred to this when he pointed out the need to be born again from the inside, to discern the signs of the times and to value people and things differently from how the rest of the world values them. "But you are not to be like that" is shorthand for the Christian principle. For the Jews, the cross was madness, but for the Christians it became the symbol of salvation. The world has traditionally adored gold and money, the *Mammona iniquitatis*, but for Christ the rich risk not passing through the eye of the needle. We are certainly good people, but often the Lord asks us to walk

and behave differently. Even our way of being in the world and of handling power requires some radical reappraisal. Only service justifies power, only by serving others, the needy first of all, will we be capable of following the Master. At times the faithful have intuited that, by simplifying his lifestyle, how he behaves, and talks in his new role, Francis has opted for an evangelical radicalism that disturbs us so much, and that has little in common with the theatricality, honor, and glory to which we have become accustomed.

7. A giant oil pipeline crossing a shantytown on the edge of a third-world city. The growing inequality in the availability of resources between the rich and the poor is the most shocking fact of recent history.

APPENDIX: SHARED GENEROSITY

If God is love, then every human being carries the imprint of their creator's love in their DNA; but it is Christ who reveals God the Father's incommensurable love, and it is Christ who reminds us that his disciples have to remain marked by this immense love, which culminated in the Incarnation. We therefore know that all Christians, merely by being Christians, are asked to demonstrate their affection and generosity towards all people—in other words towards all their brothers and sisters—both individually but also via local communities, parishes, dioceses, and the universal Church. This commitment to generosity requires a laborious organization that can set up various community services and organizations, all of them sharing the same single aim.

As we have seen in previous chapters, these innumerable concrete Christian works would not be enough if we could not perceive love of humanity in them, a love and a generosity nourished by our encounter with Christ. This is why in each of the charitable works presented in this book, particular attention is paid to human beings, to their spiritual needs, and to their deepest fears. In the same way, in addition to professional competence, we also find in all the great episodes in the history of charity surprising examples of Christian life and splendid examples of generosity, which always come from Christ.

In the last century, enormous changes have taken place in our complex and contradictory world regarding the concept of the state's social responsibility. This has been due to the extraordinary development of health policies in particular, to the extent that many displays of traditional charity have ended up becoming drastically secularized. Around the globe, numerous associations and organizations with charitable aims have been set up, both nationally and internationally; they are often set against each other and appear to be in competition not only with each other, but also with the more traditional, generally religious organizations.

Nowadays, those who want to make a donation to help children in the third world no longer have to do so through a missionary or Church organization. Catholic organizations have been joined by many other organizations that offer charitable services both within and beyond the nation they belong to. In a certain sense charity has become an institution and a project among many others. Furthermore, various governments cooperate internationally on a significant scale to help poorer nations, working together in various ways with both Catholic and other organizations to reach their objectives. In fact, it is only thanks to these huge public financings that many of the Catholic organizations' activities, both at home and abroad, can reach their objectives.

This is the cause of three phenomena that we should reflect on: professionalization, bureaucratization, and an occasionally stronger identification with the state, where its financing comes from, than with its Christian inspiration and bedrock, to the extent that charity often runs the risk of losing part of its original Catholic inspiration. It is a situation that we need to be well aware of and which believers have to face rationally and coherently in order to help the greatest number of needy possible without losing charity's original raison d'être. Christian charity conserves its profound specificity, as we have seen in previous chapters. It never reduces itself to a social interest, but arises from the figure of Jesus and his revelation of Divine paternity.

In his encyclical letter *Deus caritas est*, Benedict XVI outlined some principles that characterize the fundamental nucleus of the aforementioned problem: 1) Charity is originally a Christian experience in the

1. Educating for a better world photo by Paolo Cardone (Shoot4Change) for VIS.

sense that its origins derive directly from Christian revelation; 2) For the Church the exercise of charity is an essential and unavoidable dimension of its identity; 3) The Church is the subject of charity and the charitable organizations constitute its work; 4) Charitable work, in that it is part of the Church, is constitutionally linked to the liturgy and to evangelization, and depends on the bishop of each diocese; 5) In the Church's charitable work we see its capacity to show faith in Christ, through whom God shows himself to the world.

We cannot mention all the Catholic organizations created by the Holy See, dioceses, religious congregations, and Catholic groups around the world to promote generosity, love, and charity, but there is no doubt that we are talking about an extraordinary explosion of charity, intelligence, and Christian creativity. To mention a few: Caritas Internationalis, the federation of diocesan Caritas; the numerous organizations that have sprung from religious institutes, such as VIS of the Salesians, VIDES of Daughters of Mary Help of Christians or the Jesuit Entreculturas; institutions created by national episcopates, such as Misereor and Adveniat in Germany, Migrantes in Italy or Manos Unidas in Spain; the many organizations created thanks to the faithful, such as the Conferences of Saint Vincent de Paul, the Confraternities of Charity, Communion and Liberation's AVSI, the Emmanuel Community's Fidesco or Focolare's Youth for a United World.

Love and fraternal charity are part of the aurora borealis of so much love and union that exist in creation, in which God embraces humanity in his love for Christ, to receive in turn humankind's embrace full of tenderness.

NOTES

1. *Epistula ad fideles* 9.
2. We find the frame and appropriate reference points for the history and the reflections we make in the study of the great classic works. In Spanish: Bernardino Llorca, Ricardo García Villoslada, Juan María Laboa, *Historia de la Iglesia Católica*, 5 vols. (Madrid: BAC, 2005); in English: Hubert Jedin, ed., *History of the Church*, 10 vols. (New York: Crossroad, 1981–1990), which has been frequently reprinted and updated; in French: Louis-Jacques Rogier, Roger Aubert, M. David Knowles, eds., *Nouvelle histoire de l'Église*, 5 vols., (Paris: Seuil, 1963–1975).
3. Pierre Ceyrac, *Pellegrino delle frontiere* (Milan: Jaca Book, 2005); Dominique Paturle, *Questi poveri che interrogano la Chiesa* (Milan: Jaca Book, 2008).
4. Joseph Ratzinger [Pope Benedict XVI], *Jesus of Nazareth* (London: Bloomsbury, 2008).
5. Thomas of Celano, *Saint Francis of Assisi, First and Second Life of Saint Francis with Selections from the Treatise on the Miracles of Blessed Francis* (Chicago: Franciscan Herald Press, 1988).
6. Dolores Aleixandre, *Contar a Jesús* (Madrid: CCS, 2008).
7. Davide Caldirola, *La compassione di Gesù* (Rome: Ancora, 2007).
8. Krzysztof Dunin-Wasowic, "La Vie religieuse dans les camps de concentration allemands, 1939–1945, en tant que forme de la résistance," *Miscellanea Historiae Pontificiae* 9 (1984): 547–570.
9. Maximus the Confessor, *On Charity*, second century.
10. Vincenzo Monachino, *La cura pastorale a Milano, Cartagine e Roma* (Rome: Analecta Gregoriana, 1947) and *S. Ambrogio e la cura pastorale a Milano nel secolo IV* (Rome: Pontificia Università Gregoriana, 1973).
11. "Fragment of a Letter to a Priest," from *The Works of the Emperor Julian*, vol. 2, trans. Emily Wilmer Cave Wright (Cambridge, MA: Loeb Classical Library, 1913).
12. "Letter to Arsacius, High-priest of Galatia" from *The Works of the Emperor Julian*, vol. 3, trans. Emily Wilmer Cave Wright (Cambridge, MA: Loeb Classical Library, 1913).
13. Eusebius of Caesarea, *Ecclesiastical History*, 4, 23, 10.
14. Ferdinando Ughelli, *Italia sacra* (Venice, 1720).
15. San Colombano, *Le Opere* (Milan: Jaca Book, 2001), xv–xli.
16. *Cuadernos franciscanos* (Chile 25 [1991]).
17. Christopher Dawson, *Religion and the Rise of Western Culture* (New York: Sheed & Ward, 1950).
18. Juan María Laboa, *Atlante storico del monachesimo* (Milan: Jaca Book, 2002); *Los monjes y los estudios* (Poblet: IV Semana de Estudios Monásticos, 1961); (Poblet: Abadía de Poblet, 1963); Terryl N. Kinder, *I Cisterciensi. Vita quotidiana, cultura, arte* (Milan: Jaca Book, 1997); Philippe Baud, et al., *La vita cisterciense. Ieri e oggi* (Milan: Jaca Book, 1998).
19. Émile Zola, *The Three Cities: Lourdes* (London: Dodo Press, 2007); René Laurentin, *Visage de Bernadette* (Paris: Lethielleux, 1978).
20. Julien Ries, *L'homme et le sacré* (Paris: Cerf, 2009); Gérard-Henry Baudry, *Le baptême et ses symboles. Aux sources du salut* (Paris: Beauchesne, 2003).
21. Jacques Le Goff, René Rémond (ed.), *Histoire de la France religieuse*, vol. 1 (Paris: Seuil, 1988); G. R. Evans, *The Thought of Gregory the Great* (Cambridge, UK: Cambridge University Press, 1986).
22. Paolo Giuntella, *Il fiore rosso* (Milan: Edizioni Paoline, 2006).
23. Thomas of Celano, *The Lives of Saint Francis* 130.
24. *Fonti francescane. Scritti e biografie di san Francesco d'Assisi, cronache e altre testimonianze del primo secolo francescano, scritti e biografie di santa Chiara d'Assisi*, 3rd ed., (Padua-Assisi: EMP-Movimento Francescano, 1980); Julien Green, *God's Fool: The Life and Times of Saint Francis* (New York: Perennial Library, 1987); Giovanni Joergensen, *San Francesco d'Assisi* (Assisi: Porziuncola, 1988); Jacques Le Goff, *Francesco d'Assisi* (Milan: Biblioteca Francescana, 1998).
25. Marcel Pacaut, *Les ordres monastiques et religieux au Moyen Âge* (Paris: Armand Colin, 2005).
26. Humbert-Marie Vicaire, *Historia de Santo Domingo* (Madrid: EDIBESA, 2003); Guy Bedouelle, *La fuerza de la palabra. Domingo de Guzmán* (Salamanca: Editorial San Esteban, 1987); Agostino Gemelli, *Il Francescanesimo* (Città di Castello: Porziuncola, 2000); Lázaro Iriarte, *Historia Franciscana* (Valencia: Editorial Asís, 1979); Joaquín Smet, *Los Carmelitas* (Madrid: BAC, 1995).
27. Vincenzo Paglia (edited by), *Confraternite e Meridione nell'età moderna* (Rome: Edizioni di Storia e Letteratura, 1990).
28. Jacques Monod, *Chance and Necessity: An Essay on the Natural Philosophy of Modern Biology* (New York: Random House, 1971).
29. *Problemi di vita religiosa in Italia nel Cinquecento* (Padua: Antenore, 1960); Ernst Troeltsch, *Le dottrine sociali delle Chiese e dei gruppi cristiani* (Florence: La Nuova Italia, 1941); André Vauchez, *Les laïcs au Moyen Age. Pratiques et expériences religieuses* (Paris: Cerf, 1987); AA.VV., *Cofradías, gremios y solidaridades en la Europa Medieval* (Pamplona: Gobierno de Navarra, 1993).
30. Gaspar de Torres, *Regula et constitutiones obm de Mercede*, declaration, VI, f. 15, (Salamanca, 1565).
31. Francisco de Castro, *Historia de la vida y sanctas obras de Juan de Dios*, in Manuel Gómez Moreno, *Primicias históricas de San Juan de Dios* (Madrid: Provincias españolas de la Orden Hospitalaria, 1950), 46.
32. José Sánchez Martínez, *Kenosis-Diakonía en el itinerario espiritual de san Juan de Dios* (Madrid: Fundación Juan Ciudad, 1995).
33. *Carta de identidad de la Orden Hospitalaria de san Juan de Dios* (Rome, 2000).
34. Angel Fernández Collado, *Los informes de visita "ad limina&" de los arzobispos de Toledo* (Cuenca: Ediciones de la Universidad Castilla-La Mancha, 2002); José Luis González Novalín, *Las visitas "Ad Limina" de los obispos de Oviedo (1585–1901)* (Oviedo: Instituto de Estudios Asturianos, 1986); José Antonio Rivas, *Miedo y piedad: testamentos sevillanos del siglo XVIII* (Seville: Diputación Provincial de Sevilla, 1986); Manuel Martín Riego, *Diezmos eclesiásticos* (Seville: Caja Rural de Sevilla, 1990).
35. Severino Giner, *San José de Calasanz. Maestro y fundador* (Madrid: BAC, 1992), 387.
36. Calasanzio, "Dichiarazioni alle Costituzioni"; cfr. György Sántha, *San José de Calasanz. Obra pedagógica* (Madrid: BAC, 1984), 295.
37. José María Prellezo García, ed., *Don Bosco en la historia* (Rome: LAS, 1990); Pietro Braido, *Don Bosco prete dei giovani nel secolo delle libertà* (Rome: LAS, 2003).

38. Jesús Álvarez Gómez, *Historia de la vida religiosa,* vol. 3 (Madrid: Publicaciones Claretianas, 1990).
39. Llorca, Villoslada, and Laboa, *Historia de la Iglesia Católica,* vols. 4 and 5; Luigi Mezzadri and José María Román, *Historia de la Congregación de la Misión* (Madrid: La Milagrosa, 1992).
40. Hugh McLeod, *Religion and the People of Western Europe, 1789–1970* (Oxford: Oxford University Press, 1981); Robert Bezucha, ed., *Modern European Social History* (Lexington, UK: Heath, 1972).
41. Claude Langlois, *Le Catholicisme au feminin* (Paris: Cerf, 1984).
42. Servatius Hermann Scholl, ed., *150 anni di movimento operaio cattolico nell'Europa centro-occidentale (1789–1939)* (Padua: Gregoriana, 1962); Paul Misner, *Social Catholicism in Europe: From the Onset of Industrialization to the First World War* (London: Darton, Longman & Todd, 1991); Emil Ritter, *Il movimento cattolico-sociale in Germania nel xix secolo e il Volksverein* (Rome: Cinque Lune, 1967).
43. Suor Emmanuelle, *Confessioni di una religiosa* (Milan: Jaca Book, 2010).
44. Dorothy Day, *The Long Loneliness* (London: HarperCollins, 2009); William D. Miller, *Harsh and Dreadful Love: Dorothy Day and the Catholic Worker Movement* (New York: Darton, Longman & Todd, 1973); Ana Colomer, *Dorothy Day* (Madrid: Fundación Emanuel Mounier, 2010); Jim Forest, *All is Grace: A Biography of Dorothy Day* (Maryknoll, NY: Orbis Books, 2011).
45. Georges Bernanos, *The Diary of a Country Priest* (New York: Carroll & Graf Publishers, 2002).
46. José de Broucker, *Les nuits d'un prophète* (Paris: Cerf, 2005).
47. Jan Grootaers, *I protagonisti del Vaticano II* (Cinisello Balsamo: San Paolo, 1994), 158–170; Giacomo Lercaro, *Per la forza dello Spirito. Discorsi conciliari* (Bologna: EDB, 1984).
48. Giuseppe Alberigo, ed., *Storia del Concilio Vaticano II* vol. 2 (Bologna: Il Mulino, 1996), 226–230, 370–372.
49. Hélder Câmara, *Roma, due del mattino. Lettere dal Concilio Vaticano II* (Cinisello Balsamo: San Paolo, 2008), 336
50. Ibid., 381–382.
51. Ramón Hernández Martín, ed., *Relectio di Indis de Francisco de Vitoria* (Madrid: Consejo Superior de Investigaciones Cientificas, 1989).
52. Lyon: Les Éditions de l'Abeille, 1943.
53. Joseph Wresinski and Gilles Anouil, *The Poor Are the Church: A Conversation with Fr. Joseph Wresinski* (Mystic, CT: Twenty-Third Publications, 2002).
54. Gilbert Cesbron, *Saints in Hell* (Garden City, NY: Doubleday, 1953).
55. Joseph Wresinski, in Jean-François Six, *Les Droits de l'homme en question* (Paris La Documentation française, 1989), 225.
56. Antoine Chatelard, *Charles de Foucauld: Le chemin vers Tamanrasset* (Paris: Karthala, 2002).
57. René Voillaume, *Seeds of the Desert* (Notre Dame, IN: Fides, 1964). This is the book that inspired thousands of young people, and told the world about the founder of the Little Brothers of Jesus.
58. Little Sisters of Jesus, ed., *Magdeleine of Jesus* (Walsingham, UK: Little Sisters of Jesus, 1990).
59. Abbé Pierre, Padre Pedro, *Per un mondo di giustizia e di pace* (Milan: Jaca Book, 2005).
60. Bernadete Toneto, *L'avvocato dei senza-terra. Henri Burin des Roziers* (Milan: Jaca Book, 2003).
61. Esohe Aghatise, Richard Poulin, et al. *Prostituzione: globalizzazione incarnata* (Milan: Jaca Book, 2006).
62. By co-development, I mean the form of cooperation in which immigrants become factors in the development of the countries they come from.
63. Joseph Wresinski and Gilles Anouil, *The Poor Are the Church: A Conversation with Fr. Joseph Wresinski* (Mystic, CT: Twenty-Third Publications, 2002).
64. Suzanne Chantal, *Jérôme Manni le Vénitien: saint, guerrier et protecteur des orphelins* (Paris: Sand, 1989).
65. Ferdinando Castelli, *Volti di Gesù nella letteratura moderna* (Cinisello Balsamo: Edizioni Paoline, 1987); G. Cinà, ed., *Dio è amore. Ma può soffrire?* (Turin: Edizioni Camilliane, 2008).

INDEX OF NAMES

Page numbers of names that appear in captions are in italics.

Adam, *14*
Adelelmus of Burgos, Saint, 133
Agilbert of Paris, *79*
Al-Kamil, 83
Alcuin of York, Blessed, 117
Alexander VI, Pope, 177
Alfonso X (the Wise), King of Castille and León, 110, *111*
Alphonsus de Liguori, Saint, 118, 159, 196
Ambrose of Milan, Saint, 22, 54, *58*, 121
Ananias, *31*
Angela of the Cross, Saint, 121
Ann, mother of Mary, Saint, *197*
Anne of Austria, Queen of France, *163*
Ansgar, Saint, 132
Anthony the Abbot, Saint, *120*, *138*
Anthony of Padua, Saint, 69
Aristotle, *178*
Arrupe, Pedro, 179
Arsacius, 50
Athanasius of Alexandria, Saint, *53*, 179
Augustine of Canterbury, Saint, 83
Augustine of Hippo, Saint, 47, 56, 76, 96, 128
Averroës, *178*

Bacchin, Giorgio, *171*, *190*
Baldanzi, Alessandro, *155*
Balmes, Jaime, 168
Balthasar, Hans Urs von, 117
Barat, Madeleine Sophie, Saint, 157
Barré, Nicolas, Blessed, 155
Basil of Caesarea, Saint, 51, *53*, 57, 58, 96, 179
Baudouin, Louis-Marie, 74
Beatus di Liébana, *10*
Beauvois, Xavier, *42*

Bellarmine, Robert, Saint, 92
Benedict XV, Pope, 122
Benedict of Nursia, Saint, 96, *100*, 114
Benedict XVI, Pope, 228, 232
Benozzo di Lese (Benozzo Gozzoli), *178*
Berceo, Gonzalo de, 110
Bergoglio, Jorge Mario, *167*; see also Francis, Pope
Bernadette Soubirous, Saint, 106
Bernanos, Georges 162, *176*, 177–178, 220
Bernardine of Siena, Saint, *194*, 195
Bernini, Gian Lorenzo, *224*
Bethune, Ade, *173*
Bhatti, Shahbaz, 43
Bismarck, Otto von, *169*
Bles, Herri met de, *221*
Bonaventure, Saint, 117, *123*
Bonhoeffer, Dietrich, 41, *42*
Boniface VIII, Pope, 133
Boniface, Saint, 131
Bosco, John, Saint, 156
Bosco Penido, Joao, 42
Bresson, Robert, *176*
Bruno, Saint, 117
Bulfinch, Charles, *167*
Burin des Roziers, Henri, 210–211

Caesarius of Arles, *112*, 114
Cain, 15
Callahan, William, *175*
Cajetan of Thiene, Saint, 66
Calvin, John, 36
Câmara, Hélder Pessoa, 84, 172, 179–180, 185–186, 188, 195
Camillus de Lellis, Saint, 150, *151*, 152, 195
Caravaggio, Michelangelo Merisi detto il, 119

Carducci, Vincenzo (Vicente Carducho), *90*
Carpaccio, Vittore, *56*
Casaldáliga, Pedro, 42, 172, *211*
Catherine of Siena, Saint, 174
Cervantes, Miguel de, 141
Cesbron, Gilbert, 190
Ceyrac, Pierre, *211*
Chaminade, William Joseph, Blessed, 157, 179
Charles V, Emperor, 84, 87, 146
Charles VIII, King of France, 61
Charlemagne, Emperor, 168
Cignaroli, Giovanni, *66*
Cinquin, Madeleine (Sister Emmanuelle), *212*
Clare of Assisi, Saint, 124
Clovis I, King of France, 76, *79*
Cobbe, Valerian, 41–42
Colantonio, Niccolò, *120*
Colin, Jean-Claude, 157
Columbanus, Saint, 104, 116, 131
Comboni, Daniel, Saint, *75*, 84
Conant, Kenneth John, 99
Congar, Yves, 165, 179
Congdon, William, *204*, *206–207*
Consalvi, Ercole, 168, 178
Cornelius the Centurian, 9
Cornelius, Pope, Saint, 44, *46*
Constantine the Great, Emperor, 36, 48, 131
Constantine II, Emperor, 48
Constantius, Emperor, 48
Cottolengo, Giuseppe Benedetto, Saint, 208, 220
Courbet, Gustave, *139*
Cyprian of Carthage, Saint, 39, *46*, 58
Cyril of Jerusalem, Saint, 52, 179

INDEX OF NAMES

Damasus I, Pope, Saint, 179
Daniel, Yvan, 189
Dante Alighieri, 126
David, King of Israel, 179
Day, Dorothy, 173–176, *207*
De Nobili, Roberto, 87
Degas, Edgar, *161*
Delacroix, Eugène, *167*
Diana, Giuseppe, 188
Dionysius of Alexandria, Saint, 39, 57
Dionysius of Corinth, Saint, 57
Dionysius, Pope, Saint, 57
Dix, Otto, *193*
Domenico di Bartolo, *62, 139*
Domingo de la Calzada, Saint, 133
Dominic Guzmán, Saint, 69, *73*, 126–127, *128*

Eadfrith of Lindisfarne, *82*
Egeria, *130*, 131
Eiximenis, Francisco, 128
Elizabeth, Mother of John the Baptist, Saint, 110, *197*
Elizabeth I, Queen of England, 36
Erasmus of Rotterdam, *221*
Eulalia of Mérida, Saint, 39
Eusebius of Caesarea, 44
Eve, *10, 14*
Ezekiel, prophet, 24, *79*

Fabian, Pope, Saint, 35
Felicity, Saint, 39
Felix of Valois, Saint, 141
Ferrer, Vincent, Saint, 69, *120*
Filarete, Antonio Averlino detto il, *147, 151*
Filippini, Lucy, Saint, 156
Fleury, Michel, 42
Florensky, Pavel, 40
Foucauld, Charles de, *104*, 195, 198–202
Fra Angelico, 34
Francis of Assisi, Saint, 8, 26, *28*, 69, *73*, 83, 122–124, 127–128, 152, 165, 179, 195, 204, 209, 224, 226
Francis, Pope, *167*, 224–231
Francis de Sales, Saint, *194*
Francis Solano, Saint, 73

Francis Xavier, Saint, *87*
Frassati, Pier Giorgio, Blessed, 118
Fructuosus of Tarragona, Saint, 39, 104

Gibbon, Edward, 48
Giotto di Bondone, *28, 124*
Giovanni Cignaroli, *66*
Godin, Henri, 189
Grande García, Rutilio, 187
Green, Julien, 220
Gregory the Great, Pope, Saint, 33, 44, 83, 114
Gregory of Nazianzus, Saint, 52
Gregory VII, Pope, Saint, 177
Grignion de Montfort, Louis-Marie, Saint, 159, 179
Grouès, Henri (abbé Pierre), 209–210
Guérin, Paulin, 179
Guillermina, (Franciscan Sister), 40

Hallé, Noël, *194*
Helen, Saint, 131
Hierro, (Franciscan missionary), 73
Hincmar of Reims, 136
Hippolytus, Saint, *128*
Homer, Winslow, *169*

Ignatius of Antioch, Saint, 39
Ignatius of Loyola, Saint, 87, 117, 179
Innocent III, Pope, 126
Ireneaus of Lyon, Saint, 33, 39, 117
Isaiah, Prophet, 31

Jairus, *28*, 219
Jane Frances de Chantal, Saint, *194*
James, Apostle, Saint, 76, 92, *135*
James of Perugia, Saint, *132*
Jean de Brébeuf, Saint, 84
Jerome Emiliani, Saint, 219
Jerome, Saint, 61
Joachim of Fiore, 126, 133
Joachim, Saint, *197*
John, Apostle and Evangelist, Saint, *10, 14*, 56, 69, 76, 192
John the Baptist, Saint, 24, 119
John Chrysostom, Saint, 36, 52, *53*, 179

John of Ávila, Saint, 146, 179
John of Capistrano, *127*
John of the Cross, Saint, 179
John of God, Saint, 120, 146, 152, 195
John of Jerusalem, Saint, 150
John of Montecorvino, Blessed, 83
John Paul II, Pope, Saint, 41, 183
John XXIII, Pope, Saint, 179, 181–182, 213, 228, *229*
José de Anchieta, Blessed, 83
José María de Jesús Crucificado, 121
Joseph Calasanz, Saint, 117, 153, 156, 179
Juan de la Matha, Saint, 141
Juan Diego Cuauhtlatoatzin, Saint, 106, *107*
Julian the Apostate, Emperor, 47–50
Julius Constantius, 48

Katz, Jeff, *171*
Killian, Saint, 132
King, Martin Luther, 179–180
Kolbe, Maximilian, Saint, 41, 121

La Salle, John Baptiste de, Saint, 155
Las Casas, Bartolomé de, 83, *84*, 87, 178, 188, 195
Labouré, Catherine, Saint, 208
Lamennais, Hugues-Félicité Robert de, 140, 168, 179
Lawrence, Saint, 34, *39*, 68
Lazarus of Bethany, Saint, *22*, 106
Leo of Assisi, Blessed, 8
Leo the Great, Pope, Saint, 44, *46*, 47
Lercaro, Giacomo, 180, 181–182
Lezcano Guerra, Isidoro, 121
Liénart, Achille, 191
Liuvigild, King of the Visigoths, *77*
Llull, Ramon, 83, 162
Loew, Jacques, *188*, 189
Louis-Phillipe of Orleans, King, *167*
Louise de Marillac, Saint, *163*
Lubac, Henri de, 179
Lubich, Chiara, 180
Luther, Martin, 36, 61

Maciel, Marcial, 228
Maestro Nicolo, *10*

237

INDEX OF NAMES

Magdeleine of Jesus, *104*, 202
Mandela, Nelson, 180
Manzoni, Alessandro, 92
Marcellina, Saint, 22
Marie Javier, Franciscan Missionary, 40
Maritain, Jacques, 92, *173*
Martin of Braga, Saint, 76
Martin of Porres, Saint, 83
Martin of Tours, Saint, *112*, 113–114, 120
Mauriac, François, 190
Maurin, Peter, *173*
Maximus the Confessor, Saint, 46
Melania the Younger, Saint, 46
Menni, Benedict, Saint, 152
Mindszenty, József, 189
Monchanin, Jules, *211*
Monod, Jacques, 140
Montesinos, Antonio de, 87, 178, 188
Montini, Giovanni Battista, 190; or Paul VI, Pope
Morone, Giovanni, 179

Nabil, Gabriel, 216
Newman, John Henry, Blessed, 178
Nicodemus, 18, *19*, 31, 93

Odilo of Cluny, Saint, 104
Origen, 117
Orione, Luigi, Saint, *172*, 208, 220
Orwell, George, 174
Ossó y Cervelló, Henry de, Saint, 157
Ozanam, Frédéric Antoine, Blessed, 159, 168, 208

Palladio, Andrea di Pietro della Gondola detto, 150
Pascal, Blaise, 119, 217, 220
Paul of Tarsus, Saint, *31*, *39*, 57, *59*, 76, *218*
Paul VI, Pope, 92, 183, *184*, 186, 190, 191
Peckham, John, 178
Péguy, Charles, 191
Perpetua, Saint, 39

Peter, Apostle, Saint, 9, *39*, 57, 76, *89*, 131, 135, *218*
Peter Claver, Saint, 83
Peter the Deacon, *114*
Peter Nolasco, Saint, 141
Petrus Comestor, *6*, *10*
Pinianus, Valerius, 46
Pius XII, Pope, 36, 161, 228
Plato, *178*
Polk, Margaret, *175*
Polycarp of Smyrna, Saint, 39
Poveda Castroverde, Pedro, Saint, 157
Pozzo, Andrea, *155*
Prat, Loïc, 190
Prisset, Luc, 190
Puglisi, Giuseppe "Pino," 188

Querbes, Louis-Marie, 157

Radcliffe, Timothy, 211
Rafaela of the Sacred Heart, Saint, 179
Rafols, María, Blessed, 157
Rahner, Karl, 40
Raphael, *46*
Reccared, King of the Visigoths, 76
Ricci, Matteo, *87*
Roger of Taizé, 180
Romanus, Saint, *114*
Romero, Óscar Arnulfo, *186*, 187–188, 217
Rosmini, Antonio, Blessed, 168, 179
Rosselli, Francesco, *128*
Rubens, Peter Paul, *89*

Saint-Exupéry, Antoine de, 116
Samuel, Prophet, 18
Sano di Pietro, *194*
Saul, King of Israel, 18
Savonarola, Girolamo, 177
Scalabrini, Giovanni Battista, *74*, 75
Schutz, Roger, *105*, 179
Schweitzer, Albert, 84
Serra, Junípero, Blessed, 84, *85*

Seton, Elizabeth Ann, Saint, 208
Simon the Pharisee, 22
Soter, Pope, Saint, 57
Stephan the Protomartyr, Saint, 35, *36*
Subleyras, Pierre, *151*
Suhard, Emmanuel, 189
Sulpicius Severus, 113

Tempesta, Antonio, *147*
Teresa of Avila, Saint, 31
Teresa of Calcutta, Blessed, 180, 203–208
Theodechild of Jouarre, Saint, *79*
Theodelinda, Queen of the Lombards, 76, *80*
Theodoric, king of the Ostrogoths, *112*, 114
Thérèse of Lisieux, Saint, 31, 117
Thomas, Apostle, Saint, 76
Thomas Aquinas, Saint, 117, *128*, 178, *179*
Thomas of Celano, 26, 124
Turibius of Mogrovejo, Saint, 83

Urban II, Pope, 135
Urban VIII, Pope, 158

Valentinian II, Emperor, 22
Valéry, Paul, 15
Venerini, Rose, Saint, 156
Vianney, John (Curé of Ars), Saint, 118, 195
Vieira, António, 84
Vincent de Paul, 150, 152, 158–159, 161, 162–164, 168, 196
Vitoria, Francisco de, 188
Voillaume, René, 198, *201*, 202
Volvinius, *54*
Vouet, Simon, *163*

Waldo, Peter, 126
Weston, Dorothy, *173*
William I of Aquitane, 96
Willibrord, Saint, 132
Wresinski, Joseph, *190*

PHOTO CREDITS

Numbers in parentheses indicate illustration number.

© Alice Cambournac, Marie-Julie Maille, 43
© Archives of Fratelli Alinari, 62–63, 193
© Archives of Jaca Book/Lunwerg, 77 (2)
© Archives of Lunwerg, 78
© Archives of Lunwerg/Museo Archeologico, Madrid, 77 (1)
© Archives nationales du monde du travail—Emmaüs International, 210
© 2014 Biblioteca Apostolica Vaticana—by permission of the Biblioteca Apostolica Vaticana, all rights reserved, 7, 10, 12, 31, 115, 147 (2)
© Bibliothèque nationale de France, Paris, 39
© Jaca Book/BAMSphoto—Rodella, 16–17, 29, 37, 38, 45, 67, 101–103, 112, 113, 143, 148, 152, 156, 222–223
© Photo by Emmanuel Anati, 199
© Giorgio Bacchin, 191
© Caritas International, 214–216
© Alberto Cerrodine, 91
© Koldo Chamurro, 211 (2)
© Photo by Elio Ciol, 68–69
© Photo by Patrick Gurham, 198
© C. Lavayén, 187 (3)
© Marc Llimargas Pons, 137
Photo © Vatican Museum, 34 (1), 35, 47, 225
© Oronoz Fotografos, 90, 111, 142
© Photothèque Zodiac, 196–197
© Photothèque Zodiac. Abbey of la Pierre-qui-Vire, 123
© Pedro Querejazu, 144 (6);
© Marco Ravenna, Correggio, 81
© Roma Capitale, Museo di Roma, 151 (4)
© A. Stabin, 186 (2)
© The Nelson-Atkins Museum of Art, Purchase Nelson Trust, Kansas City, Missouri, 86

© Foto Han Walker, 182
© Servizio Fotografico de *L'Osservatore Romano*, 226
Courtesy Henry Beck, 175 (7)
AA. VV., Europa, Mercator Fonds, Brussells 2002, 166
Archives of Marquette University, 173, 175 (4–6), 176
Archivio Centro Studi per la Cultura Popolare, Bologna, 107 (1, 2), 108–109, 112
Archives of the Daughters of Charity of Saint Vincent de Paul, Turin, 164
Archives of Jaca Book, 6, 13, 15, 19, 20, 21, 24, 25, 28, 46, 50–53, 56, 66, 70–75, 79, 80, 82–85, 87, 89, 99–100, 107 (3), 114, 120–121, 127–130, 134, 138, 140, 144 (5), 147 (1), 153, 155, 157, 160, 161, 163, 167 (3), 169, 171–172, 178, 179, 189, 194, 200, 204, 205–207, 212, 218–219, 227, 230–231
Archives of Jaca Book/photo by Massimo Capuani, 95
Archives of Jaca Book/photo by Elio Ciol, 125
Photo Archive of the Community of Sant'Egidio/Lucia Gardin, 195
Photo by Paolo Cardone (*Shoot4 Change*) per VIS, 233
Archives of Martin Noël, 118
Design by A. Baldanzi, 154
Biblioteca Nacional de España, Madrid, 11
Daniela Blandino, 34 (2), 58–59, 75
Provincial House of the Daughters of Charity, Cagliari, 158 (2)
Centro S. Chiara Audiovisivi, Rocca di Papa, Roma, 180
International Auschwitz Committee, 41 (5)
Azienda U.S.L. ROMA-E—Complesso Monumentale dell'Ospedale di Santo Spirito in Saxia, Roma, 151 (5, 6)
Hessische Landes—and Hochschulbibliothek, Darmstadt, 27
Foto Fabio Lusini, Siena, 64–65, 138–139
W. Horn, E. Born, *The Plan of St. Gall*, Berkeley, 1979, 98
Illustration by Carlo Jacono, 159
Institut Catholique de Paris, Paris, 18, 22, 26, 30
Nando Lanzi, Archivio Centro Studi per la Cultura Popolare, Bologna, 132–133, 135
Montecassino, Abbey Archives, 97, 98
Musée du Louvre, Paris, 49
Fot. Pais/archive of Rodrigo Pais—CEUB Università di Bologna, 183
Panstwowe Muzeum Auschwitz-Birkenau, 41 (1)
The Little Sisters of Jesus of Charles de Foucauld, Generalate, Tre Fontane, Roma, 105 (15, 16), 202
Photo by L. Prat, 190 (2)
Photo by L. Prisset, 190 (3)
Rivista viscontiana, Roma, 158 (1)
Photo by Sandro Scarioni. From the book *Altare d'oro di Sant'Ambrogio*, edited by Carlo Capponi, Silvana Editoriale, 1996, 54–55
Union Suisse d'Archéologie Copte, Geneva, 93
Universitätsbibliothek, Erlangen, 9, 32
www.caritas.org, 60
www.jesuscaritas.it, 201 (6)
www.logifranchi.it, 204